DISMANTLING PRIVILEGE

DISMANTLING PRIVILEGE

An Ethics of Accountability

Revised and Updated

Mary Elizabeth Hobgood

THE
PILGRIM
PRESS
Cleveland

For my grandchildren,
Jonathan Thomas and Addison Claire,
and in memory of Eleanor Humes Haney, 1931–1999

The Pilgrim Press
700 Prospect Avenue
Cleveland, Ohio 44115-1100
thepilgrimpress.com

Library of Congress Cataloging-in-Publication Data

Hobgood, Mary E., 1946–
    Dismantling privilege : an ethics of accountability / Mary Elizabeth Hobgood.
      p. cm.
    Includes bibliographical references and index.
    ISBN 0-8298-1374-8 (pbk : alk. paper)
    ISBN 978-0-8298-1823-9 (alk. paper; Revised edition)
    1. Elite (Social sciences) – United States. 2. Social stratification – United States.
  3. Social ethics. 4. Sociology, Christian. I. Title.
HN90.E4 H63 2000
305.5′12′0973 – dc21   99-056633

5   6   7   8   9   10   15   14   13

Contents

5. Relational Labor and the Politics of Solidarity 136

6. Intellectual and Political Struggle:
An Agenda for Accountable Disciples 150

Preface

This book explores the ethical foundations of contemporary U.S. society by examining systems of routine, systemic, unearned advantage. I uncover the "commonsense" assumptions and institutional power arrangements that accompany the class, race, and sex/gender locations of dominant groups. My goal is to make people like me recognize our unearned privilege and explore our membership in overadvantaged groups. As privileged people seek to honor ethical requirements for accountability, we need to uncover the terms of our participation in multiple sites of unearned advantage.

While this work can never be exhausted in any one study, I build on the work of others as I examine how those with privilege are embedded at the intersection of various power relations that overadvantage us at the expense of subordinate social groups and the environment. It is true that privileged groups are not responsible for systems we did not create. Nevertheless we are accountable to others for the unearned advantages these systems routinely give to us, as well as for how we contribute (often unwittingly) to the reproduction of these systems. We are also accountable to ourselves for how these systems distort our human potential and erode justice even for us.

I argue that privileged people are morally damaged, spiritually impoverished, and put physically at risk by a society structured to give unfair advantages to the few while it dismisses everyone's needs for respect, affection, just communal relations, and a healthy ecosphere. Drawing upon resources from the Christian tradition, this book seeks to offer the privileged an alternative framework for understanding self and others to the one provided by the liberal ideology of heterosexist, white supremacist, market capitalism. In ethically evaluating social systems with a primary focus on privilege rather than oppression, my goal is to foster Christian solidarity. By unearthing the structural links among diverse systems of privilege and oppression, I hope to foster the formation of alliance politics and a more inclusive democratic practice. This requires that privileged people grow in awareness of what is at stake in the struggle for justice, not only for subordinate groups, but for us as well.

My journey with oppression and privilege began in childhood. Although both of my parents were white, their class backgrounds were starkly different. Their interclass marriage during World War II meant that I spent much time in my early years shuttling between two loving grandmothers who lived in completely different worlds — though, as I was later to realize, worlds that were intimately connected. My father's mother was a sharecropper who labored from dawn to dusk in the red clay fields of Mississippi. My mother's mother was a woman of leisure in high-society New Orleans. No matter their economic resources, however, both grandmothers had black women working for them. And to greater or lesser degrees, both experienced disadvantages because my grandfathers were dead.

Although they would not be fully articulated until decades later, fundamental questions were raised for me as I took turns living with these two women and was repeatedly immersed in such starkly contrasting environments. One month I would be swimming and dining at the country club, and the next picking cucumbers, slopping hogs, and gathering eggs that the undisciplined chickens laid under the house. As a small child, I was concerned and confused about work and poverty, about racial hierarchy and gender subordination, about fairness and justice. These were questions about which the adults around me seemed uninterested or unaware.

I spent my later childhood and adolescence in the relative isolation of suburban America, but these questions reemerged for me in adulthood when I joined a religious community. Working in poor neighborhoods and schools of New York City, while studying the documents of Vatican II and liberation theology, made suffering from exploitation and oppression a daily reality. It also made my privilege, especially as a religious with a vow of poverty, even more apparent.

After I left the convent and married, my ongoing academic work in feminist liberation ethics has helped me see that an exploration of oppression must also be an exploration of privilege. Along with others in my field, I have been encouraged to link my social location to my membership in white, affluent, heterosexual groups. But even more important, feminist liberation ethics must make the connections between the unearned advantages routinely acquired by privileged groups, such as mine, and the unearned disadvantages that are increasing today for persons in groups subordinated by class stratification, white racism, and male dominance.

This work remains pressing to me not only because of my academic commitments but also because of the people in the diverse neighborhoods my family has lived in and the organizations to which I belong. Living in urban neighborhoods, for example, makes it harder to be oblivious to privilege when some of your neighbors lack necessities. Such folk have insisted that I become a good ally to them in their struggle for greater justice. Learning how to do this is my ongoing challenge and commitment.

In this process I work with students who, whether they come from elite backgrounds or not, are preparing themselves to enter the ranks of the privileged as adults. With other teaching colleagues, I struggle not only to help students think more critically about privilege, but also to develop forms of pedagogy that will encourage them to take risks in the community. As students make important connections between themselves and others, they develop moral courage and a political agenda, including accountability to the ecosphere, which may soon be unable to sustain life.

Classroom and field work should help us grow in our understanding of how diverse people are intimately connected through a political economy that uses some groups to benefit others. Linking living and learning in the educational process should help privileged people grow in our understanding not only of how social systems exploit and oppress others as they destroy the ecosphere, but also of how they intensify danger even for elites. As we explore dimensions of mounting peril even for privileged groups, we grow in clarity about what we value, what we oppose, and what we are willing to fight for. We can become more sophisticated in what can be done today to open up small spaces of freedom that will lead to greater emancipation for all social groups and for the environment tomorrow. If we are to take moral responsibility for our lives, we must become aware of the various dimensions of our overprivilege so that we can become accountable for them. I hope that educating elites like myself about our privilege and how it works against justice even for us will make a contribution to this process.

Acknowledgments

First Edition

Publishing captures a moment in a continuing conversation. Many people helped me with this piece of the conversation. I am grateful to the College of the Holy Cross for a junior leave semester that initiated this book. The Northeast Consultation in Feminist Ethics provided a sounding board in the early stages. To ease the burden of teaching and writing, Jim Nickoloff intercepted and took on work before it reached my door. Jerry Lembcke gave support at a particularly vulnerable time and suggested my working title *Ethics for Elites*. Carolyn Howe is a dialogue partner who always pushes me forward. Alice Laffey and Sara DeMeo helped without knowing it. And deadlines could not have been met without Suzanne Sylvester.

At the Pilgrim Press, I am grateful for Tim Staveteig's kindness and his enthusiasm for this project and for Ed Huddleston's careful attention to details.

I am especially indebted to two Christian ethicists — Elizabeth Bettenhausen and Marvin Ellison — who spent hours reading earlier versions of the manuscript and helped me improve its form and content. As theorists, educators, and activists as well as human beings who are always ready for a good time, they provide enormous inspiration. I am grateful for their friendship, their good company, and all that they have to teach me.

On the home front, I give thanks to the men I live with, the three loves of my life. Nathan dropped encouraging notes and telephoned support from afar. Luke and Tom persevered through a long and grueling time of living in a small apartment with a writer.

Finally, I am grateful to Ellen Marie Keane, R.S.H.M., who first nurtured my critical eye on this world, and to Joan M. Martin for expecting me to do this work.

Revised Edition

For the continuing conversation represented in the second edition, I thank my students at Holy Cross. Their insights in both the classroom and in their work in the Worcester community have helped me better understand my work. I am also grateful for their research and writing that informs directions taken in chapter 6. Their enthusiasm for liberation readings of Scripture, tradition, the daily newspapers, and their own personal and civic experiences is a constant source of joy.

The conversation that informs this book was also supported by a grant from the Eleanor Humes Haney Fund, which provided opportunity for a consultation in Red Bud Springs, North Carolina, in 2008 with my mentor Beverly W. Harrison, whose seminal theoretical work informs my own, and Pamela K. Brubaker, colleague, collaborator, and friend.

Finally, I am grateful for Timothy Staveteig, Joan Blake, and the editors at Pilgrim Press for their sustained enthusiasm for this project over several years. Most recently this includes John Eagleson for his careful attention to the second edition.

Introduction

Theological Grounding for Dismantling Privilege

I T HAS BEEN SAID that the work of building justice is the core theological metaphor of Christian life.[1] This requires that our communities be "rightly related," that is, that shared power and mutual respect inform the social relations between persons, groups, and the ecosphere. As we will explore in subsequent chapters of this book, seeking justice and rightly related community includes dismantling unjust forms of privilege and suffering. This is the moral response to revelations of the nature of God found in the central biblical traditions of both the Hebrew Bible and the New Testament. These include Exodus, the Jubilee tradition of Leviticus 25, the Prophets, and the ministry of Jesus. These traditions are intimately connected. Governed by love of self and neighbor, all focus on the struggle for more just social relations as the site of God's presence and primary concern. In addition, as we shall also explore, much in subsequent Christian tradition also sees the work of creating justice as the very heart of Christian life. That God is justice-love is a theological, not "only" an ethical claim. Because God is found primarily in the struggle for justice and love, working for justice is never an ethical sideshow of religious life.

However, since justice is the goal, not a strategy, we can develop meaningful ways to achieve justice only when we understand how the systems that inform our lives actually work to create injustice. Through critical social analyses of the class, race, and sex/gender systems, for example, we are able to devise strategic plans to interrupt injustice, especially if we understand where these systems are vulnerable. We are motivated to do critical analysis and to develop strategies that move toward shared power and mutual respect because a liberation reading of Scripture and tradition reveals that creating just social relations witnesses to the very nature of God. Seeking effective strategies that create justice, therefore, requires engagement with complex forms of social analysis about how the world works, because how the world works is a theological matter.

Because most Christians and other ethical people have little idea how unjust power permeates and impoverishes social relations, we need critical social analysis to map out the general organization of these relations. Critical social analysis focuses on the ways power is monopolized by the few, and

1

imagines ways to realize the yet-to-be-claimed power of the many. Seeking justice is not for the faint-hearted because it involves challenging mainstream thinking about class, race, and sex/gender power structures, the major ones that inform our lives-in-relation. The central thesis of this book is that, in order to do the theological work of constructing rightly related communities as a response to the God of justice and love, social relations informed by structures that promote an unjust distribution of power and privilege must be dismantled and transformed. This involves not only learning social analysis, but also engaging in political struggle. In large part, as we will see, justice struggle involves developing subversive micro-practices at multiple sites of oppression. This is difficult for many reasons, including the ubiquity of ignorance about how unjust power informs social relations, as well as the lack of multicultural competence of the privileged.

In the eight years since the first edition of this book appeared, few if any privileges that come from a monopolization of power have been dismantled in the primary social relations that constitute our lives. Rather, the class structure of late capitalism has required the United States to become more indebted, more deeply mired in unjust wars, more threatened by terrorism and ecological crisis, more unfaithful to the U.S. Constitution, and more unequal. Since 2000, the U.S. political economy has intensified inequality and unfairness while the earth is even more gravely ill. This is also true for the world economy under "globalization" because capitalist social relations continue to enable the largest corporations to harness the most powerful states in their service. These states use neoliberal economic policies and military interventions to promote corporate interests at the expense of world majorities and ecological welfare.

Since 2000, the engine of the capitalist system, which generates corporate production of profits without limit for relatively few investors, especially when aided by conservative government policies favorable to the wealthy, has intensified war, ecological destruction, and economic polarization in the United States and around the world. In recent years this has included the production of increasing impoverishment and economic crisis (including the 2007 collapse of the global banking system), an eroding middle sector, and soaring increases in income for the highest sectors of the U.S. class system. In this Introduction to the second edition, I use three events — Hurricane Katrina, war in the Middle East, and intensified ecological destruction/global warming — as recent "barometric pressure points" for understanding increasing economic meltdown and ecological devastation wrought by the global political economy. They also serve as further illustrations of the analyses in this book.

Hurricane Katrina

The hurricane that ravaged New Orleans in 2005 gave a stark microcosmic picture of the larger U.S. reality that supports the critical discussions of class and race in subsequent chapters. Katrina provided occasion for the public to view the U.S. class system in its naked horror, particularly as class immiseration was intensified by public policy that abandoned concern for the commonweal. It also was a wake-up call to those who downplay the environmental crisis and the effects of global warming on the increasing intensity of weather patterns, including hurricanes.

However, this prominent city was devastated, not primarily by Katrina and the betrayal of flood victims in its aftermath, but by the social relations of the class structure that thoroughly harnessed the race system, and by government policies that have starved the infrastructure of most U.S. cities (including the New Orleans levee system) since 1980.[2] Government betrayal and the primacy of profits for the upper class are also demonstrated by the fact that the U.S. Congress used Katrina to reward the elite who elected them by inflating pork-barrel politics that continue to allow shoddy engineering projects, designed to control nature rather than preserve wetlands, making the situation even worse.[3] New Orleans is no safer today because profits for engineering, oil, shipping, timber, and other corporate interests, rather than public safety and the preservation of nature, have been and continue to be the priority there as it is everywhere else when government is a political economy, one elected primarily to promote the interests of the economically powerful. In short, what is happening to New Orleans is a *writ-large version* of what is happening everywhere in the United States when public housing, education, transportation, health care, above poverty wage jobs, infrastructure renewal, and other commonweal projects are eroding in quality, being increasingly privatized, or disappearing altogether because the public treasury is hijacked by the military-industrial complex and other corporate interests.[4] This situation endangers everyone, even those who receive immediate privilege and profits.

As a lens on the larger political economy, Katrina also provided opportunity for Americans to see how the racial system is employed to hide the reality of class exploitation, and how this dynamic serves the government's abandonment of the commonweal. For example, impoverished whites could not leave the city while affluent blacks did. But few noticed, and it was easy for local and federal governments to remain idle, because the structure of racism ensured that most poor people, and therefore most of the abandoned in New Orleans, were black. Writer Christopher Shea points out that we better understand the priority of the class structure when we realize that "in a world without racism, black and white poor people [would have been more equal in number but] would still have drowned when the levees broke; in a world without poverty everyone might have gotten out alive."[5] As will be discussed in subsequent chapters, the invisibility of white impoverishment, and the class system itself, guarantees that racism, sexism, and nativism displace outrage at the social relations of class privilege and subordination and destroy the solidarity necessary between women and men of all races, most of whom share class subordination but are usually unaware of it. Consequently, while New Orleans currently has twelve thousand homeless people, the majority who inhabit this devastated city (less than two-thirds of the pre-Katrina population) are wealthy and upper-income homeowners who have access to private insurance and other sources of income that make them less dependent on the eviscerated commonweal.[6]

War

The seemingly endless wars in Iraq and Afghanistan, and on terrorism more generally, give another picture of the more recent U.S. class structure, this time on an international canvas. With only 5 percent of the global population, the United States is responsible for half of the entire planet's trillion dollars in military spending.[7] The soaring profits of the military-industrial complex, including the largest U.S. corporations, which, however diversified, make most of their profits from military and military-related products and services, explain why we have a permanent war economy. In addition, when the corporate media does not give the public access to information about the government's exploitative, immoral, and illegal actions abroad, Americans easily view events like 9/11/01 as totally unprovoked and are ready for war.[8] With $10 billion of taxpayers' money being spent on the war every month, war is making a relatively few U.S. defense contractors and other investors even more wealthy than they already were.[9] In short, when war is this profitable, we are sure to have a lot of it. The profitability of war and the need by the economically powerful to control global resources, in this case the oil and gas in the region of Iraq, have led to the normalization of enemies, public lies, torture, prison camps, wire-tapping, and the erosion of civil liberties. The so-called "war against terrorism" makes war a political relation, not between states, but between "enemy" organizations and populations, a relation not governed by the rule of law. In this new and unjust relation, war has become a routine, police operation against anyone, U.S. citizen or not, who arouses the government's suspicions. Law professor Michael E. Tigar writes that the war on terror represents "a qualitative rupture with the claimed system of constitutional governance."[10]

The needs of defense contractors and other corporate interests have also justified the further dismantling of progressive aspects in the U.S. tax system. In the last thirty years, the tax burden has been transferred from large corporations to individuals, from the wealthy owners of assets to low- and middle-income wage earners, and from the federal government to (mostly starving) state and local governments, whose taxes are the most regressive.[11] To pay for war, government policies shift the economic burden, even more than the class structure itself already does, from the top to the middle and lower sectors of the U.S. population, whose services are cut, children die in war, and tax burden increases in relation to the wealthy above them.

In addition, the tens of thousands of U.S. soldiers killed or maimed in body and spirit, and the hundreds of thousands (if not over a million as of this writing) of Iraqi children, women, and men killed, injured, imprisoned, or homeless further illustrates the claim made in subsequent chapters that liberal democratic ideals are *not* the engine of this political economy. The media hides that Congress, both Democrats and Republicans, and the corporate interests Congress serves, have destroyed, not only a viable New Orleans, but *civilizations* in the Middle East, even though most Americans have been opposed to the war since 2005.[12] No politician of a major party questioned the $620 billion Pentagon budget for 2008. While candidates can call (however belatedly) for withdrawal from Iraq, no one expecting to win the U.S. presidency can challenge the military-industrial complex, the core of the profit-making engine of U.S. capitalism.[13]

Given this reality, I suggest that examples of the treatment of U.S. soldiers provides an instructive lens on the U.S. political economy's war against everyone else, including the earth itself, in order to further profits without limit for relatively few investors. For example, the claim that the government supports the troops is belied by many realities, including the following. Men and women who are on the front lines (of whom 13 percent are teens and 66 percent are twenty-five years old or younger) make about the same salary as a Wal-Mart clerk, and over twenty-five thousand military families are eligible for food stamps.[14] Because items that offer personal support and protection are less profitable to make than other forms of military equipment, it is well known that the U.S. military does not provide adequate provisions, from linens to body armor to safe vehicles, for the troops. Yet another indicator of the government's lack of troop support is that psychiatric care and other forms of medicine are cut or unavailable to many soldiers who need them.

But deliberately harmful policy goes even further than this. Even when the wounded are at serious risk of harm to themselves or others, medical treatment is often denied. In fact, it appears to be standard procedure that those soldiers most in need of medical treatment are precisely the ones who do not receive it. Many of the most seriously untreated and wounded, if they do not commit suicide first, are dishonorably discharged so they are not eligible for benefits.[15] Why? Colonel Katherine Scheirman, a retired Air Force physician who served as chief of medical operations in the Air Force's European headquarters from 2004 to 2006, explains it this way: "It's all about money.... [For example] every kid that gets [excused from active duty] with PTSD [post traumatic stress syndrome] is going to be a lifetime of disability payments for the government. Every kid who gives up and kills himself [costs the government] nothing."[16]

When it comes to the extent of the federal government's abandonment of our wounded men and women (mostly young, disproportionately of color, and from lower-income families), it is difficult to overstate the case. In addition, federal abandonment of combat-broken soldiers is not new and is found to be true in the experiences of many Vietnam veterans as well. If this is the treatment the U.S. political economy gives to Americans who put their lives on the line, how much more likely will unjust treatment be given to everyone else.

Ecological Crisis

In addition to increasing class polarization, imperialism, and war, ecological devastation advances as well. There has been increasing attention in the past few years to the health of the planet, in particular to escalating climate meltdown. Ecological crisis, however, is in large part due to pollution by the military, an inconvenient truth that even Al Gore's award-winning documentary fails to discuss. In fact, war and the capacity to make war are rapidly becoming one of the greatest threats to the environment. Military projects are inherently environmentally destructive, including the production and testing of nuclear weapons, aerial bombardment of terrain, dispersal of land mines and buried ordnance, and the use and storage of chemical toxins. The military produces more hazardous waste annually than the five largest international chemical companies combined. Not only are the 25 million acres of land the military controls in the United States riddled with toxic sites, but also the abandoned toxic contamination from military bases overseas threatens the health of communities around the world. This is in addition to the tens of thousands of nuclear, chemical, and biological weapons that remain (sometimes in vulnerable locations) in the United States, Britain, France, Russia, and Chinese arsenals today.[17]

In addition to military pollution, the planetary ecological crisis is the result of the intensified penetration of the global capitalist system into every corner of the globe. This process, often called "globalization" and believed to be inevitable, is a deliberately constructed form of intensified neo-colonialism that gives economic elites power over states and their economies, including access to resources everywhere. The capitalist process of globalization harnesses the power of international financial institutions, like the World Bank, the International Monetary Fund, and the World Trade Organization, to implement neoliberal economic policies that make regions playgrounds for the investment needs of the wealthy as they destroy local economies, privatize public goods, cut social spending, and make national populations and their governments increasingly subservient to the interests of outside elites. Faithful to the inherent dynamics of capitalism, this war on people cannot be separated from the war on the planet itself.

As we review in subsequent chapters, the many processes of global capitalist production destroy planetary ecosystems, leading to the destruction of the ozone layer, climate meltdown, the rising rate of species extinction, and increasing toxins in our air, food, water, and bloodstreams. This includes the bioaccumulation of human-made radioactive isotopes in the environment and in *all* human bodies since they were introduced into the environment with intensive military nuclear testing between 1946 and 1958.[18] The United States continues to sustain capital accumulation for the few at the top at virtually any human or ecological cost. As early as 1962, Rachel Carson, in her pioneering book *Silent Spring*, recognized that "the principal causes of ecological degradation" were "the gods of profit and production." She critiqued a society where "the right to make a dollar at any cost is seldom challenged." A scientist and a writer, Rachel Carson devoted her life to contesting "chemical and radioactive warfare" on all living things in capitalist political economies, and her work is even more pertinent today than it was in the mid-twentieth century.[19] As we will discuss further in the final chapter, because governments primarily serve the interests of the elite, it remains to be seen how effective any government will be, without massive mobilization from below, in limiting the scope and intensity of our current ecological crisis by moving beyond cosmetic remedies. For humans to live in a sustainable and more just relation to nature, economic production — and profits — must be fundamentally altered. As geography professor Joshua Muldavin writes: "We must focus on the real root of the problem: a highly unequal and unsustainable international system of production, distribution, and consumption."[20]

In summary, in its total embrace of the so-called "logic of the free market," the neoliberal domestic and foreign policies of globalization have intensified the unjust structural dynamics of capitalism in recent years. These dynamics require that most of the benefits of the labor force go to those at the top, and the assault on most people is matched only by the assault on all living things. Capitalist neoliberal policies intensify these dynamics by dismantling the welfare state, privatizing public goods, starving the infrastructure and other components that serve the common good, as well as engaging in imperial conquest and control.

Nations that have resources like oil, diamonds, copper, cacao, coca, timber, beef, flowers, and bananas become subject to civil wars of resistance (often dismissed as "tribal hatreds") because their corrupt governments function as colonizing powers, working in tandem with large corporate interests to export the wealth, impoverish the country, and sicken the environment.[21] Thus our environmental crisis is sociologically grounded, because the destruction of persons waged by the class, race, and sex/gender systems is mirrored in the destruction of ecosystems themselves. In other words, if we live in systems that don't respect and share power with the neighbors we do see, how can we respect the environment and take seriously the greenhouse gas emissions and other toxins we do not see?

Economic Polarization and Post-Democracy

Political scientist Colin Crouch has written: "We are living in a distinctively post-democratic age [in which] a powerful minority of interests have become far more active than the mass of ordinary people."[22] World leaders and the minority elite in their countries are pressured (especially through the neoliberal economic policies of the International Monetary Fund and the World Bank, so-called free trade agreements, and threats of military invasion) to become part of a vast network that promotes the interests of the world's economically powerful at the expense of the majority in their own countries.

In the day-to-day activities required by such arrangements, the burdens of global neoliberal policies fall disproportionately on women and girls. Christian ethicist Pamela Brubaker writes: "When governments cut social spending, families become more responsible for health, education, and other social services. Since in most societies women traditionally are the care-givers, these responsibilities fall to them,...increasing an already heavy workload."[23] In addition to increasing unpaid and low-paid work, such policies often result in girls dropping out of school and the further marginalization of women.

Even though women collectively bear the worst from the negative fallout of globalization, women are the "glue" that keeps what is left of families and neighborhoods together. For example, a group of 1,000 women from 153 countries were among the nominees for the 2005 Nobel Peace Prize because of their unique contributions to world peace. Often operating under the radar screen of the media and public consciousness, women are "building houses, working for access to clean water, fighting for universal education, reintegrating prisoners and former child soldiers and people with AIDS into society."[24] These 1,000 represent millions more women who are unacknowledged and underutilized in "reconnaissance, negotiations, disarmament and governance."[25] Given these realities, rightly related community is hard to find.

With most nations today existing as neocolonies of these elite corporate interests, the economic fallout of globalization is predictable. The UN World Institute for Development Economics reported in 2000 that the richest 1 percent in the world owns 40 percent of the planet's wealth and the next richest

9 percent own 45 percent of the world total of global assets. Of the most extremely wealthy, more than one-third live in the United States, 27 percent live in Japan, 6 percent in the UK, and 5 percent in France.[26] Such figures do not consider the rising sector of 3 million new capitalists from China, India, and the former Soviet Union who are becoming major economic players in most parts of the world.[27] At the same time, half the world's adult population owns barely 1 percent of global wealth.[28]

The world's economically powerful often maintain that if they do well, income and wealth will "trickle down" to everyone else who is willing to work hard. They claim that if impoverished countries open themselves to the surplus of global capitalists they will "develop." New York University professor Kim Phillips-Fein maintains that "these ideas have their own attraction [because] the market model suggests that individuals exercise tremendous power over their own destinies."[29] People are susceptible to mainstream economic thinking and market ideology because, whatever the market's actual results, these ideas give people a sense of power.

A careful analysis, however, reveals that "trickle down" is hardly the case. The New Economic Foundation reported in 2006 that the share of the benefits from world economic growth dropped 73 percent for the world's poorest in the last decade.[30] This reality is also reflected in the fact that, according to the United Nations, the net transfer of capital from impoverished countries to wealthy ones was $784 billion in 2006, up from $229 billion in 2002.[31] Not only is "trickling down" from rich to poor a myth, but the reality is rather "gushing up" from the impoverished to the affluent and the wealthy at the top.

Mainstream economic thinking, which promotes growth through policies that benefit the wealthy as a solution to poverty, needs revision not only because of the reality of intensified economic polarization and meltdown through a global capitalist process of "gushing up" as discussed above, but also because of environmental sustainability. Not only is the one tiny "spaceship Earth" we inhabit becoming more gravely ill all the time, but for everyone in the world to live at the current European average level of consumption, we would need more than twice the bio-capacity actually available, or the equivalent of 2.1 planet earths. If everyone consumed at the U.S. average rate, we would need nearly five planet earths to sustain us.[32]

Such rising global inequality and growing privilege for those at the top at the expense of everyone else is also indicative of the United States. Although I expand on this in some detail in subsequent chapters, suffice it to say here that, since 2000, there has been continued erosion in economic security for most Americans while those at the very top have become even wealthier. A primary reason for the existence of economic growth in tandem with increasing economic vulnerability, both nationally and globally, is that the formal labor sector is eroding, especially due to the pervasive mechanization of work.[33] To put it simply, increasing numbers of people are becoming superfluous to the (legal) economy since more profits for relatively few investors can be made by de-skilling (that is, breaking work down to routinized components) as well as lowering the wages of work, outsourcing it to lower-wage countries, or mechanizing it altogether. This explains the fact that, even though productivity has roughly doubled in the past three decades, most U.S. workers' wages have stagnated or eroded.

Since the publication of the first edition of this book, this is now even truer of the highly skilled, highly educated workforce. Yale political scientist Jacob Hacker writes at the end of 2006: "*all* well-educated workers, even those at the top, are at a much greater risk of economic reversals than they used to be [and] the ranks of the long-term unemployed . . . are disproportionately professional and well educated."[34] Even the hard working and the well educated in the United States are vulnerable to the dynamics of this current stage of capitalism.

In contrast to the vulnerable economic situation of the overwhelming majority of American workers, a small group at the top, the upper 5 percent of workers, currently have earnings that are up 9 percent since 2005, and the 10 percent at the top of the U.S. population have a share of national income equal to the bottom half.[35] Clearly, we see the phenomenon of "gush up" not only globally but also in the United States as the gains from the productivity of the U.S. workforce as a whole are going only to the top. We also see that rising numbers of privileged people are becoming vulnerable, and they also have an urgent stake in social transformation.

At the expanding bottom of the economy, as we will discuss in subsequent chapters, the number of workers making poverty wages, or those making 100 to 200 percent above the official poverty line but are still poor, has also increased since 2000. Even before the economic meltdown that began in 2007, poor or near poor were about 94 million, or almost one-third of Americans.[36] About one-third of these impoverished Americans are children who are growing up suffering the violence and abuse of hunger, homelessness, and lack of a decent education, health care, or dental care.[37] In the wealthiest country in the world these children, now at least one-third of the bottom third, are also trying to survive the abuse of shame. For example, in some cities in my home state of Massachusetts, hardly one of the poorest states in the union, as many as one in five public school students are homeless or likely to become homeless, and teaching can take a back seat as teachers give time to handing out extra clothes and trying to make sure students are fed.[38] Meanwhile, in affluent neighborhoods in Massachusetts, children are being abducted, and parents fear that if children scream, no one will hear them.[39] Homeland safety and security erodes for all citizens when affluent communities are segregated and isolated, and when increasing numbers even in so-called "good times" (before 2007) suffer the trauma of impoverishment and other forms of violence.

It seems apparent that the U.S. political economy, the powerful alliance of government and business interests that runs the United States and has been controlling (at least up until now) much of the rest of world, is at war with everything and everyone that stands in its way. Whether in New Orleans or Iraq, or in impoverished, polluted, and strife-torn neighborhoods in increasing places everywhere on the globe, things are being destroyed and not being repaired because these conditions are good for business. They insure the control of outside investors while the citizenry, isolated in affluence or struggling for survival, provides little organized resistance. Or as international organizer Sasha Chanoff says, politicians may deliberately engineer violence by exploiting racial or tribal differences to promote the self-destruction of the idle and distract people from the global vested interests at work.[40] As Michael Fitzgerald says in his article "Militarism and the American Way of Life," things are not fixed because "they are supposed to be quagmires . . . the wars will remain. The longer they last the more steroids for the economy."[41] In other words, the more dictatorship, the more corruption, the more impoverishment, and the more social chaos in any given country, city, or region, the easier it is for economic elites, including U.S. multinationals, to control and plunder the country without accountability. These are the dynamics of global capitalism and the global class structure, no matter how many U.S. leaders talk about spreading "democracy."

Challenging the Adequacy of Our Ideology

We must keep challenging the destructive myths and assumptions of the national and global political economy that help to reproduce the unjust social relations of the class, race, sex/gender, and ecological systems and the escalating suffering they reproduce. These include challenging assumptions that progressive taxes are bad, that policies promoting nurture and care create wimps, that government accountability to the common good is quaint, that people are impoverished because they don't work hard enough, that education is always the answer to impoverishment, that people of color and "illegal aliens" are less human than whites, that military force and torture, not police work, diplomacy, and above all greater justice, are the solutions to terrorism and civil war, that economic growth and profits for the few benefit everyone, and that the current economic system is the only possible one.

These and other myths and false assumptions that prevent the establishment of rightly related community are explored in this book. Such myths must be challenged because they promote unjust relations that shape us as people who tolerate enormous human suffering and social and ecological cruelty. Theologian Robert McAfee Brown wrote about the need "to suspect ideologies [or ways of interpreting the world] that permit us to remain complacent in the face of human suffering."[42] Scholars have observed the facility with which capitalism has courted such complacency, whether in its merchant, industrial, or current "global" historical periods. Historian Marcus Rediker writes of the slave trade of early merchant capitalism: "Learning cruelty was intrinsic to learning the trade itself.... [For the slave ship captain it was] a requirement of the job and of the later economic system it served."[43] Eric Hobsbawm wrote of the industrial robber barons during the second historical period of capitalism: "None had noticeable scruples, or could afford to have, in an economy and an age where fraud, bribery, slander, and if necessary guns were normal aspects of competition.... Most would have regarded the question of whether they were honest as considerably less relevant...than the question whether they were smart."[44] Former businessman and recent ex-empire builder in the current global economy, John Perkins, writes:

> Is anyone in the U.S. innocent?...Millions of us depend on the exploitation of [impoverished countries] for our livelihoods. The resources and cheap labor that feed nearly all our businesses come from places like Indonesia and very little ever makes its way back. The loans of foreign aid ensure that today's children and their grandchildren will be held hostage. They will have to allow our corporations to ravage their natural resources and will have to forego education, health and other social services merely to pay us back.... Does the excuse that most Americans are unaware of this constitute innocence? Uninformed and intentionally misinformed, yes — but innocent?[45]

Because a Christian social ethics of accountability requires that we interrogate the adequacy of our ideologies, I invite you to wrestle with the analyses in the chapters that follow. They serve as a counternarrative that challenges dominant ideology or normative thinking and "innocence." The analyses of critical social theories explored here seek to move past the misinformation and erroneous assumptions that ground the unjust social relations in this political economy. They offer an alternative reading about our national and global realities so that we can understand why justice and rightly related community are scarce, and *why they don't necessarily have to be so.* Sadly, as the above statistics demonstrate, the analyses in the following chapters are as pertinent now, if not more so, than when this book was first published.

Chapter 6 is an addition to the original volume and pays introductory attention to growing experiments in more just community building in Latin America and South Africa. These provide examples of grassroots initiatives that have formed in recent decades to resist the chaos and suffering from the neoliberal economic policies of global capitalism. Such stirrings of popular discontent challenge the right of government and business to charge people for the privilege of living. Behind these stirrings are thousands of very ordinary, courageous people who take risks that make a difference in creating more just social relations every single day. Their novel and complex political strategies are worthy of attention and study by people who are engaging in social change work in the United States.

It is vital to our continuing evolution as human beings, and to our capacity as moral agents, that we study the unjust social relations of class, race, sex/gender, and ecological destruction that create us to be the people we are, often far too comfortable with business as usual and growing injustice. It is vital for our continued survival and well-being that we begin to *imagine what kinds of people we would like to become* and what kinds of communities we wish to build. We have to create new kinds of social relations that will shape us into the people we want to be.

In order to develop creative ways to interrupt injustice and transform our society, we can continue to study, hopefully beyond the brief introduction in chapter 6, those who attempt to transform unjust political and economic arrangements here and abroad. This is essential to developing strategies that are accountable to the divine mandate to love ourselves well, including loving and caring for all those communities on whom we depend for survival and flourishing. Theologically speaking, if God requires that Christian life be fundamentally rooted in building more just social relations and communities, then creative possibilities for a common good *really do exist* because God does not require the impossible. Practically speaking, the common good must be served, and justice is required, not only for the flourishing of all creation, but also *for our very survival*. May the second edition of this book contribute to the creation of such justice-seeking, ecologically accountable communities, and may it support the increasing multitudes, both in this country and around the world, that believe things can be better and work in whatever way they can to make them so.

ONE

An Ethical Agenda for Elites

How can we come to understand the ethical obligations we have to one another not only as individuals but as members of groups?
— PETER J. HAAS

ON SEPTEMBER 3, 1991, the Tuesday after Labor Day, the Imperial Foods chicken processing plant in Hamlet, North Carolina, caught fire. Fifty-six of the 200 workers were seriously injured, and 25 workers, primarily women and disproportionately African American, died. Like the 146 workers of the 1911 New York City Triangle Shirtwaist fire, the Imperial Foods workers went to their deaths in a sweatshop-style industry that disproportionately exploited white women and people of color. Unlike the Triangle Shirtwaist fire, however, which elicited a hundred thousand people to march down Broadway in a protest that provoked the unionization of garment workers, the Imperial Foods fire received little media or political attention.[1]

These stories of workers, disproportionately female and of color, who suffer and die while the world barely notices are common in our society and around the world. Such events are juxtaposed against the reality that, even though productivity has doubled in the last three decades, average paychecks have remained the same. While the incomes of the richest 300,000 Americans, adjusted for inflation, more than tripled between 1970 and 2000 because of the productivity of the U.S. workforce, wages were either flat or falling for nine out of ten Americans. In addition those earning more than $100,000 (top 10 percent in 2005) own more than three-quarters of all stocks and the richest 1 percent (those earning more than $348,000) have a share of national income equal to the bottom 50 percent.[2] These events are also juxtaposed against the reality of a political economy that, on the one hand, exploits (pays back less than the wealth created) and oppresses (politically silences) increasing numbers of workers at the lowest tiers of the working class and, on the other hand, offers benefits and unearned advantages primarily to white workers in the upper tiers of the labor market. The work of this book is to pay attention to the story of the Imperial Foods disaster and others like it and to analyze the realities of class exploitation, racism, and sexism that deeply structure these events. However, more is needed for an ethic that guides people for living in the real world in this

14

new century. What is also needed is an ethical framework that connects the growing misery of many to the privilege of a relative few in the society.

My analysis is indebted to Peggy McIntosh, whose seminal essay about "unearned privilege" has helped many of us begin to analyze our membership in groups that grant routine advantages about which we are meant to remain oblivious.[3] We have been socialized to see privilege as a just reward for superior talent and effort and disadvantage as a result of individual inadequacies. Consequently, we are not tutored in uncovering the way society reproduces unshared power arrangements that are often at the root of these privileges and disadvantages. As will be discussed, my analysis assumes that unshared power is at the root of injustice and that uncovering social relations of class, race, and sex/gender that reproduce unshared power and routine unearned advantage for some is the work of ethics.

Although most readers of this book may not be in the richest 10 percent of the population, they are likely to belong to the relatively small percentage of people in our society who, while not necessarily of the upper class, nevertheless enjoy significant unearned advantages because of the privileged groups to which they belong. This study invites all readers to do an ethical analysis of social power and privilege. Those who have relatively more amounts of power and privilege in the class, race, and sex/gender systems are called "elites" in this study. I especially encourage these more privileged readers to make connections between their relatively advantageous social location and the human vocation to create a moral world. I write from an explicitly Christian ethical perspective; however, I hope that my analysis will be helpful to others of differing faiths and of no particular faith tradition.

In the chapters ahead I address people who are unaware they have unearned benefits through the class, race, and gender systems that impact almost every dimension of our lives. I address people like myself, a white professional woman who, while not among the most powerful in society, nevertheless routinely receives unearned advantages. We comprise a global minority if we are white and enjoy relative economic affluence. Among us some enjoy other aspects of privileged status in this society that are associated with being able-bodied, heterosexual, or male.

An analysis of group membership reveals that privilege does not come randomly. Having privileged access to the benefits in society is usually not a matter of having good luck or of being fortunate. Neither is privilege solely a matter of personal effort. Routine privilege is largely due to our membership in elite class, race, and sex/gender groups that enjoy unshared power in our society. I will argue that contrary to what most people have been taught, the power of privileged access to social benefits is not distributed primarily through good luck or individual merit. Rather, privilege comes as a result of our dominant positions in interlocking class, race, and sex/gender systems.

As we shall see, unearned benefits come when our group has the power to increase the social burden on other groups.

Working Definitions

Differences by way of race, gender, and even class are often considered natural or biologically determined. I follow a different logic: these differences are social in nature.[4] They are constructed in culture and laden with ethical meanings. I will construct class, race, and sex/gender as ways of distinguishing people according to the vested interests of more powerful groups. These systems construct different identities through unjust power arrangements. These systems are patterns of relations that elites reproduce through their ownership and/or control of the major institutions in the society. Class, race, and sex/gender are not natural or essential attributes of who we are as human beings. Contrary to dominant assumptions, they are not like hair or eye color or blood type. Rather, class, race, and sex/gender distinctions are artificial constructions that mutually condition one another. They have been created historically by the most powerful social groups to serve their interests as these interests change over time. Patricia Hill Collins notes that dominant knowledge assumes that differences lie in the groups themselves rather than in the unjust power relations that construct class, race, and sex/gender difference.[5]

Social constructions of class, race, and sex/gender divide people into groups in order to treat them differently and unfairly in social institutions. These institutions include families, neighborhoods, labor markets, businesses, the medical and legal professions, government, the media, schools, prisons, and churches. Class, race, and sex/gender relations promoted by these institutions have been carefully constructed by persons with power in the society to routinely give advantages to their groups while increasing the social burdens on others. I will argue that a relative minority in the society use economic, political, and cultural and financial institutions to promote their vested interests at the expense of the majority.

Powerful groups are called "elites" or "the privileged" or "dominants" in this study. For our purposes here, the most powerful group in the society includes those with the greatest advantages in all three systems. They belong to the capitalist class and are overwhelmingly white and male. The capitalist class, roughly 2 percent of the U.S. population, is the corporate elite that will be explained more fully in chapter 3.[6] Most of this group's income is made not from wages and salaries but from income-producing properties. This group makes the major decisions that drive the economy, the political process, and major cultural and financial institutions. The power of this group includes the ability to define the economic interests, cultural values, and patterns of social behavior that are imposed on everyone.[7] This group and the wealthy immediately below it who do not control capital enjoy most of the benefits in the society and create unjust burdens for the majority.

Immediately below the top 10 percent (of capitalists and other wealthy groups), however, are the affluent sectors to whom this study is addressed: especially those earning high salaries (top 20 percent of earners) who since 2003 have been rapidly outpacing middle- and low-wage workers (70 percent of earners).[8] We are elites who enjoy some of the class, race, and gender benefits of the most privileged. As we shall see, we enjoy unearned benefits to the degree that we are essential to the work of reproducing the class, race, and sex/gender systems. We enjoy relative social power even though we may also occupy subordinate social locations. For example, we may be white and also gay, economically affluent and also female, white heterosexual male and also disabled. We must therefore acquire a sense of our relative power within a variety of dominant/subordinate relations.

For purposes of my argument, the elites addressed here enjoy more dominance than we suffer subordination. We are disproportionately white, heterosexual, and male. We are not members of the capitalist class, but like them, we derive unearned benefits and advantages from the lower tiers of the working class. We are professionals and managers in the upper tiers of the working class (sometimes called "middle class" or "upper middle class"), or those preparing to enter those tiers. Most of us are not, *at least yet,* subjected to a significant erosion of our relative control over work or the disappearance of our jobs, which has been endemic to the lower tiers of the working class. We gain status by separating ourselves from other workers and calling ourselves "middle class." We separate out as middle class even though, like all workers, we have only or primarily our productive abilities to sell for a wage in order to sustain ourselves and our families. At the same time we do not acknowledge that our income, compared to most wage earners, is anything but middle. We include those whose incomes have been steady or rising, whose households in 2006 earned as much as $97,000 or more and thought of ourselves as middle class even though almost 80 percent of U.S. households earned less than we did.[9]

It is my purpose to show ways in which those in privileged groups, ourselves included, use institutions to socialize people into "proper" dominant and subordinate class, race, and sex/gender identities and roles. These proper identities and roles shape what people think and value, how they act, and the degree to which they feel entitled to the benefits of society or blame themselves for disproportionately bearing its burdens. Such identities enable elites to enjoy, to greater or lesser degrees, selective access to the material and symbolic benefits in the society. Most damaging of all, these socially constructed identities oblige most people in the society to act against their long-term interests so that elites can receive short-term benefits.[10]

This situation is constantly reproduced when unequal power relations are hidden within "commonsense" assumptions that mystify our class, race, and gender locations.[11] Our society has successfully normalized the social relations that comprise class, race, and sex/gender systems and the unshared power arrangements they reproduce. As a consequence, poor female workers of color routinely suffer and die in sweatshops, and such events get buried in the back pages of newspapers. We experience the social relations that mediate class exploitation and gender and race oppression as normal and natural. We do not notice how the patterned behaviors we engage in daily, either as individuals or as affiliates of institutions, exploit, silence, disable, or marginalize some as they confer status, profits, and other benefits on elites.

My task in this book is to analyze the class, race, and sex/gender systems and to challenge our customary assumptions about them. I will argue that the identities and roles reproduced at various institutional sites, such as families, labor markets, and the media, often reinforce one another and maintain a class-stratified, white supremacist, heterosexist, and male-dominant society. Analysis of institutional sites of human interaction that mediate class, race, and sex/gender power is for a distinctive purpose: to encourage alternative ways of acting and the *creation of new social systems* where power is more equitably shared.

Groups that are disadvantaged by the class, race, and sex/gender systems, called "subordinates" in this study, are usually aware, at least to some degree, of how institutions work to disempower them and how they carry a disproportionate share of the burdens in the society. It also remains true that, although power may be disproportionately waged by a few groups, elites never monopolize it totally. While they wield massive institutional and ideological control of subordinates, as our investigation will uncover, the most privileged groups also depend on the cooperation of subordinates, including those like ourselves who enjoy some dimensions of elite status, to maintain the status quo. Since every dependency is in reality an interdependency, the better we understand the way class, race, and sex/gender systems work, the more we see where dominants are vulnerable and where subordinates have at least some power under some conditions.[12] Some subordinates are aware of this and exercise their power to resist their subordination. As we shall see, the work of solidarity is extremely important, since the costs to subordinates when they claim their own power are inversely proportionate to the numbers who engage in resistance.

My focus in this book, however, is not on subordinate groups but on those who enjoy relatively more amounts of social privilege than they suffer subordination. As I have noted, most people in privileged groups have little notion that systems mediating disproportionate advantage to them even exist. Since class, race, and sex/gender systems make unearned advantages for dominants and unearned disadvantages for subordinates seem normal and natural, they are "commonsense" to elites.

Thus, I am not concerned with what dominants *intend,* for many people privileged to greater or lesser degrees by class, race, and sex/gender have only good intentions and wish harm to no one. Rather, I am concerned with what privileged groups *effect* through their ownership, control, and reproduction of the major institutions in the society.[13] I wish to address people like myself, who occupy dominant positions in at least some of the three systems examined here. How various institutions reproduce our class, race, and/or sex/gender privilege becomes visible to us only when we work to analyze them. Demonstrating the connection between unearned privilege and unearned disadvantage is essential if we are to understand more realistically our responsibilities as Christian moral agents.

Why the Privileged Should Dismantle Privilege

As a Christian ethicist, I am concerned with the institutional dynamics that reproduce systems of privilege for the few, not only because these systems are unjust for subordinate groups but also because they promote cultural values and social relations that damage everyone. Class, race, and sex/gender systems enable those values to achieve normative status in the society that serve only the vested interests of the few while they limit everyone's choices and impoverish the quality of all relationships. Such "values" include the work ethic of discipline, overwork, and managerial control over increasing sectors of labor. They include the sex/gender pseudovalues of entitlement for men and self-sacrifice for women, and a highly regulated marriage ethic for everyone. These values also include an ethic for white normative status that reinforces dominant class and sex/gender values by requiring obsessiveness about work and restrictions on mutual emotional and sexual expression even for elites.

Obsessiveness about work, managerial control over work, and restrictions on friendship, intimacy, and community violate nonnegotiable aspects of human beings that I believe social systems must honor. As discussed below, these aspects or characteristics are grounded in our fundamentally communal nature. They include the need for self-awareness, affection, respect, sexual fulfillment, and self-management over one's activities, especially one's work.[14] When social systems reproduce ignorance about the connections between self and others, when they isolate people from one another and destroy community, when they stigmatize erotic desire and restrict friendship and intimacy, and when they intensify managerial control over work, they are harmful to everyone. This applies also to elites even when such systems bring unearned advantages to them.

In addition, the class, race, and sex/gender systems, as well as the values that sustain them, are dimensions of ecological domination that jeopardize everyone's survival and well-being. As class, race, and sex/gender are social constructions made by the powerful to condone the unjust treatment of "inferior" categories of human beings, so the nonhuman world is identified with inferior groups and is subject to injustice. The relations of elites to less-powerful human groups are also reflected in their relations to the biosphere, which is plundered, exploited, raped, and regulated like those in subordinate classes, races, and genders.

Consequently, while we might be tempted to think that only those routinely disadvantaged by class, race, and sex/gender structures would wish to change them, I argue that *everyone should want to change them* because these systems, and the values and social relations they promote, harm even the privileged. We need to investigate not only how class, race, and the sex/gender systems confer undeserved privilege on elites, but also how they confer pseudovalues, impoverished social relations, limited consciousness, and ecological destruction that diminish elites. Therefore, a Christian ethic worthy of the name must investigate how dominant behavior patterns and cultural values deeply distort and impoverish all relationships, even those of the privileged. Political theorist Michael Parenti says, "The power of the system operates even over those who are its more powerful participants."[15] The system imposes its necessities even over the needs of individual elites.

Yet privileged groups are largely uninterested in analyzing these structures, perhaps because they mistakenly believe they have only their privileges to lose. When elites analyze systems, as in liberal political theory or neo-classical economic theory, their point of view typically justifies the status quo. Because I am interested in showing how elites are also damaged, I wish to analyze social systems from a critical rather than a self-justifying point of view. Therefore, I am grateful to the analyses developed by subordinate groups and their allies whose perspective is informed by an alternative consciousness. They do not benefit from class, race, and sex/gender dominance but must bear unjust social burdens as a result of them.

Privileged people need to become familiar with critical social analysis because it increases self-awareness and offers a moral assessment of social relations. People are like soft putty, shaped by the repeated impact of persons, events, systems, and institutions. Critical social analysis helps us discern how we are constructed as persons through patterned and very ordinary relations of domination and subordination. We can gain some control over the persons we wish to become only if we use social analysis to make a moral evaluation of how unshared power is continually misshaping us and our relations with others. Understanding the workings of class, race, and sex/gender systems is basic to an ethical life because these systems, and the institutional interactions that reproduce them, deeply condition the morality of our lives-in-relation.

In sum, ethical analysis should help us in the project of discerning unjust power arrangements in our relationships with persons, creatures, and the planet itself. This is a first step in a longer process of struggle to change these arrangements. Analysis should also help us understand how unshared power damages us all, including the moral damage suffered by those who seek to monopolize power. Even though groups are harmed in significantly different ways, everyone is profoundly damaged by these fundamental social systems that limit our choices, treat people unfairly, destroy community, and impoverish most aspects of our lives. In addition, we need to discern how class, race, and sex/gender interactions condition us to accept the massive exploitation and destruction of the earth and the environment. Basic cultural literacy, including our self-understanding as socially constructed persons and our ability to morally evaluate social relations, is at stake in this work, for elites as well as nonelites.

The Moral Ambiguity of Being Elite

Systems of privilege and the values they promote damage the privileged themselves, so much so that elites suffer a moral pathology. At the same time, the moral responsibility of most elites is complex and ambiguous. For one reason, most elites occupy locations of dominance and subordination simultaneously. Insofar as we belong to one or more subordinate groups in the class, race, and sex/gender systems, we may be tempted to deny our role as dominants in reproducing economic exploitation and political and cultural oppression for others. For example, we may have compassion for people of color, white women, or gays and lesbians, but lack awareness of our participation in exploitation, oppression, and self-righteousness as affluent people, whites, or males.

Insofar as we occupy multiple social locations, the lack of power and freedom we experience from our membership in subordinate groups may blind us to the power we have as members of dominant groups. Our moral situation is complex. We must acknowledge both our pain and our privilege, both how we are constrained and where we have power, if we are to attain responsible moral agency.

Our moral responsibility as elites is further complicated by our relatively sheltered lives. In order to maintain benefits not accessible to others, we value innocence in the forms of ignorance, arrogance, and isolation. We live largely within class- and race-segregated environments in which it is easy to assume that the advantages and resources at our disposal are accessible to others. Ignorance, arrogance, and isolation protect our unearned benefits while keeping us in conformity to the status quo.

However, ignorance, arrogance, and isolation as ways of being in the world also violate the fundamental characteristic of who we are as human beings — selves-in-relation. The ambiguous dimensions of our moral situation become apparent as we become aware of how the roles we play and the values we live by are shaped by systems that, because they isolate us, deeply impoverish the quality of our social relations with people, earth creatures, and the ecosphere.

As the political economy polarizes society even further, and especially since the beginning of the economic emergency in 2007, privileged groups are experiencing erosion in privileges and status. The moral ambiguity of our situation is revealed when we see that some of this erosion includes loss not only of unfair advantage but also of entitlements, such as decent work, nutritious food, and adequate health care that a just society should make available to all. In addition, when our whiteness or maleness no longer protects us from the harshest fallout of the status quo, and we do not understand the dynamics of our social system, we are ready to believe that conventional scapegoats are the cause of our problems. Fiercely waged by the religious and political Right, scapegoating has intensified in recent decades as it becomes even more necessary to divide dominant groups from the subordinated groups whose ranks we may soon be joining.

Investigating moral pathology and the ambiguity of our moral situation is a difficult task because what most of us know about ourselves and the world has been largely shaped by people who have vested interests in preserving the status quo. Such knowledge is developed by people in the privileged class, race, and sex/gender groups who have power in the institutions that shape cultural practice. Italian Marxist Antonio Gramsci defined "hegemonic knowledge" as knowledge developed by dominant groups in the society to further their own monopolization of power.[16] It is often the only knowledge available to people because it supports conformity to the status quo. This knowledge is transmitted through families, schools, churches, businesses, the media, government, and the medical and legal professions. Dominant groups with power in these institutions create discourses, including the myths, symbols, language patterns, and knowledge through which we understand ourselves as "properly" — that is, hierarchically — classed, raced, and gendered persons. They also shape cultural practice, such as the work ethic and sexual behavior, further regulating fundamental aspects of our lives.

The most powerful are also deeply conditioned by these values and institutions that rarely reveal how power is inequitably shared in the society. Powerful groups shape institutions and cultural values, which in turn shape and misshape them. Consequently, people remain ignorant about precisely how some groups have privileged access to resources at the expense of others. People are also ignorant about how most people, even members of privileged groups, are in danger of losing resources that a just society would make available to all.

People who spend long years exposed to dominant knowledge, values, and behavior patterns believe that the status quo represents the natural order of things. The elites I address here are intensely indoctrinated into the logic of the system since such education provides the resources that elites need for the task of reproducing the society. Another dimension of the complexity of our moral agency is that we often lose power when we challenge unjust systems. Elites maintain their privilege only insofar as they conform to the status quo and make significant contributions to promote it.

What we learn to think about ourselves and others is limited by our unique circumstances of personal biography, by our social location, including our dominant positions in some or most of the class, race, and sex/gender groups, and by our intense exposure to the knowledge created by those who are most powerful in these groups. We are largely unaware that the framework of meaning that informs our consciousness as moral agents has been created by those whose concern is not to enlighten us about how unshared power permeates and impoverishes social relations. As a consequence, many of us suffer ignorance about the way the world is experienced by people in the subordinate positions of the class, race, and sex/gender systems. Their knowledge of the social world is not easily available to us.

Those who seek to monopolize power in class, race, and sex/gender interactions are the minority in the U.S. population. Those who exercise relatively less power in homes, neighborhoods, labor markets, businesses, schools, government, the media, the medical and legal professions, and the churches are the majority. They include working-class/working-poor people; many white women; people of color; gay, lesbian, bisexual, and transgendered people; people with disabilities; children; other creatures; and the ecosystem itself. These groups, which overlap at many points, do not hear or read much that describes the world from their point of view. The perspectives of the economically exploited, politically oppressed, and culturally marginalized majority are certainly largely unknown to the minority in dominant positions.

The ambiguity of our moral agency as privileged people who have little access to subordinate knowledge and suffer relative social isolation is illustrated by an article that appeared in my local newspaper. A front-page story tells of the release of a Canadian drilling company owner after ninety-four days of captivity in Latin America. Norbert Reinhart was held hostage by a Colombian revolutionary group struggling for peasant agrarian reform. Reinhart was owner and chief executive of a company that was subcontracted by a Canadian mining company to search for gold in the Angostura region of Colombia. Reinhart gave himself as a substitute hostage for an employee who had been captured by the Revolutionary Armed Forces of

Colombia. Reinhart, justly hailed as a hero who risked his life for another, made little of his efforts and pointed to the suffering of his family and friends who agonized about his survival and well-being. He said his captivity was simply a moral response to the situation of his employee.[17]

I think most people would agree that Norbert Reinhart is a human being who manifests exemplary courage and compassion. We deeply admire his compassion for his employee and his willingness to do what he believed was just and right, even at enormous personal risk. We also need to notice that although Reinhart was attuned to the well-being of an employee in an extraordinary way, he seemed little attuned to his captors. They were the men, women, and children who were dispossessed of the land upon which his company was mining. He described them as decent folk who allowed him to subsist on rice and beans.

Reinhart feels responsibility to his employee but not to thousands of hungry and homeless families whose ancestors once farmed land now confiscated by foreign businesses. As a drilling company owner, he also does not have critical consciousness of how mining dangerously impacts the ecosphere. Without critical social analysis Reinhart lacks awareness of the relationship between the suffering of human and nonhuman nature and the lucrative profits made by his company. Without analysis of class and race, without knowledge of how these systems are embedded in the historical processes of colonialism, neocolonialism, current neoliberal economic policy, and ecological destruction, justice-oriented people like Norbert Reinhart are not tuned in to or responsive to injustices.

It is easy for people in dominant positions to remain ignorant about how systems work to advantage a privileged few and deeply disadvantage the majority. This ignorance directly feeds arrogance when we assume that the world works for others the way it works for us. People with an arrogant sense of entitlement, built on ignorance of how their entitlement comes at the expense of others, suffer a moral pathology in need of relief and repair.

Elites living in ignorance, arrogance, and relative isolation from other groups are also deprived of friendship and community with people, other creatures, and the earth. Reinhart's relatively superficial encounter with the men, women, and children who were his captors shows the normalcy of using others for our purposes or dismissing them as irrelevant to our lives. Knowledge created by dominant groups and promulgated by such institutions as schools, churches, government, and the media anesthetizes our minds and hearts by keeping us from interrogating the structures that mediate our privilege and understanding how privilege is connected to other people's suffering. We become further isolated when others see us as moral pygmies because, in order to deny that we are engaging in preferential treatment, we resist fundamental questions of politics and ethics.

Avoidance of responsible moral agency is easy for elites who occupy ambiguous locations of both privilege and subordination, live relatively isolated lives that support ignorance and arrogance, are overexposed to education that naturalizes the status quo, and risk losing privileges when we challenge business as usual. That is the bad news. The good news is that our potential for moral agency is enhanced when we explore how systems of privilege hurt others and distort the minds and hearts of the privileged. What is adversely affected is not only our knowledge of the world, but also our fundamental humanity as communal beings created to live in interdependence with others and in accountability to them.

Social Theory and Christian Ethics

Christian vocation has fundamentally to do with making justice in the world. However, to act justly in the world, we need to know how the world works. We need a better grasp of the interlocking structure of class, race, and sex/gender systems. We need to know how these systems mediate social interactions. Only then can we evaluate them in light of Christian principles of justice and solidarity. Only then will we be in a position to form alliances with others and address unshared power arrangements and social injustice.

Christian ethicist Beverly Harrison writes that all theological ethics have to do with questions of power.[18] Power is good when democratically shared in the service of the commonweal. Democratically shared power promotes critical self-awareness, self-management, and responsible interdependence. Democratically shared power promotes justice and the flourishing of the whole creation. Power is unjust when elite groups define economic interests, cultural values, and patterns of social behavior that are imposed on others to the benefit of elites and the destruction of the natural world.

Ethics has to do with the moral evaluation of social relations as they are mediated in and through systems that reproduce unshared power. Ethics needs critical social theory that challenges rather than justifies present arrangements. Critical social theory "names and maps out the general organization of social relations" so that people can better understand their relationship to unshared economic, cultural, and political power.[19]

Critical social theory helps us explain the systems that structure our personal and collective experience. It helps us analyze class, race, gender, sexuality, and ecological dynamics that mediate unshared power and define our social reality. These systems, often invisible to those who benefit from them, put powerful constraints on the majority of people in this society who are socially constructed as subordinates and restricted in their ability to live dignified human lives. These systems are intimately interconnected and mutually shape and reshape one another. They are interlocking and they reinforce one another even as they sometimes work in contradiction.

As the following chapters will make evident, it is difficult to analyze one without looking at the others.

Some social theories, such as liberal political theory and neoclassical economic theory, support these systems. They "innocently" maintain that current economic, political, and cultural arrangements are inevitable. Other theories, including those drawn upon in this book such as feminism, neo-Marxist economic theory, and anti-racist analyses, are critical of current social arrangements. They seek to demystify how human constructs such as the class, race, and sex/gender systems function so that we can intervene and resist reproducing injustices in our lives. Representing the world from the point of view of subordinate groups, critical forms of social theory help us in the struggle to discern what we need to do to become makers of justice. They help us to critically evaluate our social location so that we, the privileged, can begin to see how we are related to less privileged as well as unprivileged others.[20]

These social theories challenge our social world so that we can act together to reshape it in a way better suited to Christian visions of justice, shared power, and the universal purpose of the earth and its resources. For example, these theories help us see that other people are not simply extensions of ourselves with the same goals and opportunities. Rather, systems of unearned advantage and exclusion separate us into groups with unequal levels of assets (in society's terms) due to our unequal levels of social power. Critical analysis of these systems helps us see how privilege and oppression do not simply coexist side by side. Rather, the suffering and unearned disadvantages of subordinate groups are *the foundation* for the privileges of dominant groups. The social theories I draw upon help us see that social relations we often take for granted, such as a disproportionate number of people of color in menial jobs and women in charge of housework, are really abusive relations. These commonsense relations involve unshared power, the disproportionate carrying of society's burdens by some groups, and the monopolization of benefits, such as free maid service and more enjoyable, better paid work, by dominant groups.

Social theories that foster this ethical work represent the standpoints of persons excluded from unearned advantage. They often see what is going on in our social systems better than we, the privileged, could ever do by ourselves alone. To study unearned advantage is to stand outside dominant thought patterns and to know something we could not have known without the tools of the outsider's point of view. These interpretations are important, not because they are the only ones, but because they yield alternative perspectives about dominant groups and how social systems work on our behalf. These theories show how the social world is experienced by the majority of people in the world, those who are poor, female, and people of color.

My debt is to the subordinated groups and their allies who have produced such critical social theory and whose knowledge is usually marginalized from mainstream theory, education, and much Christian ethics. My purpose is to explore what we need to know to be moral agents, to gain a perspective on the social relations of advanced white supremacist, male-dominant capitalism, and to become allies with subordinates in strategizing meaningful change.

The Autonomous Self and Invisible Group Power

Why is unshared power taken for granted in our society? One reason that inequality in class, race, and sex/gender power remains invisible is that dominant groups have shaped a cultural ideology, or worldview, based on liberal political theory.

When liberalism analyzes the social world, it focuses on individuals, not social groups. For example, liberal social theory views people who are poor and people who are wealthy as individuals whose different situations are primarily determined by their personal choices and abilities or the effects of random good or bad luck. Affluent and poor groups are not viewed as connected by a common political economy. People in the class system are seen as only accidentally grouped together because of individual choices or unique circumstances. Unlike critical social theory, liberal theory does not acknowledge *social power,* the power people exercise (or do not exercise) as a result of their group memberships. Nor does it acknowledge a structural relationship between those who enjoy economic, political, and cultural privilege because they are male or white, or have relative economic security, and those who do not.

Liberalism's devotion to the so-called autonomous individual has been dominant in the West since the Enlightenment period of the eighteenth century. In part a response to the constrictions of hierarchical feudal social relations and mean-spirited communal traditions, the myth of individualism inaugurated other kinds of oppressive structures and practices. Emancipation from the control of popes and kings was achieved at the expense of treating others in objective and instrumental terms. It gave dominant groups, especially the new emerging merchant class, the freedom to economically exploit, politically oppress, and culturally marginalize nondominant groups.

In the United States, subordinate groups such as indigenous peoples, African slaves, and "white savages" or "black" immigrants were "civilized" by being wrenched from their communal settings and turned into an isolated and easily controlled workforce for the business class. At the same time, the white affluent male whose group monopolized social power was divorced from a communal setting as well. His group created what psychologist Philip

Cushman calls a "masterful, bounded, empty self," an identity that was primarily understood in terms of what it was not. The "masterful, bounded, empty self" was *not* the properly subordinated and objectified "other" who was poor, or female, or of color.[21]

Liberal theory has taught dominants that their value lies precisely in not being like others, the actual majority in the world. Subordinate others, on whom dominants depend for labor, entertainment, sexual, and other social services, are thought to need privileged groups to control their lives. Elites consider this arrangement beneficial to both groups. The empty selves of privileged groups, devoid of friendship and community, are then filled up with the services and material goods of consumer society.

Liberal theory ignores the imbalances of power between dominant and subordinate groups as it focuses on individuals who enjoy democracy in the voting booth. It is true that the long, slow move out of the feudal world of the sixteenth century into the modern period of the Enlightenment promoted formal political equality for some. This is seen in the eighteenth-century rallying cries of the French Revolution, which promoted "liberty, equality, and fraternity," and the American Revolution's support for liberty and justice for all. However, even though the liberal theory that backed these revolutions was critical of monarchy, feudalism, and a hierarchical view of self and society in the political sphere, modern "democratic" societies rest on a vast network of unacknowledged invisible hierarchies built on the backs of subordinated others.

As I will show in the succeeding chapters, the autonomous public "I" of liberal theory who supposedly enjoys democracy in the political sphere is also a person who occupies the dominant position in the class, race, and sex/gender systems. As political theorist David Harvey says, what is rational for liberal social theory is what is male, white, and economically secure.[22] Ethicist Elizabeth Bounds citing Jon Gunnemann and others observes that when we consider how society actually works, privileged groups are hardly autonomous since they are buttressed by an invisible foundation of subordinated "others."[23] These subordinates do the work in so-called private homes and private industries to materially sustain and maintain the public status, lifestyles, and profits of the dominant groups.

People who enjoy economic affluence, especially those who are white, heterosexual, able-bodied, and male, are supported by whole armies of subordinate groups in so-called private homes and workplaces. These groups in the lower sectors of the working class include disproportionate numbers of people of color and white women who build, clean, and service their houses, offices, and vacation spots. These subordinate others make and clean the clothes of the dominant groups; pick, package, and cook their food; clean up their messes; take care of their children; service their cars, planes, appliances, hospitals, and schools; and collect and process their garbage.

Through a regressive tax structure, subordinate groups maintain a disproportionate share of the social infrastructure that sustains us all. If they are not unemployed to keep the general wage level down, these subordinate groups often work at little or no pay with inadequate benefits in order to maintain the political economy within which elites work, play, and accumulate profits. Those in privileged positions in the class, race, and gender systems, however, are taught that their hard work maintains the economy and provides jobs and the good life for everyone else. Because elites have more status and more of the good life than others, they believe this is justly and richly deserved due to their own merits.

In the liberal view of political economy, the home and the business world are thought to comprise the private sector so that domestic and industrial structures are not subject to democratic notions of accountability and shared power supposedly at work in the political sphere. This private sector work includes the unpaid reproductive and domestic labor of women in the family and the exploited low-wage labor of subordinate classes, races, and genders in the workplace. It is no wonder that ethicist Jon Gunnemann observes that the autonomous dominant individual of liberal social theory is in reality a parasite.[24]

When privileged groups are inculturated into the ideology of liberal individualism and meritocracy, we are socialized not to see the people whose work maintains our lifestyles or grasp the economic system that gives us access to better jobs and, for a few, stock market profits. Rather, we consider that our work and its opportunity for leisure primarily sustain society. Both before and after the Enlightenment period, traditional ethical discourse has made it seem normal and natural that privileged groups take care of their own needs first so that the rest of society will prosper. This is reflected in the medieval church's view that wealth and social hierarchy are ordained by God for the right ordering of society and the promotion of the commonweal. This is certainly the basis for the acceptance of liberalism in modern Christian ethics, including the legitimation, however qualified, by official Christian bodies of the pursuit of private profit and self-enrichment through the capitalist market.[25] This principle of self-interest is the central concern of liberal economic theory, political democracy, and the philosophy of individual rights.[26]

In the social and economic worlds, liberal theory's view of self and society functions to separate "I" and "others" by the process of objectification. People in dominant groups objectify others, that is, deny them their capacities for self-determination and their rights to shared power in the society. Elites do this in part because they fear losing their dominant position. Because elites are taught by liberal social theory that they are separate individuals and radically disconnected from others, they fear that others will not be responsive to them. So they use coercive power to make sure their needs will be met.[27] Coercive power is necessary when autonomy and scarcity and competition, not reciprocity, interdependence, and accountability, are understood to be our fundamental social reality. These notions and practices, which separate us from others and make us feel that we cannot depend on them, breed insecurity and feelings of vulnerability, and insecure people seek to manage and control every aspect of life.

This brings us full circle to the reality that people manage and control others through systems of domination and subordination, especially those of class, race, gender, and sexuality. Subordinates are not viewed as the unique subjects that elites believe they themselves are. Instead, people who are subordinated become objects of imposed definitions so they can meet the needs of insecure elites. These definitions separate others into groups by socially constructed differences, such as class, race, and gender. These socially constructed different identities are often, although not always, tied to physical characteristics, such as skin pigment or reproductive systems, or forms of personal presentation, such as speech or dress. Constructions of class, race, and gender distinguish subordinate groups from dominant groups in order to justify their unequal access to cultural, political, and economic power and their becoming means to the ends of privileged groups.

This "othering" has enormous significance for how we understand our relationships to one another and what is required of ethical persons. Traditional Christian ethics has often assumed that this radical disjuncture between myself and others means that egoism (self-interest) and altruism (other-interest) are opposed. The opposition between egoism and altruism assumes a fundamental disconnection between myself and the social world of others, including human beings, animals, and the biosphere. Either I am focused on myself, *or* I am focused on the other. If I am focused on the other, then I experience doing this at the expense of myself. In addition, when I think of others as radically different from me or separate from me or opposed to me, I can justify their subordination and my privilege. I can also justify my need at times to be altruistic toward others who sometimes need my "help" and are deserving of my self-sacrifice, but never warrant a mutual or reciprocal relationship with me. However, is the self-other split, along with the human-natural world split, an accurate representation of reality?

The Self as a Self-in-Relation

An alternative to liberalism's autonomous and separate "I" is a view of the self as fundamentally in-relation-to-others. We are what we have been able to do (some of us laboring under far more constraints than others) with the cultural ideology, personal relationships, and material structures of our historically specific selves. We are constantly interacting with and mutually reshaping one another, other earth creatures, and the ecosystem itself. What is in the food we eat and the water we drink and the air we breathe is also in us.

In this view there is no radically distinct *ego* whose opposite is *alter.* This view is indebted to social theories that challenge the individualism of liberal social theory. The notion of a fundamentally relational self comes from an analysis rooted in the point of view of those who are located in the subordinate positions of the class, race, sex/gender, and ecological systems. The goal of these theories is to make visible the unacknowledged relations between social groups and between people, other creatures, and the earth. They articulate the perspectives of women of all races, men of color, working-class/working-poor people, and endangered natural systems that are often very clear about the myriad ways that dominant men, whites, and affluent sectors depend on them! An analysis of the privileged individual who is sustained by the invisible labor and resources of others can be unearthed by these social theories. They ground a worldview insisting that there is no autonomous I, that every I exists fundamentally as a self-in-relation.[28]

According to this alternative moral vision, I am radically dependent on all the persons, creatures, and the earth itself who have contributed to my very existence and my continual sustenance in this world. I am a fundamentally social species-being. Who I am is what I have made out of all the social and ecological relations that have impacted me both before and after my birth.[29] The list is endless, but it includes the social relations that have attended to my physical and emotional/spiritual needs and have shaped my political consciousness. It includes my caregivers and all the people, social forces, and material environments impacting them and making it easier, or more difficult, for them to care for me. Since my well-being (or lack thereof) from even before birth is intimately connected to all these humans, creatures, and the earth, what helps them flourish is also good for me. But interdependence goes farther than this. Not only is our well-being dependent on everyone else's, but we mutually define and redefine one another in unending relational process. Ethicist Elizabeth Bettenhausen observes, "Because of Holy creativity, all that constitutes the Earth is interdependent — from the wood tick to the blue whale, from the virus to the mountain. . . . As social creatures we are not only wholly dependent on the entire planet, but are also always creating and maintaining each other." Human and nonhuman nature are in constant interaction, mutually shaping and reshaping each other. "Security on this earth," says Bettenhausen, "is a function of this interdependence."[30]

This radically relational view of self is the one I assume in this book. This view is indebted to feminist theorists who have long been critical of abstract individualism and who in various ways richly analyze the self-in-community. In her review of selected feminist theories, philosopher Kristin

Waters notes that Patricia Hill Collins sees healthy autonomy as radically dependent upon interconnections. While feminists have called for a woman's right to control what happens to her physical and emotional self, this is always viewed within a context of responsible interdependency. In a view that is in harmony with other feminist approaches, Collins regards an individualistic notion of autonomy not only as inadequate, but as social pathology.[31] This social pathology is rooted in the dangerous notion that we are fundamentally disconnected from others and must coerce them to get what we need.

The view of the self as fundamentally relational also converges with many ancient teachings of this planet's people, including strains of Taoism, Hinduism, and Buddhism; the mystical teachings of Judaism, Christianity, and Islam; and the worldviews of many indigenous peoples.[32] The notion of a distinct and separate "I" is not ethically sound because it conceals the process by which we stand in *radical interdependence and mutual re-creation* within an enormous intricate web of social and environmental supports. Since this web is responsible for and necessary to our survival and flourishing, we must be accountable to it.

Since I as a self-in-relation am in some real sense also a "we," ethical relationship, including the security of all, requires that all social groups share cultural, political, and economic power. In this social theory or worldview, solidarity, not altruism, describes the valued moral standpoint since no opposition exists between "I" and the "others," between my self-interest and the commonweal.[33] Given the radical interdependence that is the foundation of our lives and well-being, when I work for the common good, I also work for my own interests. Conversely, without a viable common good, I am in jeopardy. When the air is polluted, when we cannot insure the safety of the global food supply, when there is no tax base to sustain a literate population and a rich culture, when economic restructuring devastates formerly upper-income families, everyone, even privileged groups, suffer.[34] Similarly, when my welfare or the welfare of any other group is at risk, the commonweal suffers since all groups interact to reshape the whole.

Further, if solidarity is a natural capacity of our radically interdependent nature, solidarity is not something we decide to create so much as it is something we learn to *extend*.[35] Social transformation, then, is not a utopian ideal but a viable and necessary moral project. This very project of creating structures to serve the commonweal is not something we need to have imposed from without, but something that emanates from who we are as social beings, radically interdependent on one another and the earth. Moral understanding is learning to uncover and feel bound by the just demands that proceed from our inherently relational nature.

Moral and Political Tasks

The political task at hand, one that is essential to create a moral and secure society, is to fashion a social world that "amplifies benefits and diminishes burdens."[36] It is to fashion a society that can not only feed the hungry, clothe the naked, shelter the homeless, and provide reasonable life chances for everyone, but can also bring community to the lonely, provide meaningful work and play, nurture human creativity, and sustain diverse forms of species life, both in the human community and in the ecosystem.

Many cringe when they hear such a list. Such goals may strike us as naive, if not totally impossible. Because we have been thoroughly indoctrinated with the liberal myth of the autonomous individual competing in the midst of scarcity, we believe that there is not enough — not enough jobs, money, education, health care, or love — to go around.[37] The analysis contained in this book holds, however, that the only scarce thing is natural resources (which we are told will never run out!). The moral question is, in fact, a political one: How do we transform the structures that mediate our economic, political, and cultural relations so that these goals, grounded in our species-nature, can be better accomplished?

We begin by uncovering and addressing the dynamics of unearned advantage and oppression that are all-pervasive in our society. What must be made visible is how elites stand upon the shoulders of large sectors of subordinated others in the so-called private spheres of home and work. Deepening awareness of our social location is vital in the struggle of privileged people to become ethical. However, since it is also true that we usually lose at least some privileges whenever we resist the status quo, social commitments even more than social geography determine who we are. Evaluating how we participate in elite status and what we need to do about it is important work, morally and politically.[38]

Taking responsibility for privilege, letting our social commitments rather than our social geography determine our identity, involves becoming newly accountable to others as we become aware that we are not isolated individuals but selves-in-relation. Exploring systems of monopolized class, race, and gender power helps us to analyze our experiences in relation to pervasive social patterns and systems. According to educator Suzanne Pharr, our personal experiences contain political truth, but we do not comprehend their meaning without the critical information necessary to discern linkages.[39] As we examine the dynamics of systems of class, race, sex/gender, and ecological destruction, we can better discern the specific claims that others may have on us. Discerning our social location within a web of economic, political, and cultural systems is essential to evaluating our responsibility to others.[40] It is only at this point that we can start to frame, with others, an ethics of accountability.

Privilege and Christian Ethics

Since the fourth century C.E., the meaning of Christianity has been largely determined by Scripture scholars, theologians, and ethicists from the dominant social groups in the West. Therefore, creating a moral agenda through an examination of privilege has not been a Christian priority. However, since the mid-twentieth century, Christianity's center of gravity has been shifting from the First World to the Two-Thirds World (large sectors of Latin America, Asia, Africa, and growing poor sectors in the First World), not only demographically but also theologically.[41] Since the meaning of Christianity is determined through a dialogue between believers and the historical tradition, and since believers bring to the dialogue concerns from their own social location, subordinated groups are bringing concerns to the dialogue about the meaning of Jesus, Christianity, and ethics that privileged groups have not had. As is true of other forms of cultural perception, those who suffer from poverty, racism, male dominance, and other forms of subordination see things in Scripture and tradition that those who enjoy privilege often miss. For example, liberation theologians with roots in the Two-Thirds World have claimed that salvation in Jesus includes material liberation and freedom from this-worldly oppression as well as spiritual redemption.[42]

As scholars from the overconsuming First World learn from the underconsuming Two-Thirds World, and as new methods of interdisciplinary study help Scripture scholars understand the social world that gave birth to Christianity, emerging work in North America also supports this focus on the material world as a site of redemption. Oppressed Christians in the Two-Thirds World, often working out of movements for their own liberation, and new work by North American scholars on the dynamics of Christian origins are transforming our understanding of Jesus and the movement that became Christianity.

Traditional views of Jesus incorporate notions that he only appeared to be human and was unconcerned with politics and the social world. For many believers influenced by Western dualistic thought, Jesus has been a God who "came down to earth" to ransom individual souls through a historical act of self-sacrificial love. The altruistic ransom that Jesus accomplished is perpetually dispensed to Christians through the sacraments of the church. This view of Jesus did not necessarily challenge the entitlement of the privileged and the suffering of the subordinated because the material world was viewed primarily as a waiting room for the next, and whatever wrongs were experienced here would be corrected in the spiritual world — after death.

Jesus is now understood by an increasing number of Scripture scholars in North America as a radical social critic and a teacher of subversive wisdom.[43] Like many of his fellow Jews who emerged out of the richness of first-century Palestinian Judaism, he challenged a highly stratified society.

Jesus, like many Jewish reformers of his day, challenged a society deeply divided between urban elites and the exploited peasantry, polarized by gender and patriarchal family values, and regulated by religious purity laws that legitimated and enforced all the social hierarchies.[44]

This more recently developed view understands that Jesus was crucified because he was passionately involved in the struggle to transform the unjust social world of his day. Therefore, the Jesus movement was a fundamental threat to the status quo. It was not a *political* revolution but a far more radical *social* revolution, a change from the bottom up.[45] Drawn from all sectors of society, the Jesus movement not only preached a new vision. It also lived a confrontational lifestyle, including having open table fellowship with outcasts, touching and healing outsiders, calling religious and political leaders to task, and treating women and slaves as equals. More than annoyances to dominant groups, these behaviors and practices were in fundamental opposition to the religious, cultural, political, and economic hierarchies of the time.[46] They challenged the very foundations of the social order.

Emphasizing the humanity of Jesus, many Scripture scholars and theologians today view him not as an isolated hero, but as one who rode the crest of a wave of renewal in first-century Judaism. Jesus was thoroughly Jewish, and Christians misread him if they do not understand his deep embrace of the Exodus, Jubilee, and prophetic traditions of Hebrew religion. As one shaped by the traditions of his ancestors, Jesus modeled courage in the face of social injustice and invited his followers to live as he did.

The implication for Christians is that we ought not to honor respectable hierarchies. The Jesus movement required that people live unconventionally, as though God's reign of radical equality and mutuality had already begun on earth as it is in heaven. Like the prophets of Israel before it, the Jesus movement denounced ideologies and systems that justified and blessed unshared power. It refused to sanction the privilege of dominant political, economic, and religious groups held at the direct expense of others.

In contrast to an older view that Jesus is the exception to the human condition, alternative perspectives understand Jesus as the blueprint for understanding who God is and for understanding who we are.[47] If we wish to better understand what it means to be Christian, we need to look at this outrageous convention-flaunting Jesus movement comprised of folks from both dominant and subordinate groups. People took responsibility for their own power, whether or not it was affirmed in the public sphere. They lived and died in the struggle for the flourishing of all.

As Elisabeth Schüssler Fiorenza writes, in the process of building a discipleship of equals where there were no excluded ones, the early Christians experienced an extraordinary quality of life for themselves. In their struggle to break down social barriers between persons and groups and create an alternative community, the fullness of God's life was "already experientially available" to them as they were engaged in a this-worldly transformation of social life.[48] Whether rich or poor, slave or free, male or female, Jew or Gentile, they refused to honor conventional social boundaries. They believed that an injury to one was an injury to all and that their concrete commitments in this world, not finally their social location, determined who they were as Christians. The Jesus movement not only critiqued the status quo; it trusted sufficiently in the possibilities of human community that it actually began to embody it.

As contemporary Christians develop a power analysis in order to connect religious norms to a course of ethical practice, we have Scripture as a resource for these norms, and we also have church tradition. One stream in church tradition is modern Catholic social teaching, which includes the documents of bishops and popes that have been periodically issued since the late nineteenth century and address issues of justice, especially economic justice.

Even though some of the social analysis and most of the social policies identified by Catholic social teaching are in harmony with the goals of capitalist liberal society, it is also clear from other strands of analysis and policy prescriptions that this tradition offers a fundamental challenge to economic business as usual. For example, Catholic social teaching has identified values that point to the need for structural change. These include the need for all persons to participate in their society with dignity, the need for democratic values in the economic sphere, the priority of laboring people over the wealth they produce, and the preferential option for a resisting poor who struggle to create new, more just cultural, political, and economic structures.[49] At these points, Catholic social teaching is at home with the ethical sensibilities at the center of Christian origins. This is especially evident in the 1971 document of the World Synod of Catholic Bishops, *Justice in the World*. The bishops challenge "networks of domination" and claim that action on behalf of earthly liberation is at the very heart of the gospel.[50]

Why Christianity Has Avoided Examining Privilege

Despite the above-mentioned resources, Christian ethics, like all symbol systems in the political economy, has been rooted in the material systems of class, race, gender, and sexuality that reproduce inequality. To achieve widespread support, much Christian ethics, like Christianity itself, has not always been faithful to liberation perspectives in its origins or to radical critiques in the subsequent development of its tradition. To be consistent with wider social values, traditional Christian theology and ethics adopted the dualism and hierarchy of the Western philosophical worldview. This worldview predates Enlightenment liberal theory and continues to permeate the cultural values, if not the narrowly political values, of post-Enlightenment societies.

As noted earlier, some strains of Christian theology and ethics have been critical of liberal democratic theory, especially with regard to the unregulated capitalist market.[51] But the majority of Christian teaching has been very much in harmony with the unshared power in family and work arrangements and with the nondemocratic social values that liberal capitalist societies depend upon, but do not acknowledge.

Along with liberal notions of an autonomous self, both philosophical and Christian ethics have supported hierarchies by adopting a metaphysical dualism that conditions people to divide reality into distinct and opposing spheres. One part of the divide is dominant (superior) over the other subordinate (inferior) one. Consequently, Western ethics and the worldview of many people are based on a hierarchical and binary system by which reality is described and values are expressed. Binary opposition is a fundamental process of how Westerners think.

Binary thinking splits the whole person into mind and body and makes the mind dominant. It makes men, whites, Christians, and heterosexuals, for example, dominant over women, people of color, Jews and adherents of other religions, gay people, and the earth itself. These latter are subordinate because, unlike dominants who are identified with the mind and rationality, subordinates are overidentified with their (inferior) bodies, including a deviant sexuality. Binary thinking regards the spiritual realm as dominant over the material earth; it values the eternal as more important than the historical. Binary thinking supports the dominance of church and state authorities over ordinary people, rich people over working-class and poor people, and human beings over other earth creatures and the earth itself. The binary opposites of divine and human have been at the root of doctrinal struggle over who Jesus is. What would it mean for us to consider Jesus (and ourselves) outside binary, hierarchical ways of thinking?

Whenever ethics, including traditional Christian ethics, has been hierarchical and binary, it has operated to support the status quo. For example, Christian ethics has often interpreted Scripture and tradition to affirm the dominant values in the culture. Examples include the consistent theological tradition of ascribing inferiority to people overassociated with their bodies, such as women and Jews. Examples also include the affirmation of slavery by most Christian churches during the centuries of its legalized existence. Still another is the Christian just war theory, which largely operates to affirm the national interests of more powerful states. Ethicist Gloria Albrecht contends that the Christian narrative has always functioned to honor "the master sex, the master race and the master class."[52] We see where this can lead when we look at the Nazi ethic of Aryan supremacy, also rooted in a system of hierarchy and dualism. Deeply indebted to the intellectual history of the West and supported by Christian teaching, Nazism maintained that what is perceived as a threat to the status quo can be justifiably destroyed — primarily Jews but also gays, Gypsies, criminals, and disabled persons.

An Agenda for the Privileged

Not all theology, ethics, and Christian practice have been based on a world-view of binary opposition and hierarchy. As is true in many parts of the world today, there have always been Christians who have joined others in resistance to domination and injustice. Resistance movements demonstrate that those who are subordinates in the cultural, political, and economic spheres are never only victims who suffer domination. They are also people who have enormous creativity and power to resist their subjugation, and they have managed to find resources for their liberatory projects in Christian Scripture and tradition.

Ethics developed from liberatory practice in the social world recognizes that those with monopolized power and privilege are also damaged. The system allows us to be ignorant about subordinates, arrogant in our assumptions about ourselves, and blind to how institutions work on our behalf. We need to explore the impact of internalized oppression on subordinate groups and the impact of *internalized entitlement* on dominants. We need to expose ourselves not only to alternative views about subordinates, but also to new views of ourselves. We need to expose the pathology that comes from enjoying unearned advantage and unshared power at others' expense.

An ethical agenda for people in dominant social locations includes taking responsibility for the beliefs we absorb in an uncritical and unexamined way. These beliefs promote and extend systems of unearned and unshared privilege. An ethical agenda includes taking responsibility for the ways we become (often unwitting) conduits for passing these systems on to others, reproducing and intensifying the monopolization of social power. We need to work hard to break out of our socially constructed identities as class-stratified, male-dominant, white supremacist, and heterosexist people. We need to question our roles in the family, the neighborhood, the church, the workplace, and the political system.[53] The requirements of living an ethical life include being attentive to our particular histories and belief patterns, many of which are explored in the following chapters, that have legitimized our dominant positions and the privileges we receive from them. The moral basis upon which we define ourselves and our relations to one another is the foundation by which we recognize what is just and unjust, what is good and evil.

Taking responsibility for transforming our lives-in-relation requires developing a critical self-consciousness regarding *how power operates in society*. This challenging, difficult work may produce uncertainty and debate by asking us to leave our comfort zones behind and take on the burdens of "uncertainty, dissension, and critical debate."[54] New ways of seeing and acting involve "crossing borders" as we understand the world and self through the eyes of people we have made "other." This work entails exposing ourselves to a variety of interpretations about ourselves and the way the world works.

Why should we struggle to transform systems of class, race, sex/gender, and ecological destruction? I argue that we do this not only to be just toward others and to insure the planet's very survival, but also to become truly human. As the previous discussion of our radical interdependence suggests, our very capacity to achieve our human/godlike potential is conditioned (and limited) by the larger social collective. Political theorist Stanley Deetz says that our moral agency is challenged when we realize that "the collective is the upper limit of what a person can be rather than the lowest common denominator. The capacity and richness of the individual is limited by the collective capacity — not the other way around."[55] We can be only as human — as moral — as the communities from which we come.

We create ourselves through daily social practices received from our society. What kind of selves are being created? What kind of selves do we want to become? What established practices do we want to resist? What new practices need to be imagined, created, and embraced? What kind of people do we want to be, and how do our cultural and religious structures facilitate or frustrate our capabilities of becoming these particular kinds of persons? Isn't this the fundamental moral question: Who will we either willfully or unwittingly become as human beings?

Perhaps most important, we can critically analyze where we have been, what we are now, and who we really want to be only if we have hope for a better way. Hope is perhaps less difficult for subordinates to imagine since they have only their unearned disadvantages to lose. It is more difficult for people in privileged groups since the immediate rewards of unearned advantage from being white or male or heterosexual, or using the earth as a supply house and sewer for economic gain, keep us from seeing our more fundamental moral disfigurement and social peril. We have to work hard to see what others see so easily. To many subordinates, people in dominant positions present themselves as "tiny spirits hiding behind large egos."[56]

When we come to terms with how we are damaged, we can take courage from the fact that, like many in the Jesus movement and in resisting Christian groups throughout history, there have always been people in dominant social locations who have "border crossed." These are people whose moral commitments rather than social geography have defined them. In earlier Christian history, these include renewal movements in monasticism and the Reformation churches. In recent history these include such movements as Christian-based communities, the Catholic Worker and Sanctuary movements, and Christian support of the labor, civil rights, peace, and feminist movements. Throughout the ages, Christians have insisted that social and economic injustice is a distortion of God's creation and have embraced life-enhancing solidarity.[57] The Christian vocation to justice-making requires effective action against systemic, routine injustice and a moral imagination that envisions alternative structures for a better future.

Engaging in critical social analysis, moral imagination, and social action is a challenge for dominants because few of us are encouraged to reflect on the ethical foundations of the society in which we live. However, without structural analysis, ethical evaluation in light of an alternative vision, and collective action, we risk becoming dangerous conduits of injustice. After the Holocaust of World War II, philosopher Hannah Arendt recognized "the banality of evil," that is, that very ordinary people could design and execute monstrous deeds on a daily basis.[58] We are susceptible to moral evil when we fail to analyze the social reproduction of misery and injustice through interlocking class, race, and sex/gender systems that regulate almost every dimension of our lives. Since dominant social institutions and cultural practices do not support us in this analysis of preferential treatment for the few, this book will be hard work for most readers.

The work will be difficult because I ask that we think differently about our world and about our place in it. While dominant culture teaches us to individualize and overpersonalize our relationships, I ask that we think about the *social groups* we belong to and how these groups monopolize the exercise of social power. I ask that we think not only about privilege and social pain, but also about how they are related to each other and what they have to do with us as members of privileged groups.

My goal in this book is to contribute to a process whereby privileged people better understand the social systems that distort and limit our humanity. To call ourselves ethical, we must work in coalition with subordinate others to transform social systems that are detrimental to all. If we are deformed by these systems of privilege and unearned advantage, as I will show, then we can be reformed only by social transformation. This includes being faithful to the liberating vision present in our biblical and church traditions. It includes resistance to these systems collectively as well as in the ordinary daily practices of our personal lives.[59]

However deeply embedded we are in particular social locations of privilege, moral agency first, foremost, and finally depends on the ethical commitments we undertake and the ways we choose to spend our time and material resources. If we come to believe that our humanity is diminished by unfair entitlements, if we believe we have moral obligations to people in other social groups and the earth itself which sustains us, then we can join together with others to resist current social arrangements and to create new ones.

In the chapters ahead I will analyze the race, class, and sex/gender systems with an eye to how they grant routine privileges to elite groups while they also deeply damage elites. As we shall see, the ways class, race, and gender privilege damage elites are legion, but they involve no less than being alienated from ourselves, others, and the natural world. They include being divorced from our own sexuality and playfulness, from our need to deeply trust others, and from our capacities for self-management and creativity. We grow in appreciation for the ongoing personal and moral damage entailed in this state of affairs when privileged people along with others accommodate to such injustice as "the way things are."

In each chapter I will also give account of some resources in the Christian tradition for a moral evaluation of the system in question. In chapter 5 I argue that knowledge about the interlocking structure of class, race, and sex/gender systems is essential but not sufficient for ethical response. For this we need a politics of solidarity that has yet to be created and is our ongoing ethical responsibility. In this chapter I locate support for such a politics in a major discussion of the Christian tradition and the Jesus ethic, as well as in the theoretical work of such ethicists/activists as Janet Jakobsen and Sharon Welch. Chapter 6, the new concluding chapter of this second edition, examines what social change agents in the United States can learn from growing grassroots initiatives for justice in Latin America and South Africa. To ground a politics of solidarity we need both intellectual and political struggle. We need theoretical comprehension of what is at stake for us in the struggle for justice, and we also need to learn viable strategies from others who engage in the transformation of their societies. To this work we now turn.

TWO

Dismantling Whiteness

White people are trapped in a history they do not understand.
— JAMES BALDWIN

FROM THE TIME Ronald Reagan became president in 1980 until the passage of the 1996 welfare legislation that dismantled sixty years of federal entitlements to welfare, the anti-welfare media campaign in this country promulgated ubiquitous images of black women as irresponsibly sexual with poor work habits. Such images showcase the deep linkages between race, sex/gender, and class oppression. These images cohere in public consciousness because they are part of a whole, an *interlocking system* of class, race and gender components that define the parameters of most social life in this political economy. Otherwise said, white supremacy is about money (the class system) and sex (the gender system) as much as it is about any thing else. As we shall see, white racism is largely about class elitism and white erotic disempowerment, including managing white people's impoverishment, the division of labor to benefit some at the expense of others, the division of the working class as a whole, and white people's socialization in the sex/gender system to fear sexuality.[1]

Race Is Grounded In Class

Even though this volume places the discussion of the racial structure before the discussion of class (because some tend to be more familiar with notions of race privilege/oppression than with class dynamics), I wish to argue in this second edition for *the primacy of class* because it is *the material basis of all oppression* in a way I have not previously emphasized. While we must never forget that class, race, and sex/gender systems are interlocking and reinforcing in our political economy, I suggest that we pay attention to the primacy of class as the social location that deeply informs the experiences people have of race and gender. This will prevent the lumping together of "race, class, and sex/gender," often in this order, that is common in academic discourse (including much Christian ethical discourse) as *social descriptors* or markers of identity, meaning the amount of melanin, consumption status, or biological sex/sexual orientation people possess.

In contrast, I use "class, race, and sex/gender," and the order is important, to refer to the dominant and subordinate *power positions* of these systems. When one assumes "race, class, and sex/gender" as different but equal identities, they are assumed as inevitable. Perhaps most importantly the material roots of racial and gender inequality in the class system are rendered invisible, as is the enormous inequality found between classes of white people in the economy. If (theoretically) we could dismantle the race and gender systems apart from the class system, then everyone would have an equal chance of being in the capitalist class *and* in the upper and lower sectors of the working class. In other words, everyone would have an *equal chance* of being impoverished or astronomically wealthy. As Robert Boynton writes, when we treat race, class, and gender "as different but equal identities, we have decided to *manage* inequality rather than reduce, much less eradicate it" (emphasis added).[2] In short, it is dangerous to everyone's economic well-being when race is used to hide the class system.

For purposes of analysis, I believe the first goal of liberation is to reduce and eradicate inequality by transforming the class system. (In practice untangling these systems could not happen because they are interlocking, and liberation must be a *simultaneous transformation* of all the structures within the one interlocking system. I propose this only for the sake of sharpening our thinking.) Ending class exploitation would not necessarily rid society of race and sex/gender and ecological oppressions, but it would get rid of the economic system's need for these structural oppressions (for example, to divide the workforce, to provide scapegoats for low-wage white workers, to segregate jobs and pay nurturing work lower wages, to use the ecosphere as supply house and sewer, and other ways the class system harnesses the race and sex/gender systems to serve its purposes, as discussed below). Theoretically speaking, transforming the class structure would work to level the field so that we can more meaningfully address racism, sexism, homophobia, and ecological crisis.

In addition, when we do not *give the class structure its proper weight,* we encounter great difficulties when we talk about the race and sex/gender systems. For example, ethicist Elizabeth Bounds points out how discussions of racism founder when attempted between lower-income white women and affluent black people.[3]

Similarly discussions of sexism founder between impoverished men of all races and affluent women of color, discussions of heterosexual privilege founder between affluent white families and families of color, and discussions of ecological well-being break down when people's jobs are at stake.

So in order to sharpen our consciousness and communicate that class is the material basis of everyone's oppression, and the class system is always mediating and modifying the experiences of race and sex/gender privilege and oppression, I prefer the order "class, race, and gender." I also put race before gender, because most women in the world are of color and most experience being even more negatively impacted by the racial/ethnic system than by their gender.[4]

But even though we untangle the three systems for purposes of analysis, it is important to remember that the power relations of domination and subordination are components of *one interlocking system.* As a consequence, most historical struggles that have tried to target economic inequality but have not simultaneously addressed patriarchy have not been fully successful in the work of liberation (for example, Cuba and the USSR). In addition, because these systems are ubiquitous, we do not engage in pristine face-to-face individual relationships in most of our daily interchanges. Rather, class, race, and sex/gender domination and subordination, including the historical development of these unjust relations, *always mediate our interactions* with one another. While theory explores experience to help us understand it, no theory is ever completely adequate because no theory can exhaust experience. We need to work for even better theory that unveils how racism and sexism interact systemically with the class structure.

Even though in this and succeeding chapters I focus somewhat separately on each of these major components, I always try to show not only how each component works to reproduce injustice, but also how each component is intimately related to the others, reinforcing them and being reinforced by them, as well as modifying them and changing qualitatively the experience of each of them. In short, each component of the major systems that inform our lives never exists separately but is always distinctively modulated by the others.

The Race System

It is important to recognize the class structure as the material grounding of *all* forms of oppression. It is also equally important *not* to let a focus on class relations marginalize or prevent us from discerning other unjust power relations that more shared class power *will not on its own transform.* This is especially true of the race system.

The race system is a complex web of social institutions that devastates people of color economically, politically, and culturally.[5] The race system, which gives whites dominance over other racialized groups, also restricts whites emotionally and damages us morally. White dominance, or white supremacy, harms people socially constructed as white in ways most whites neither see nor understand. That said, the truth is that whites gain at the expense of communities of color, which is the primary reason for the construction of whiteness and the racial system. Elizabeth Bettenhausen writes that "race is a socially constructed category of power used to create a hierarchy of social relationships that serves the interests of white people."[6]

The effects of white dominance are so pervasive that they can be felt between people of color even when no white people are present, as well as between whites even when no people of color are present. White supremacy includes a color caste system within communities of color and the horizontal violence of people of color because they have internalized this system. White supremacy is at work in whites as emotional reserve and constraint. As we shall see, *whiteness* is achieved at the expense of internalizing the restrictions required by capitalist work discipline and patriarchal heterosexual domesticity. As a result, white racism, the fallout from the trauma of white racialization, is inextricably linked to attitudes and destructive social patterns that are *anti-poor and erotophobic.*

Most whites collude with the harm done to us by white racialization because we profit individually and as a group from the system of white dominance. When whites participate in institutions that promote white supremacy, we become deeply shaped by racism. In this sense, white supremacy is similar to pollution. By participating in white supremacist institutions, we extend white dominance, whether we know it or not, or whether we want to or not. However, as with the problem of environmental pollution, we can do much about white dominance once we study its causes and learn how it works.

A good place to start is to define white supremacy as the act of affirming, going along with, or refusing to recognize "the mechanisms of the white racial state." This definition includes a person's lack of awareness of, or indifference about, being racialized and located within the racial system.[7] The system of whiteness also includes ignorance about how white supremacy works through systems and institutions, not only through personal attitudes and behaviors.[8]

Whiteness is a white problem because white people are the ones who can afford to deny the reality of white racial supremacy. Whites are supposed to ignore the mechanisms of the white racial state while most people who do not have white status are deeply aware of them. Whiteness is also a white problem because the situation of being racially dominant deeply damages whites as it does untold harm to others.

This chapter explores two sets of mechanisms central to the *trauma* and the *overprivilege* involved in white racialization. One set generates the social, political, and economic disadvantages for the many and the privilege and unearned advantages for the relatively few who enjoy white racial identity. The other set of mechanisms, which ensues from the emotional restrictions involved in white racialization, generates erotic repression and the denial of the relational self. In short, whiteness creates unearned advantages at the expense of others while *denying dimensions of our relational capacities* as human beings. Otherwise put, the system of white supremacy is compensation for the restrictions involved in white racialization. Whiteness means suffering both moral and emotional damage even as we derive unearned benefits at the expense of others. Defining white supremacy as a refusal to recognize the mechanisms of the white racial state underscores the fact that whiteness is a problematic social construction and institutions in white racist societies promote unearned advantages for whites and erotic regulation for everyone that must be transformed.

Furthermore, this definition moves white supremacy beyond individual acts of discrimination to the fundamental web of complex, interdependent social structures. Institutional patterns constituting the mechanisms of whiteness are pervasive in this society, including the cultural repression and regulation of eros; the racialized labor market; segregated housing, schools, and churches; and the white-controlled media, medical, legal, and other corporate establishments. These reinforce the assumptions that white supremacy is commonsense, while they have devastating material and ideological fallout for communities of color. Whites cannot and will not move effectively against white supremacy until we understand how the fundamental cultural and material structures of society work together to *reproduce routine invisible privileges for us* and racist outcomes for people of color. These same structures also produce negative emotional, sexual, moral, and spiritual fallout for whites.

This chapter explores the historical creation of whiteness and analyzes how white supremacy is the necessary fallout of white racialization. The methodology here is informed by Christian liberationist perspectives, which affirm that ethical questions deal centrally with power-in-relationship.[9] Unshared power has become commonsense by routinizing the material advantages and cultural dominance of whites as a group. A historical process has created systems that reproduce monopolized power for whites even as they deny whites access to the erotic, relational self. While understanding how white supremacy damages whites is a necessary component of Christian anti-racist praxis, there are dangers in examining white racial identity. One such danger is the temptation to remain at the level of a theory of white racial identity and white supremacy. However, the goal of anti-racist Christian ethics is not only to understand white racialization and white supremacy, but, more fundamentally, to dismantle the white system. My thesis is that undoing white dominance will require multiracial, multiclass coalitions to mount a strategic and ethically imperative political response to moral evil.

What Is at Stake for Whites

We do well to investigate white racial identity and the mechanism of whiteness for at least three reasons. At stake for whites in this project is cultural literacy, including increased self-knowledge, responsible agency, and moral integrity as white people.

First, we need to put a spotlight on the history that impacts our daily lives in order to understand what it means to be members of the group known as "white." Whiteness is a major social structure that has developed historically to organize social space and individual experience, including whites' deepest understandings about ourselves and others. When I interact with someone not of my designated racial group, an entire history is embodied between us.

As an example, consider the interchange between an African American woman, Bess Smith, and a white woman, Grace Brown. Bess is a graduate of a historically white college that invited alumnae to help organize a women's studies conference at the college. Bess volunteered to organize several panels for the conference, including a presentation of black women poets and a faculty workshop on mentoring women of color. However, Grace and the other white women in charge of this event ignored her requests for information and aid. After many unsuccessful attempts to acquire needed information from the directing committee, Bess wrote a letter to Grace, stating that she was withdrawing her panels from the conference. Bess then received a note from Grace, telling Bess that she was "totally miffed" by Bess's decision.

Reducing this exchange to a personal squabble, as many on the campus did, is predictable if we do not understand the historical dynamics of white racism that have deeply conditioned the relations between black and white women. Many white women do not begin to grasp how white privilege has historically and systemically conditioned their relationships with black women and continues to shape perceptions and daily interactions. Becoming culturally literate requires a more sophisticated analysis of the historical roots and present dynamics of the racial system because this system prevents, or at least frustrates, egalitarian and empathetic relations between women who are racialized differently.

Cultural literacy also demands an understanding of the historical process that confers white status on certain people who *relinquished dimensions of their humanity*. Historically, white status has been awarded only to those of European background who gave up living close to their bodies and the natural world. As the Industrial Revolution took off in postcolonial America, becoming white was a reward given to those who successfully adapted to a highly regulated and socially repressive capitalist workplace. Common-sense racism constructs whiteness in order to accommodate the needs of an economic system built upon alienating social and political practices. As we shall see, in the United States the white self has been created to justify the exploitation of Europeans in industrialized wage labor, and to compensate them for the brutal work discipline that cut people off from their emotions, their sexual desires, and the natural world.

In addition to cultural literacy and self-knowledge, a second reason for whites to explore white racial identity is grounded in the Christian vocation to create a moral world. Whites can discern what is ethical, what we ought to do, only if we listen long and hard to people who endure racism. Christian ethicist Ada María Isasi-Díaz observes that dominants learn what we ought to do as moral agents only by listening to subordinated others and allowing ourselves to be questioned by them.[10] Feminists of color, as well as African American liberation theologians such as James Cone, have persistently called for a critical evaluation of whiteness by whites. During a time of rapid social change, including economic crisis, at the beginning of the twenty-first century, there is mounting need for whites to become responsible in dealing with increased racial hostility. Listening to and taking seriously people of color will help us see how commonsense racism is pervasive, diffused, and normalized in the culture. Racism is "commonsense" because it is built upon "the norms and forms thrown up by a few hundred years of pillage, extermination, slavery, colonization and neo-colonization."[11]

In learning from people of color we begin to adopt new perspectives about ourselves as whites. Learning to see ourselves from the point of view of the other is the only way to avoid what Iris Marion Young calls the "falsifying projection."[12] She cautions, however, that even with the best of intentions, we can walk in others' shoes *only* as the privileged people we are. As Young insists, in a culture of inequality, we "stand in relations of asymmetry and irreversibility with others."[13] In learning to heed how we misrepresent the disadvantaged situation of others as well as our own advantaged one, we better discern the contours of the moral project. Much of my own critical insight I owe to white Jews and diverse women and men of color who, for centuries, have observed dominants with a critical ethnographic gaze.

Third, repairing white moral integrity is at stake in this project. The system of whiteness has devastating effects upon people of color, and it also supports attitudes, behaviors, and institutions that deeply damage whites and violate our integrity. Our self-alienation as socially constructed white people lies at the base of our alienation from others. We need to *understand the dimensions of this self-alienation.* It is also true that while communities of color have been strengthened by collectively resisting the racialized system, the moral integrity of whites is eroded by our continuing efforts to benefit from injustice. Therefore, white racial identity bestows unearned advantages, and it damages its supposed beneficiaries. The fundamental moral project for whites is doing the work necessary to recover integrity by dismantling the white system.

The Dangers of Exploring Whiteness

On the one hand, white people need to be weaned from our attachment to white privilege and the white supremacist construction of our identities. On the other hand, confronting whiteness can have deleterious effects. These hazards include guilt, hopelessness, self-absorption, and confusion about our capacity to be allies in anti-racist work.

White people are tempted to guilt and/or hopelessness when we learn about the enormity of the racialized system and how it privileges and disables us as it disadvantages and oppresses others. Being embarrassed and feeling shame may be good insofar as they maintain our moral bearings and prompt us to develop a positive agenda for change. However, because people often feel hopeless about a legacy over which they seem to lack control, many whites become morally evasive about racial identity and escape into other aspects of social location, such as being female, gay, or Jewish.

Here clarity about blame and responsibility is needed. No one alive today is directly to blame for creating the racial system. Yet my family has been able to take for granted things that others might never have access to at all. While we are not responsible for the historical creation of racism, the fact that *we systematically benefit from this inherited system* that simultaneously disadvantages others marks the location of our personal accountability.

Perhaps the worst danger in becoming preoccupied with whiteness is that we can become self-absorbed and kept from crafting an anti-racist political agenda in coalition with others. Therefore, the message cannot be repeated too often: the solution to white supremacy is not guilt, hopelessness, or self-absorption. Rather, the solution is the democratic appropriation of economic, political, and cultural power, which can be forged only by the hard work of coalition politics. What is needed is a politics centered on making connections across differences, *a coalition politics of resistance and solidarity across racial/ethnic lines.* Simply put, although we cannot help accidents of birth, we can do something about the way we spend our time, energy, and money.

In the search for a viable anti-racist politics, whites have much work to do. We need to gain a clearer sense of how we have been racialized, how we define and enforce social categories connected to race, and how some receive more unearned advantage from whiteness than others. For example, the experience of whiteness is significantly different for a working-class lesbian and an affluent heterosexual male. It is qualitatively different for a Christian and a Jew — who sometimes benefits from white privilege but is also the target of anti-Semitism. Although class, gender, ethnicity, religion, and sexual orientation change qualitatively the experience of white supremacy, it is also true that, to greater or lesser degrees, *virtually all whites now benefit from white supremacy.*[14] In every social location whites have work to do because we have only begun to listen to the analysis of racially subordinate others, the only way to demystify whiteness and its legacy within us.[15]

One way to take inventory of whiteness is to analyze how the white system provides a twofold function for people socially constructed as white. First, whiteness provides *psychological compensation* for capitalist exploitation and the rigors of adhering to *industrial morality* and *patriarchal domesticity*. Second, whiteness provides *concrete material rewards* through a system of affirmative action for whites in the economic, political, cultural, and ecological spheres. This system is invisible to whites but blatantly evident to communities of color.

Whiteness as Wages for Industrial Morality

White racial identity has been historically constructed and reproduced in Western societies through cultural patterns anchored in the material institutions of capitalist political economy. Even though whiteness is customarily associated with skin color, whiteness is first and foremost *a social construction*. Historically, not all light-skinned people have been accorded white status. A historical analysis shows that whiteness is not primarily related to skin pigment, but is a cultural creation that serves vested interests.

Scholars have argued that white racial identity in the United States is rooted in the search of exploited European workers for economic advantage and cultural status. For example, historian Noel Ignatiev argues that the social construction of whiteness was a response to the need of nineteenth-century immigrant workers, especially the Irish, to disassociate themselves from the exploitation and oppression of slavery. After years of competing with "free" blacks for the worst jobs, the "black" Irish gained the right to become "white" by joining other European immigrant groups in excluding black workers from most industrial employment.

Forced to sell themselves piecemeal to the nineteenth-century factory owner, these workers sought to salvage their self-esteem by distinguishing themselves from former slaves. Workers accomplished this by establishing segregated unions, thereby rendering most forms of industrialized labor as white preserves. In this way, white workers tried to convince themselves that if blacks were excluded from certain forms of labor, the demeaning work they endured was not actually wage slavery. Selling oneself piecemeal became dignified (white) work if people of European origin were the only ones allowed to do it. Ignatiev argues that the very construction of the U.S. working class depended on the construction of whiteness, such that "the distinction between those who did and those who did not have access to the most dynamic area of the economy became a principal element defining 'race' in the North."[16]

While Ignatiev focuses on the type of labor monopolized by groups constructed as white, historian David Roediger focuses on the cultural characteristics required of workers in a white-only industrial workplace. Notions of whiteness are rooted in the industrial morality of hard work, self-discipline, and strict sexual regulation required by the long hours, intense supervision, and uninterrupted pace of capitalist work. To survive a brutalizing, unstable economy, industrial workers who had been torn away from agrarian life rejected preindustrial patterns of being human. Among these norms were being in touch with the erotic, including nature's rhythms and one's own sexuality, and being able to enjoy a more simple, carefree, and noncommercialized style of life.[17]

The construction of blackness — and racism — is the other side of socially constructed whiteness. Deprived of relationship to the land and access to the natural world, and subjected to extremely routinized work, rural-born immigrants were shoved into densely populated urban slums and dangerous, overcrowded factories. Their anxieties due to severed relationships with nature, leisure, and their own bodies were projected onto people vested with blackness, who came to be perceived as oversexed and irresponsibly playful. The social construction of white and black created a relationship of fascination and repulsion, of longing for what was lost and hatred for the preindustrial (black) self.[18]

Both Roediger and psychologist Philip Cushman agree that minstrel shows and whites' appearing in blackface were tools in the creation of whiteness. These popular theatrical forms were developed by Europeans frustrated by the enormous social dislocations of industrialization. Minstrelsy and blackface allowed an angry, exhausted working class, as well as the prim-and-proper Victorian entrepreneurs, to indulge in and mockingly reject the "black" part of themselves that loved music, dancing, clowning, relaxing, and sex.[19] A new industrial morality of whiteness, imposed on upper- and lower-working-class sectors alike, was constructed over against the blackness of the "savage, lazy, sexual, communal" American Indian, the enslaved or free Negro, and the newer European immigrant.[20] As a component of a more expansive racist folklore about the lazy, erotic, careless, and carefree black, these cultural forms of minstrelsy and blackface allowed people with white status to indulge at least momentarily in these longed-for attributes and escape the harshness of their lives. Like Ignatiev, Roediger argues that the even more exploited black "other" allowed those with whiteness to sublimate their own economic exploitation and social oppression. Like Cushman, Roediger argues that *whiteness developed as a disciplined industrial morality* and held together diverse immigrant groups in a relatively homogenized but empty capitalist culture. White racist capitalism has required sexual and social regulation and has placed in opposition those who attained whiteness and those who were excluded.[21]

Critical theorist Herbert Marcuse shows how industrial morality intensified its authority in the twentieth century. In his analysis of the social controls of modern industrial society, Marcuse argues that preindustrial characters who were noncompliant and disruptive, such as the artist, adulteress, rebel-poet, and the fool, were replaced in the new technological world. Their successors are freaks, such as the beatnik, the neurotic housewife, and the gangster. These character-roles do not challenge the intensified social control of industrial society.[22] Disruptive figures who once helped people imagine an alternative to the status quo have been deprived of any antagonistic force by being made into commodities that are sold everywhere and incorporated into everyday reality.[23] Using Marcuse's analysis, one could argue that in this century, the social creation of whiteness also co-opts and trivializes images of other ways of life and thereby makes unimaginable the rebellion these alternative images imply.

I think it is important for whites to recognize that white racial identity is an identity created and sustained under duress. Achieving white status requires people to adopt the "personal rigidity, loneliness, isolation, and lack of imagination, humor and creativity" necessary to function in the technologized workplace.[24] It requires isolated, predictable personalities who perpetrate killings in the market, in the concentration camp, and on the battlefield. As Scripture scholar Walter Brueggemann observes, people fully accommodated to the social controls of technologized capitalist society can implement almost anything and imagine almost nothing.[25]

In the process of becoming white, whites have lost access to themselves. For example, white people have had to become numb to the suffering within and around them. They have learned to divorce themselves from their bodies and to despise what is particular to all human beings, vulnerability and mortality. They have learned to deny their physical and sexual needs. White culture supports contempt and outrage for children, poor people, disabled persons, and those overidentified with their sexuality, who seem unable to keep their needy bodies under strict control. In adopting a white industrial morality, people constructed as white have split off fundamental aspects of their humanity, especially their capacity for relationships. These aspects have been demonized and shunted onto black (Negro, American Indian, Irish, Chinese, Latino, Jew, etc.) "others" who are characteristically portrayed as oversexed, carnal, lazy, and irresponsible. Blackness embodies preindustrial ways of being human and the desire for leisure time and pleasures from nature and from a more spontaneous sexuality that whiteness considers uncivilized.

Consequently, blackness must be demonized precisely because a white capitalist political economy cannot accommodate these human traits and desires within the constricted parameters of capitalist culture. Profits go down without desexualized bodies as instruments of labor and profit-making. Profits go down when people can do without products to correct the deficiencies of inadequate bodies and repressed sexuality. Profits go down if people are not highly regulated and obsessed with work. Profits go down if the black erotic is not rechanneled into the service of capitalist work, the reproduction of new workers, in heterosexual domesticity, and selling products.[26] At the same time, aspects of the white self that are no longer acceptable are deeply grieved and longed for, as well as hated and scorned.[27] To become white, people divorce themselves from what feels right and good to them and lose their ability to imagine an alternative future. A white student observed, "When you analyze white people from this point of view, you can really feel sorry for us."

As Roediger argues, the social construction of whiteness over against a scapegoated black other has been essential to the stability of capitalism. The scapegoating of blacks requires most people of color to be more exploited and oppressed than most whites. If the situation of communities of color improved substantially, or if social systems such as authentic welfare reform gave some relief from economic misery, the vast majority of whites could no longer ignore their own suffering through class exploitation.[28] Both Ignatiev and Roediger draw on a wide variety of scholarship to support W. E. B. DuBois's insight that degraded and exploited workers of color have always been necessary to bolster white workers who cash in on "the psychological wages of whiteness."[29] Whiteness has cushioned workers against their hatred of capitalist work discipline and eased their fears about their dependence on wages. In so doing, *the racial system has divided and conquered the majority of workers* who sell their productive abilities for a wage.

In a similar vein, with today's increasing numbers of low-wage workers and people's escalating fears around job security, many workers distinguish themselves as reliable, responsible, and indispensable workers in contrast to the despised welfare recipient, largely perceived as a nonworking woman of color. Social theorist Ann Withorn notes that, as more people work harder under deteriorating conditions in the labor force, the thought of others collecting money without having to endure similar immiseration has become an increasingly hot zone for people. As more people endure abusive marriages and take on multiple jobs that make them sick and deprive them of time with their children, the fear that others might have some alternatives to these situations raises questions about the value (and necessity) of their own suffering.[30] The emotional volatility around welfare recipients is not about the recipients, but about the compromises that whites have been told they must make to survive, compromises that whites deeply resent.

Making Whiteness Divine to Increase White Wages

Because white status is bought at such a great price, whites try to increase the psychological wage by scapegoating others and divinizing whiteness. As we have seen, white dominance is rooted in the need to split off the vulnerable and dependent self onto racialized and impoverished others. Such marked others assuage the emotional needs of suppressed, angry whites by offering them scapegoats as well as subordinates to care for them or entertain them. Instead of facing their own exploitation and struggling to overcome white oppression in the social order, whites intensify scapegoating. This practice uses others not only to restore faith in the goodness of whites, but also to mitigate whites' own suffering.

White people's need to dominate the racialized "other" has survived de-segregation, affirmative action, and visions of racial equality, goals that a few decades ago seemed in sight. Rooted in whites' oppression, this need to dominate others is reinforced by grandiose views of white people. These views are so strong that many, perhaps most, whites believe that others view them as paragons of virtue. Whites believe that others view them as virtuous and pure rather than dirty (whites do not do their own cleaning), as kindly rather than cruel (whites kidnap people for slave ships and ovens).[31] Whites believe that whereas communities of color speak from a narrow, culturally biased viewpoint, they themselves speak from a universal, unbiased viewpoint. White morality grants sympathy to victims but never redress or *reparations to equals.*[32] White morality presumes that white people are not prejudiced, that they have earned their way through individual merit, and that being ethical requires following the forms, procedures, and due process within social systems created by powerful whites.[33] Manning Marable adds that white religion "provides an intellectual shield through which the oppressive essence of their economic and political systems are made virtually invisible."[34]

In light of this analysis, it is easy to see why "the habit of whiteness and the conditions producing it have survived."[35] For whites to construct an identity outside the racist construct, we would need to give up our socially constructed white selves and *embrace the rejected parts of our humanity* that require scapegoats. Whites would need to give up proving ourselves on the terms required by capitalist political economy. Whites would challenge the belief that it is virtuous to be body denying, desexualized, and work obsessed. Challenging industrial morality means questioning a work ethic that says it is honorable to work multiple jobs even though the wages earned can never raise one's family above the poverty line. Challenging escalating economic insecurity would require honesty about the fact that it is less than just that one can hold a relatively good job now, but cannot count on holding it in the future. Whites would need to give up the self-righteous claim that because we work hard on capitalism's terms, so should everyone else. Instead of seeking to achieve status from white capitalist morality, whites would have to challenge the rigidly moralistic class, race, and sexual system. Rather than being superaccommodating to the political economy and its institutions, whites would instead acknowledge that *we deserve better,* and so does everyone else.

In short, change would become possible only by shattering people's psychic and spiritual numbness to the misery within and around them. Change becomes possible only when whites can mourn the alienation from self and others that is the foundation of whiteness. However, given all the functions whiteness continues to serve, one scholar writes, "If race lives on today, it does not live on because we have inherited it from our forebears... but because we continue to create it today."[36]

The existence of even more impoverished and culturally marginal communities of color has been necessary to stabilize a system that has guaranteed whites some measure of ideological and material compensation for their self-alienation in this political economy. Racist practices are even more necessary to maintain the current status quo as whites' needs are increasingly subordinated within the larger political economy, which demands self-negation from most citizens, whites as well as people of color.

Invisible Affirmative Action for Whites

The wages of whiteness are not only psychological; they are also material and concrete. In addition to providing emotional compensation for the suffering involved in being faithful to industrial morality, whiteness provides invisible affirmative action for whites in the economic, political, cultural, and ecological spheres. A second major feature of whiteness is its *unequal access to power, privileges, and benefits* in all sectors of the society. Whiteness is a vast invisible system of affirmative action for whites, although truthfully speaking, what may be invisible to us is very visible to communities of color. As Paul Kivel notes, the entire system of whiteness is maintained "to construct a normative set of values which defines who is entitled to certain resources and privileges," who is denied access, and who is scapegoated for social problems.[37]

The racial system accomplishes this by homogenizing people within groups and establishing a hierarchy of absolutely distinct human populations. However, the historical process of race-making is unstable because groups are not homogeneous, and more overlap than difference exists between racialized groups. White supremacy is, in part, an effort to *undermine the commonalities* among peoples whose differences must be exaggerated if some groups are to maintain unfair advantage. White dominance in the political, economic, and cultural spheres denies that the various communities of color are as diverse as whites and, equally telling, that they share commonalities overlapping with whites.[38]

On the individual level, educator Peggy McIntosh describes white affirmative action as an invisible package of unearned assets that whites cash in daily, but about which we are meant to remain oblivious.[39] These privileges include not living in fear for our own or our children's safety, having greater access to better jobs and educational institutions, receiving fair representation in the media and the court system, being assumed to be financially reliable in business transactions, and having social permission to be ignorant of other people's cultures.[40] When those without these race-based advantages fail to measure up to white standards, they are then penalized and required to bear a greater share of society's burdens while simultaneously receiving unequal access to society's benefits.

On the institutional level, the system of routinized unfair advantages in favor of whites means that the absence of overt discrimination will not, by itself, make up for unequal schools, redlined neighborhoods, segregated job markets, and exclusionary banking and housing policies. A lack of overt discrimination by individuals will not compensate for unfair treatment by theological doctrines, the media, the medical and legal establishments, or the criminal justice and social welfare systems. Institutionalized racism means that visible affirmative action for individual people of color is a drop in the bucket compared to the pervasive, yet unacknowledged, affirmative action for whites as a group, in every dimension of the political economy.

Accurately drawing a picture of affirmative action for whites requires unpacking white racial advantage as it is manifested in economic and political privilege, cultural hegemony, and ecological apartheid. The following brief inventory uncovers only the tip of the iceberg, but it may identify pressure points to be targeted by coalition work in dismantling whiteness and building a more just, anti-racist society.

Economic Affirmative Action for Whites

In differentiating whites from exploited others, the system of white racial identity also secures economic advantage for whites. As we have seen, white supremacy has created and historically maintained systematic inequalities in work and in meeting material needs in order to compensate for the economic struggle of most whites in the class system.

Whiteness, however, keeps most whites ignorant of the fact that the very existence of communities of color in the United States is due to conquest, colonialism, and the deliberate importation of cheap labor for purposes of profit-making for whites. A primary example is that, as a group, African

Americans have perhaps paid the highest price in their service to the evolving U.S. economy. They have worked as slaves, forced breeders of slaves, and sharecroppers, and, more recently, they have been disproportionately represented at the lowest rungs of industrialized labor, including prison labor and the unemployed.[41]

African Americans are not alone in overserving the economy. In the mid-nineteenth century, Spanish-speaking peoples entered the United States in large numbers as their homelands were colonized by U.S. forces expanding markets for U.S. business. In addition, American business recruited Chinese to help replace abolished slave labor. More recently, Latino/as have arrived to serve the need for labor in the Southwest as a result of the U.S. blockade of Cuba, interventions in Haiti, and U.S.-sponsored dictatorships in Central America and South America.[42]

A current example of the exploitation of immigrants by (mostly white) stockholders is the U.S. meat-packing industry, which depends largely on Laotian and Chicano workers. These immigrants are recruited, exploited, and exhausted in dangerous jobs that are typically sustained for less than a year. When workers are let go or suddenly expelled by the U.S. Immigration and Naturalization Service (INS), their employers avoid having to pay health benefits. In this way, the INS keeps labor transitory and invisible, and industry is guaranteed an inexhaustible supply of impoverished workers of color.[43]

A historical analysis of labor markets makes clear that whites collectively enjoy much of the capital accumulation, infrastructure, agriculture, food processing, child care, housecleaning, cooking, and basic maintenance of the society that has been disproportionately performed by slave labor and low-wage labor of men and women of color. Granted, whites have also worked hard, but they have had access to schools and universities, school loans, VA loans, housing and auto loans, unions, job contracts, and farming programs, all of which have excluded peoples of color and sometimes white Jews as well.[44] White dominance has built a global capitalist system through the disproportionate labor of workers of color and their children, who have been exploited through the systems of slavery, colonialism, neocolonialism, and now the intensified system of global low-wage labor, which is deepening even in the United States.

Another way the race system maintains the economic status quo is the use of "the race card" to conceal class analysis and the overlap in the impoverishment of poor and working-class whites alongside communities of color.[45] At the beginning of the twenty-first century, especially given the global banking crisis that began in 2007, escalating economic vulnerability is the lot of increasing numbers of people across the color line. Whiteness no longer protects the way it once did. Consequently, those at the top of the economic hierarchy find racism especially important in maintaining the status quo. Promoting hostility between racial groups keeps white workers and workers of color divided, both nationally and internationally. Even as they share common positions at the bottom of the economy, their lack of unity promotes the smooth functioning of the global economy.

Finally, while it is true that the subordination of people of color within the workplace is a significant dimension of white dominance, *class relations do not exhaust racism.* For example, in apartheid South Africa, the "color bar" at times was allowed to inhibit profit-making. When making maximum returns for investors collided with the apartheid system, the whites in charge of the economy tolerated a latitude of inefficient operation. In order to maintain white supremacy, they even worked against their immediate economic interests.[46]

Cultural Affirmative Action for Whites

White cultural affirmative action requires that white language, values, images, history, literature, music, and religion are constantly reflected as normative to everyone in the society. At the same time, whites expropriate the culture of racialized others by distorting, packaging, and marketing whatever cultural elements suit the purposes of white pleasure, profit, and escape from the repression and boredom of whiteness.[47] As the primary shapers and beneficiaries of a bureaucratic and hierarchical culture of consumption, affluent *whites decontextualize other cultures,* which are then consumed as exotic. In the process, whites are guaranteed not to be confronted or changed by an encounter with the "other."[48]

At the same time that the white system consumes the culture of others, it uses the media and other white cultural forms to scapegoat the people to whom these cultures truly belong. A politics of representation blames peoples of color rather than the U.S. system of white supremacist inequality for our culture of violence. For example, television programs and movies blame Asian American and Jewish economic success, as well as African American poverty, for the troubles experienced by poor and working-class white people.[49] In this way whites objectify and define the other as the source of societal ills rather than as the primary recipients or, more significantly, as resisters of the violence created by white capitalist society. The process of scapegoating keeps whites from paying attention to the source of their own exploitation and oppression.

Political Affirmative Action for Whites

Political power is monopolized by whites, who are elected by those who control the economic and cultural spheres. In the political sphere, white supremacy means that public policy is often intentionally coupled with a racially charged perspective in order to gain support for the policy and elicit the collusion of whites across class lines.[50] For example, although more people on welfare are white rather than African American, policy for dismantling welfare is racially coded so that the typical welfare recipient is inaccurately portrayed as a black woman.[51] Most illegal drugs are manufactured and sold by whites, and more than three out of four drug users are white, accounting for 80 percent of cocaine consumption. However, white supremacist criminal justice policy places predominantly poor people of color in jail for drug use.[52]

White political hegemony is further illustrated when nondominant groups attempt to focus public attention on their concerns, but whites steal the center. For example, when white women equate sexism with racism, gender oppression typically receives center stage. The experiences of women of color are rendered invisible, as illustrated in the Anita Hill–Clarence Thomas televised hearings. Many white feminists assessed the problem as sexual harassment "pure and simple," and yet many African American women recognized a more complex and familiar white-racist drama. As noted earlier, the social construction of whiteness involves oversexualizing black women and men. For many people of color, the Hill–Thomas hearings were spectacles for whites to project their fears, fantasies, and repressed desires onto scapegoated blacks.[53]

These insights are difficult for many whites to assimilate, especially if they do not comprehend the mechanisms of the white racial system. Similarly, Ida B. Wells, a nineteenth-century social reformer, observed that white women did not recognize lynching as a feminist issue because they did not understand their white-racist participation in the oppression of black men. Today, few white feminists understand why anti-rape "Take Back the Night" campaigns also require efforts to oppose disproportionately severe criminal sanctions, including stiffer prison sentences, for men of color.[54]

Knowledge of white political oppression is also necessary to make sense of the interchange cited earlier between Bess Smith and Grace Brown. White women, for example, are often less aware than black women of how white women have occupied the roles of both economic exploiter and political oppressor in relation to black women. Interactions between black and white women are never free of the history of black women as slaves and servants to white women. Neither are they free from more recent patterns of servitude in which white women have built professional careers from the subsidies provided by the low-wage labor of women of color in white homes and in white factories across the globe. Interaction between Bess Smith and Grace Brown is not free of the history of betrayal that women of color suffered in the women's suffrage movement because of white women's refusal to take women of color seriously as equal partners. Because this sordid history shapes white women's perceptions of black women and vice versa, it is no surprise that black women have reason not to trust us.

Understanding the mechanisms of the white racial system helps white women see that comparing race and gender oppressions is highly suspect, although whites often do so. By claiming others' experience as our own, we do not have to comprehend their actual experience or be fully accountable to it.[55] Deepening our understanding of the mechanisms of white racism helps white women respond to bell hooks's insight that "as long as white and black women are content with living separately in a state of psychic social apartheid, racism will not change."[56] As the interchange between Bess and Grace illustrates, however, white women will not be ready for solidarity until we learn from black women, including how not to crumple in the face of conflict.[57]

Another way whites avoid coming to terms with other groups' experiences is often through political language about multiculturalism. The rhetoric of multiculturalism may be popular, in part, because it lumps all communities of color together so that whites are not required or expected to take seriously each group's specific claims. It allows whites to construct an imaginary symmetry in which all races "appear and are treated as though they occupy a *common* position in relation to each other and the state."[58] *The racist absence of shared power,* which gives rise in the first place to the need for multiculturalism, is never addressed.

Ecological Affirmative Action for Whites

The construction of whiteness results as well in ecological alienation and insensitivity to nature and its rhythms. White elites monopolize the use of land and natural and human resources while destroying the earth and its atmosphere. The long-term consequences of environmental destruction will, of course, be fatal for all. In the meantime, ecological affirmative action for whites means that communities of color (and poor nations) are more likely than affluent white areas to be sites of pollution production and hazardous waste facilities. Geographer Joni Seager writes that "race is one of the most significant variables in determining the location of commercial, industrial and military hazardous waste sites."[59]

For example, south-central Los Angeles, 59 percent African American and 38 percent Latino, is the dirtiest community in the state with more than 33 million pounds of toxic waste dumped there in 1989.[60] Similarly, major hazardous waste sites in the nation include Sumter County, Alabama, and the southeast side of Chicago, which also have predominantly African American and Latino populations.[61] In addition, the greatest producer of toxic waste is the military, whose nuclear bomb testing sites in the continental United States are all located on Native American lands, mostly on

Shoshone territory in Nevada.[62] While *more than half* the U.S. population currently resides in areas with uncontrolled hazardous waste sites, communities of color are predominantly targeted. This is true both in the United States and in the Two-Thirds World, demonstrating continuing patterns of imperialism, colonialism, and racism.[63] As a result, children of color suffer disproportionately from lead levels in the blood, respiratory diseases, cancer, and other health problems. It is no surprise that primarily men and women of color and white women, understanding the connections between poverty, racism, and sexism, are leaders in the struggle for ecological justice.[64]

Moreover, the white supremacist global economy creates both the degradation of poverty and the assault of affluence. Each threatens the earth's life-support systems, though in exceedingly different ways. White supremacy will not protect even whites, for as Larry Rasmussen warns, "If this situation continues, we will not."[65]

How Whites Are Hurt by White Privilege

While hardly suffering the devastating costs that accrue to diverse communities of color, whites bear significant economic, emotional, and spiritual suffering because of the white system we have been carefully trained to accept as normative. What costs do whites bear? Consider the following:

As previously mentioned, whites suffer alienation of the white self from the erotic, including the divorce from the natural world, from one's own sexuality, and from spontaneity, playfulness, and creativity. The system of whiteness restricts and constrains our relations with other white people. Capitalist culture and its system of profit-making cannot accommodate people having access to their full selves for fear they will become assertive about what feels right and good to them. Perhaps most sobering of all, white alienation from ourselves and others lies at the origin of our alienation from nature as planetary destruction threatens the sustainability of all life-forms.

Whites suffer arrogance in believing that knowledge, including moral knowledge acquired through a white racial lens, is the measure of all things. We also live with an inaccurate picture of history and politics, including ignorance of the crimes and practices of white people.

Whites are hurt by our outstanding ignorance about the white racialized state and how *our systematic unearned advantages permeate every aspect of our lives.* Ignorance of the historical record, including how white people have betrayed people of color, is central to failed communication, which frustrates coalition work.

And how do we begin to calculate the loss to society of the contributions of communities of color, had they not been burdened with systematic unearned disadvantage and oppression? Equally painful is the loss of our own ethnic cultures insofar as white racial identity is defined over against the racialized other who embodies all that must be rejected from the self as white.

Whites are hurt, too, by the lack of friendship and intimacy that capitalist culture inflicts on people in order to sell products that appeal only to those who are insecure in community life. Whites suffer the loss of friendship with people of color in our largely segregated lives. A related problem is the confusion and helplessness whites feel when confronted by angry people who do not share white privileges. White racism disempowers whites by blocking us from the increased power we would gain in forging alliances with communities of color.

In addition, whites sometimes lose the friendship of other whites, even in our own families, in confrontations over racism. We are taught to live in fear of people of color, although they are the ones at risk from white supremacy. If we are not wealthy, we remain ignorant about our own exploitation by (Christian) whites who control the economy and teach us to blame economic troubles on Jews and people of color. If we are women, we remain ignorant about the real source of personal violence in our lives, which is white men we live with or near, not the stranger of color.[66] White privilege ensconces whites in immaturity and incompetence. From their vantage point as servants, black women have often regarded white women collectively as "willful children, pretty children, and mean children," but not as very competent.[67]

Perhaps most important, *white privilege leads to moral bankruptcy.* Because white status depends on denying the deepest parts of the relational self, our humanity is impoverished, and our capacity to be moral — in right relationship with others — is diminished. White supremacy produces trauma, pain, fear, ignorance, mistrust, and unshared vulnerability, and for this reason, white moral character is warped and undermined.[68] Our integrity is necessarily damaged in environments that systematically promote discrimination, harassment, exploitation, and misery. Our integrity is damaged when, as participants in white culture, we are divorced from our deepest longings and capacities for creativity, and when we do not know how to intervene.[69]

White people purchase hegemonic power at the price of splitting off aspects of our authentic humanity, including our vital human need for mutual recognition and respect. In different ways everyone is assaulted, wounded, and deformed by the process of being racialized. Racialization denies our commonalities, and in the process we cut ourselves off from others. The tragedy here, as African American writer Barbara Smith points out, is that integrity of character, including moral insight and action, can come only from emotional and spiritual connection.[70]

The ethical goal of mutual recognition and shared power will not be achieved until white people understand the damage done to whites by the historical process of being racialized as white. The Boston-based Combahee River Collective says it well: "The most profound and potentially most radical politics comes directly out of our own identity, as opposed to working to end somebody else's oppression."[71]

Catholic Social Teaching and Racism

Catholic resources for addressing racism are exceedingly limited, in large part because of the racist practices of the church itself. The Catholic Church has a racist history that, along with racist U.S. society, continues to impact its organizational structures and the individual attitudes of most Catholics. This history includes (but is not exhausted by) the theological justification of slavery; the ownership of slaves; complicity in the mistreatment and genocide of American Indians; refusal to let people of color into the priesthood, religious life, and parish and diocesan leadership positions; participation in legal segregation and white flight; marginalizing Catholics who participated in the civil rights movement; the direction of church resources to suburban rather than urban areas; and the failure to teach its official stand against racism in schools, seminaries, parishes, and the public arena.[72]

The official stand of the church against racism has been made especially explicit in the U.S. bishops' 1979 pastoral letter, *Brothers and Sisters to Us*.[73] While some critics wish the bishops had detailed a more thorough structural and theological analysis of racism, this document offers resources to those concerned with dismantling whiteness.[74] The bishops write that *racism distorts the personhood of whites* by its promotion of indifference and resentment.[75] But racism not only characterizes individuals; it is deeply embedded in society's institutions and organizations. The bishops are clear that racism systemically reproduces unearned advantages for whites and unearned disadvantages and suffering for people of color when they state that society's institutions "are geared to the success of the majority and the failure of the minority."[76] The bishops exhort Christians to *learn how social structures reproduce white supremacy* and how the church has directly participated in racism. The bishops then outline specific strategies in which Christians and their churches can engage, including expanding the participation of people of color at every level of church life through a more rigorous application of affirmative action than is evident in secular institutions.[77]

Brothers and Sisters to Us was written over thirty years ago and has been reaffirmed in other Catholic documents.[78] Nevertheless, the Catholic position on racism is little known, and most of its policy prescriptions have never been implemented. Especially unconscionable is the largely unheeded mandate to publicly confess past and present wrongs, express contrition for them, and actively work to make amends.

Given this sad track record, it is clear that the church first needs to work hard on its own racism. Only then will its call to dismantle racism and white supremacy in the larger society have any impact. Working against its own racism will also entail joining with others in organizing and implementing concrete policies and structures to address racist violence, police brutality, economic exploitation, homelessness, hunger, and unequal access to education and health care. To be effective in dismantling white supremacy, the churches need to transform their own institutional practices and ally themselves with others in the larger work of anti-racist coalition politics.

Dismantling Whiteness through Coalition Politics

The institutional churches, like individual Christians, can work to understand the racial system and join with others in the project of dismantling white racialization and white privilege. While we do not choose our racial location, we can take charge of our political actions out of the knowledge that justice benefits everyone, at least in the long run. Our shame about the truth of white supremacy will not immobilize whites if, through a shared analysis of racialized power and how it works to hurt most people in this society, we can identify common benefits. It will be clear how each of us will gain through investments of time, energy, and risk-taking required in solidarity work.[79] When we analyze the system of white supremacy and understand how it is built on the trauma of white racialization and both reinforces and is supported by other processes of domination that hurt most whites as well, it becomes more evident how diverse coalition partners can have their interests met by a comprehensive altering of the status quo.[80] This precursor to systemic change is located in the subversive micropractices at the multiple sites of oppression, targeted in multiracial, multiclass coalition work.

Perhaps the most important point to remember is that white people are not doomed to be white supremacists. Historically, some courageous whites have always joined multitudes of people of color in challenging, resisting, and refusing to be overwhelmed by white dominance. We begin to dismantle whiteness when we embark on the long, hard struggle of *basing our personal identities on political consciousness and action,* not on skin color or cultural status. Personal identity is created not by the domination of others, but by justice-making in solidarity with others. As a result, defining our political commitments and what we do with our time and energy and money is more important than defining our social location in determining who we are.[81] Hope comes also from the writings and actions of people of color who insist that whites become good allies to them.[82]

Coalition politics is based on the moral knowledge that the system of white racial identity is constructed to diminish the relational capacity of whites as it reinforces other systems that hurt whites. Shared understandings of power and human need provide common ground and a positive alternative to guilt as a primary response to white privilege. Resistance to white hegemonic power is revitalizing the labor movement and community organizing throughout the country by those advocating workers' rights, civil rights, and human rights.[83] Staying in coalition with others sustains the struggle for the long haul and counteracts white people's hopelessness and impatience when social transformation does not come quickly.

Coalition politics is not easy for whites because it requires multicultural competence, participatory group process, and democratic decision-making — all fundamental elements of social justice that white supremacy (and patriarchy and capitalism) rejects. Coalition politics is hard for people taught to reject the erotic, playful, and creative self. Coalition politics is hard for people taught to live in ways that are "based on injury, insult and exclusion."[84] Coalition politics is hard for people socialized within an anti-cooperative society that is saturated with the hierarchies of business, academia, church, sports, and military training.[85]

Ethicist Elizabeth Bounds identifies a model of community in which the common good cannot be achieved apart from ongoing conflict and negotiation of difference. Here is, in my judgment, a good model of coalition work.[86] Few of us have experience with egalitarian and participatory political practices that actually welcome conflict for purposes of clarification and transformation. However, as Sharon Welch reminds us, without conflict, difference, and diversity, we lack the means for ongoing self-criticism.[87] Without conflict and negotiation, we lack exposure to the narrative of the "other," to which we must deeply listen so that the white supremacist narrative within us is changed.[88]

Learning from the beloved and despised other also means challenging docility and compliance and learning how to resist. It involves embracing the gifts of blackness. These gifts, as W. E. B. DuBois identified them, include "a sensuous receptivity to the beauty of the world" and a steadfast refusal to be the "mechanical draft horse" at the service of grim powers oblivious to its beauty.[89]

Only this kind of collective engagement and democratic experimentation begins to awaken in us a passion for justice, sustains resistance to injustice, and envisions viable social alternatives.[90] Only this kind of collective engagement and democratic experimentation can dismantle white hegemonic power.

Melanie Kaye/Kantrowitz, a Jew long involved in social justice work, concludes: "I may be secular but I know holiness when I hear it. One of its names is solidarity, the opposite of whiteness. The more you claim it, honor it, and fight for it, the less it costs."[91]

_____

THREE

An Economic Ethics
of Right Relationship

*I have to struggle with my reluctance to understand how the money
that I earn is suffused with the pain and blood of people in the past
and in the present.* — MINNIE BRUCE PRATT

O NE OF THE WORST industrial fires in the history of capitalism was the
May 10, 1993, fire at the Kader Industrial Toy Company in Bangkok,
Thailand. The official dead numbered 188 persons (most likely underesti-
mated). All but 14 were women or girls, some as young as thirteen years of
age.[1] Like the 1991 Imperial Foods fire in Hamlet, North Carolina, cited at
the beginning of chapter 1, this event was buried in the back pages of major
newspapers. As noted previously, when workers die, especially workers who
are female, young, and of color, the world barely notices.

This chapter is devoted to an analysis of the class system, a major structure at work in these industrial fires. While race and gender subordination
also deeply structure these events, class analysis is fundamental to understanding them, including how race and gender work in the economy and
society at large. Yet class is the structure most people in our society are the
least equipped to understand.

The Taboo Social System of Class

Social theorist David Harvey contrasts the spare media coverage of the 1991
Imperial Foods fire with the media preoccupation with two other events at the
time: the sexual harassment charges against Supreme Court nominee Clarence
Thomas and the brutal beatings of motorist Rodney King. Harvey observes
that gender and race oppression in non-working-class contexts are not as
hidden by the U.S. media as are class politics and economic exploitation.
Perhaps exploring issues of racism and sexism is less threatening to the status
quo than unmasking economic and political power. However inadequate the
exploration, racism and sexism can be discussed long before class issues are
ever raised, especially analysis that shows how a relative few at the top of

the economic system monopolize control over the labor process, the social wealth others produce, the system of finance, and culture and politics as well.[2]

I explore the structure of class as a way of discerning the material basis of our relationships to one another, especially the material basis of race and sex/gender relations. While many people have race and gender identities, fewer have a *class identity*. While class by no means exhausts the meaning of race and gender, we will not fully address racism and sexism until we help people form class identity. Two groups are fundamental to class relations, capitalists and workers. The capitalist class exercises the most power in the political economy because it owns and controls the means of producing social wealth (including land, factories, offices, machines, natural resources, human labor, stocks, and other assets). In addition, as direct production of goods and services has receded in the economy, capitalists have also gained control over a myriad of financial instruments (like subprime mortgages, complex bonds, derivatives and hedge funds) that have been increasingly used to generate profits for investors, both in the United States and globally. It is important to be clear that the power of this class comes not primarily from its enormous wealth, but from its *control of production and finance*. The economic power of the capitalist class means that it also controls government and cultural institutions.

The basic contradiction at the center of the capitalist system reveals itself when, in their search for unlimited profits, capitalists exhaust and destroy the very means of producing social wealth. People are worked to death, resources become extinct, the land is irradiated, and financial sectors crash, bringing economics to a halt. Capitalist control of culture and government means that, despite twenty-five years of environmental policies, "global warming, ozone depletion, species extinction, rain forest destruction, desertification, and the contamination of our land, water, and air by toxic chemicals, oil spills, radiation leaks, and pesticide use continue largely unabated."[3] As we shall see, capitalists not only exhaust the means of producing social wealth; they also increasingly eliminate the markets they need to sell the wealth. Perhaps most dangerously, as will be discussed below, financial instruments used to create capitalist profits can become so unaccountable to real value that they implode, creating financial havoc to the far corners of the earth.

The second major class in the capitalist system, the working class, has only or primarily labor to sell for a wage or a salary in order to make a living. The capitalist class, only 2 percent of the population, makes the labor of working-class people, roughly 90 percent of the population, a commodity that capitalists buy in order to make profits for stockholders.

Former secretary of labor in the Clinton administration, Robert Reich, divides the huge contemporary U.S. working class into three major groups. The top group, about 20 percent of all workers, comprises those he calls the "national and global symbolic analysts." Global symbolic analysts, many of whom overlap with the capitalist class, are CEOs of global corporations, and partners and executives in global investment banks, law firms, and consultancies. National symbolic analysts are upper-income earners like accountants, software programmers, engineers, doctors, lawyers, journalists, academics, designers, and researchers. Middle- and low-income earners comprise the rest of the U.S. working class and include factory workers (about 25 percent of U.S. workers) and service workers (about 50 percent of U.S. workers). As you can see, only about one-fifth of U.S. workers earn upper-income salaries. Half of this top group, about 10 percent of workers, have such large discretionary income that they generate the need for increasing amounts of low-wage service work in the U.S. economy (like personal trainers, masseurs, drivers, gardeners, cooks, nannies, dry cleaners, fast food services, etc.).[4]

Capitalists and the top sector of workers make sure that most of the working class (more than two-thirds of workers), who often already experience inferior status because of race and gender subordination, are low- or lower-wage earners who have little control over their labor. They represent especially lucrative labor for capitalist profit-making as well as the labor required to service the affluent few. However, it is also true that increasing amounts of the higher income labor of symbolic analysts are being shifted to places like China and India, where the highly educated are willing to work for less than professionals in the United States, thus generating greater corporate profits. It is important to remember this as we explore the fact that economic vulnerability is moving up the class ladder as the U.S. labor market generates increasing amounts of lower-wage work that is affecting even upper-income sectors of the U.S. working class.[5]

Only by exploring class relations in more detail below can we see how subordinate class position, including the threat of losing an upper-income job, unites a majority of people who are otherwise separated by attributes of difference such as income, race, gender, sexuality, and nationality. The working class is also divided by ideology. As discussed below, most, but not all, working-class people believe in the basic fairness of the capitalist system. As David Harvey suggests, this may be the main reason this culture is silent about class and yet willing (however poorly) to discuss sexism and racism. If persons with different incomes and divided by race and gender and other attributes recognized their common class position in relation to capitalists, *new alliances might be forged* that make a claim on their fair share of social and economic power, and the class system might be transformed. Consequently, it is important to the status quo that subordinate groups remain fragmented by different social identities (as professionals or laborers, as women, people of color, gays, etc.) and people remain ignorant about class.

Working-class divisions remain strong when people believe the myth that there are three, not two, classes: upper, lower, and middle. People believe that with hard work they can leave the working class and join the superior ranks of professionals and managers, mistakenly called the middle class. So-called middle-class or upper-middle class people are those who make higher salaries than the workers below them. They identify their interests with capitalists, even though most have only their labor to sell for a living. They are largely unaware of their common class position with workers in income brackets below them.

The task for Christians who enjoy privileges in the upper echelons of the working class, then, is to become tutored about class power. We lack power in relation to capitalists, but we benefit from the exploitation of the lower tiers of the working class. We need to understand better how we participate in some privileges of the capitalist class through our income, race, or gender, as well as how we benefit from a system that reproduces hardship, suffering, and sometimes death for the majority of workers. This is difficult work because, as economic actors, we are seldom taught to *evaluate economic relationships as social power relations.* Rather, we are encouraged to consume profit and pleasure as if we are isolated individuals. Moreover, even though we may presently enjoy a relatively high income and a sense of economic security, we need awareness of our increasing vulnerability as members of the working class in a radically changing economy.

Blood on Our Food, Tears on Our Clothes

This chapter explores a taboo: the reality of class. Describing the basic geography of class privilege and exploitation, I offer a brief summary of the historical evolution of the class system in the twentieth century. It is also important to make a case for understanding the history and dynamics of class as pivotal work for Christians, especially affluent ones. Since Christianity puts the *neighbor in need at the center of its tradition,* affluent Christians should know the forces at work that generate deteriorating conditions for the majority of the world's workers. These are the persons who lie behind the food, clothing, shelter, and other commodities and services that maintain affluent lifestyles, not only for capitalists but also for those of us in the upper tiers of the working class. Without this kind of investigation, privileged Christians suffer ignorance concerning how our lives of relative affluence and security are connected to others on whom we depend.

While we purchase symbols (Nikes, not shoes, BMWs, not cars), do we realize that many on whom we depend live without meeting basic human needs? The reason is the economic structure of class. A critical analysis of class, as well as resources from the Christian tradition, will help us connect the suffering of industrial fires and similar events to people like us whose salaries enable us to eat meat, wear designer clothes, and buy toys produced through that suffering.

Notions of free markets, labor contracts, and money, and the language we are given to talk about the economy make it impossible to think relationally and historically about the economy. The economy itself is conventionally viewed as a *natural system* rather than something *humanly produced* and humanly transformable. We are taught that economic actors function as autonomous individuals rather than as members of groups who interact with disproportionate amounts of power. In addition, economic concepts are presented as if they are universal, unchangeable laws. Such concepts hide how we are intimately connected to the people who produce our food, clothing, housing, and all the artifacts and services we depend on daily.

In contrast to popular understanding, the economy is not just an economic regime. More fundamentally, the economy is a *system of social relations* among groups of people, earth's other creatures, and the environment. This system of social relations has developed over time and binds us intimately, though invisibly, with others. These lived connections are hidden by notions such as markets, money, and labor contracts, which only distance us from the capitalist class above and from people in the working class below. As Christians concerned with the moral quality of our relations with one another and with the earth, we need to uncover and explicitly name the social relations of class. This analysis will help us understand the nature of the bonds between ourselves and others in this economy so that we can address economic injustice and unshared cultural and political power.

To deepen understanding about class, I will first explore how Scripture and church tradition impel Christian concern about unjust class relations. Then I will briefly describe class structure before summarizing the historical evolution of class relations in late twentieth-century global capitalism. I will then look closely into who lives, suffers, and dies behind the largely invisible structure of class. The capitalist class is making increasing profits off such lower-working-class groups as agricultural workers, sweatshop workers, prison and child laborers, and workfare recipients. However, even those of us in the upper echelons of the working class, though privileged by the class system, suffer economic vulnerability and moral damage. Finally, I offer suggestions about how to transform the structure of class.

Scripture, Tradition, and Class Power

Taking Christian tradition seriously gives ample reason for concern about class. Scripture scholar Norman Gottwald gives an account of the biblical foundations that critique class elitism. Working his way from Hebrew to Greek Scriptures, Gottwald describes three major moments of community struggle by early Jews and Christians against unshared class power. The

Exodus, a jailbreak engineered by the bottom class of the society, embodied the resistance of ordinary people to a tributary mode of production that enslaved them to maintain privilege for the few at the top.[6] Philosopher Michael Lerner adds that as Judaism developed, it ridiculed religious practices that lost touch with a God who enabled "ordinary people to triumph over the claims of entrenched ruling elites."[7]

Building on this tradition, Gottwald identifies a second wave of Jewish faith, embodied in the prophetic challenge to the kings of Israel, who pauperized the majority by expropriation of land, debt peonage, and state taxation. While the prophetic tradition can be critiqued for its negative images of women and warrior-like images of God, its class analysis is compelling. The prophets proclaimed God's outrage at a society in which wealth and luxurious living were built on the backs of those who suffered economic misery. Though largely ignored by First-World Christians, biblical tradition is clear that poverty is not a mark of having sinned, but a result of being sinned against. The ancient prophets knew that God is outraged by poverty. Not only is it unjust that some have little or nothing in the midst of plenty, but the abundance going to the rich has been gained from the deliberate exploitation and oppression of poor people.[8]

Among the thousands of verses about the poor in the Bible, Isaiah (3:13–15), Jeremiah (22:13–17), and Amos (8:4–6) provide particularly clear examples of the insight that poor people are the source of the wealth that has been stolen from them by the affluent. This claim is also present in the Jubilee tradition, or "the acceptable year of the Lord," found in Leviticus (25:1–14). The goals of Jubilee, the same goals Jesus announces for his life and ministry at the beginning of the Gospel of Luke (4:14–21), are achieved only when what has been *stolen from those at the bottom of society* is returned to them. God's justice requires economic restoration.

Gottwald states that a third wave of biblical economic ethics emerged in the Jesus movement, which reaffirmed the communitarian ethics and socioeconomic practice that Christians inherited from Judaism. Early Christians embodied a discipleship of equals that included converts drawn from diverse social classes, genders, and racial/ethnic groups.[9] Scripture scholar Marcus Borg says that Jesus perceived wealth not as a characteristic belonging to individuals but as a *product of belonging to an oppressive social class.* Jesus and the movement he founded "subverted the world of convention and imaged an alternative way of life."[10] Gottwald adds that in nearly all periods of Jewish and Christian history, voices have criticized economic injustice as contrary to God's creation. Active resistance requires diverse practices such as charity, voluntary poverty, reform, and revolution.[11]

This strong predisposition toward communitarian values continues in current teachings of Christian churches. Catholic social teaching embodies a perspective on economic justice that is shared by many Protestant denominations as well.[12] The Catholic tradition has more than a hundred years of modern teaching about economic justice that generally supports the class system, but with the qualifier that classes should not become polarized. Nevertheless, this cautionary tendency does not exhaust the Catholic legacy. Developed by popes and regional bodies of bishops since the end of the nineteenth century, this tradition also encourages elites to be critical of the class system and promote fundamental social change.[13]

One key legacy is the late Pope John Paul II's mandate "to honor the truth that private property is under a social mortgage."[14] By this the pope means that collective goods in society, which should be read to include the well-being of humans, creatures, and the ecosystem itself, "constitute the essential framework for the legitimate pursuit of personal goods on the part of each individual."[15] As the pope claims, no one can pursue individual or group goods without the support of this larger environment, including a wide range of human, animal, and ecological resources. Therefore, anyone pursuing individual goods must pay back the social mortgage on what he or she has used.

In another teaching, John Paul II says the social mortgage is what is owed by capital, or money-making interests, to labor. John Paul identifies *human work as the source of wealth* because capital is "the historical heritage of human labor." Work, not capital or money, is the major source of the real wealth in the society. The needs of workers have priority over the interests of employers and stockholders. Indeed, those who own and control capital, says the pope, are subordinate to the "right common to all to use the goods of all creation."[16]

The Canadian Catholic bishops have extended this insight about the priority of labor to include the need for "communities and working people [to] have effective control over both capital and technology." Otherwise, the bishops note, "the tendency is for them to become destructive forces in economic development."[17] The Canadian bishops support grassroots resistance to the status quo and the struggle to "acquire communal control over the necessary means of production" in order to "organize the economy to serve [the whole community's] basic needs."[18] For Latin American Catholic bishops, elites including the church can pay back the social mortgage by practicing a "preferential option for the poor."[19] Enforcing this option does not mean asking elites to share some of their goods while maintaining the status quo. Rather, the privileged are to change sides, stand in solidarity with organized poor people, and resist structures and practices of exploitation and domination that benefit elites.[20]

Official Christian teaching affirms that the thrust of biblical and other theological traditions mandates Christian commitment to more inclusive economic structures than presently in place. It is also clear that this teaching remains among Christianity's *best-kept secrets*. Beyond "diffuse sentiment and generalized moral challenge," Gottwald says, *none* of the official churches assists people in analyzing the roots of poverty or other forms of economic injustice.[21] Knowledge about how the class structure impacts groups differently is largely unknown to First-World Christians. However, knowledge about class is essential so that Christians, as moral agents, can both analyze and address how the economy promotes or obstructs the realization of biblical values and contemporary social justice principles.

Camouflaging Group Membership

In popular discourse, class is defined according to individual income or capacity to consume products and services. This notion, measuring how groups of individuals are related because they enjoy similar economic rewards such as income and prestige, is rooted in the work of sociologist Max Weber.[22] Contrary to the biblical view, which regards class as a relationship among groups, this notion perceives wealth and poverty as characteristics belonging to individuals. People who adopt this view often believe that two minorities, one very affluent and the other poor, live in a society with a middle-class majority of individuals who consume comfortably.

Even if one were to subscribe to a view of class based only on consumption capacity, this view of a comfortable middle majority could not be further from the actual incomes of U.S. households. In 2006, 20 percent of households in the United States made $20,035 or less a year; 40 percent earned $37,774 or less. This income is not enough or hardly enough to afford a modestly affluent lifestyle for two-fifths of U.S. households. In addition, many households with incomes approximating $97,000 a year or more think of themselves as "middle class" or "upper middle class" when in fact they are upper income. There is nothing "middle" about them. Almost 80 percent of U.S. households bring in less than they do.[23]

This chapter defines class not primarily according to an individual household's income level or consumption capacity, but according to group membership, including the group's relationship to the production of social wealth. Class here is defined by the relations among social groups as they go about producing goods and services rather than by consumption, an idea familiar to the biblical prophets and deeply probed by Karl Marx in the nineteenth century. Class as a *system of social relations* based on capitalist production continues to be developed by the Marxist tradition today.[24]

If the economy is fundamentally a system of social relations, it is important to understand how the two major classes relate to each other, including what each does *for* and *to* the other. For purposes of a working definition, we might say that classes are groups of people who, because of their leisure, employment, or forced unemployment, and the power they do or do not experience in relation to other groups, have a common interest in either maintaining the system or changing it.[25] While the relation of different groups to the process of production is complex and intertwined so that no paradigm can adequately reflect it, I offer the following simplified framework for defining the two major classes in U.S. society, the capitalist class and the working class. As mentioned previously, while the capitalist class is united in its control of the major economic, political, and cultural institutions of society, the working class is deeply divided, not only by income levels, but also by gender, race, and other differences.

At the top of the class structure is the capitalist class, the group that owns and controls the means of producing social wealth. The means of producing social wealth, itself primarily the product of the labor of the working class, includes the factories, offices, natural and human resources, and financial capital needed to produce profits, products, and services. In recent decades, the U.S. capitalist class has increased its control over social wealth. Constituting only 2 percent of the U.S. population, the capitalist class is the corporate elite, senior executives, and CEOs of the largest corporations and banks who are often in revolving door arrangements with the U.S. government. (Hence the use of the term "political economy.") Economist Michael Zweig identifies an even smaller group within the capitalist class that he calls "the ruling class." The ruling class includes the most powerful people in the United States, positioned not only in business and finance, but also in the three branches of government. The "ruling class" also includes influential leaders in academia (often also in revolving door relationships with business and government) who "give strategic direction to the country as a whole," and who "coordinate capitalist activity across enterprises" in order to further corporate interests. Zweig says the members of the U.S. ruling class are so few they would fit into the old Yankee Stadium, which held 57,000 people.[26]

The capitalist class, especially the top 1 percent, have been the primary beneficiaries of the doubling of U.S. productivity by the U.S. workforce in the last three decades. It is difficult to reconcile the claim by people like economist Larry Summers, a former U.S. Treasury secretary, former president of Harvard, and chief economic advisor in the Obama administration, that globalization is inevitable and good when Summers also notes that since 1979 the share of pretax income going to the top 1 percent of American households has risen by 7 percentage points, to 16 percent. Over the same span, the share of income going to the bottom 80 percent has fallen by 7 percentage points. Interviewer David Leonhardt quotes a favorite Summers statistic: "It's as if every household in the bottom 80 percent is writing a check for $7,000 every year and sending it to the top 1 percent."[27]

Income polarization in this country deepened especially in 2005. In fact, the incomes of the top 1 percent, those receiving more than $348,000 a year prior to 2005 now have incomes averaging $1.1 million each, an increase of more than $139,000. Income inequality has grown so much in recent years that the richest 300,000 Americans after 2005 received 440 times as much as the average person in the bottom half earned. In addition, the incomes of the top tenth of a percent (up $908,000) and the top one-hundredth of a percent (up nearly 4.4 million) soared by about 20 percent in one year. Here we see that the gap between the wealthy and the superwealthy has been enormous and growing.[28]

Economist Robert Kuttner has written that the astronomical increases in wealth of these minuscule groups of Americans in the capitalist class, when viewed against the reality that four out of five Americans have had "basically stagnant living standards since the mid-1970s," means that "the real 'Two Americas' are not the poor and everyone else, but the mega-rich and everyone else."[29]

The 8 percent of Americans below the capitalist class do not control the largest corporations and banks like the top 2 percent. But they also are very wealthy people who may or may not earn a salary because most of their income comes, not from their labor if they do have jobs, but from their ownership of capital and other assets. They reaped the rest of the lion's share of benefits from the productivity of the U.S. workforce that has doubled in the past three decades. Statistics that help us grasp this reality include the facts that the top 10 percent of Americans collected almost half (48.5 percent) of all reported income in 2005; the richest 10 percent own more than 75 percent of all stocks; and 80 percent of the 2006 tax cuts go to the top 10 percent of Americans.

But these statistics only point to part of the depth of the polarization between these few Americans and the bottom 90 percent. The Internal Revenue Service claims that it collects more taxes from people whose income is derived only from wages and not other assets that comprise wealth. The IRS estimates that it receives taxes from 99 percent of wage income, but only 70 percent of business and investment income that is not accurately reported by upper-income individuals. Economist Robert Kuttner says that "total taxes lawfully owed but uncollected are estimated at more than $300 billion a year — roughly the size of the federal budget deficit."[30]

As previously noted, Americans in the capitalist class, and some of the wealthy just below them, can live off the income from their assets whether or not they hold jobs. Often residing in gated neighborhoods while attending private schools and holding memberships in exclusive international clubs with other members of the world capitalist class and the global elite, many of the wealthiest Americans are building private societies apart from the majority and have largely withdrawn their money and their presence from public arenas and policies that support the common good.

In short, the capitalist class controls the economy and the major social institutions in the society. Its goal is to make the highest possible profits for shareholders (primarily themselves) from their ownership and control of factories, offices, land, raw materials, human labor, investment capital and their manipulation of various forms of (often dubious) financial instruments. The capitalist class does this by strict management of various sectors of the working class and the labor process itself along with their power to deregulate the financial sector. The U.S. capitalist class, along with the world capitalist classes, also controls the international working class through such institutions as the CIA, the School of the Americas, the U.S. military, NATO, and global financial institutions such as the International Monetary Fund and the World Bank. These institutions make sure the global arena is hospitable to the business interests of the economically powerful, including providing cheap labor, forums for investments that will increase countries' debt and bondage, lucrative contracts for rebuilding nations after war-making, the ability to harvest other countries' resources and pollute without restriction, and, perhaps most importantly, access to these countries' markets as they destroy their local economies.

Capitalists determine which products and services are generated, how and where they are made, and how the profits from these working-class endeavors are reinvested. The capitalist class also financially supports and controls the major political and cultural institutions in the society. These are run by the upper sectors of the working class, professionals and managers, to insure that social institutions remain hospitable to the status quo. Largely invisible to most Americans, the capitalist class decides how most people spend most of their time, what their living conditions will be, and how they will think about themselves and their relations to others.

The other major class, the working class, is defined by its subordination to the capitalist class since working people, whatever their income level, have only their labor or primarily their labor or productive abilities to sell in order to live. The highly diversified U.S. working class includes professionals and managers occupying its upper echelons, but constituting about 20 percent of U.S. workers. While there are different levels of income, managerial authority, and professional status in this upper-working-class group, as noted previously, it includes small business owners, doctors, lawyers, academics, journalists, accountants, designers, and some CEOs, among others. The upper tiers of the working class also include semiprofessionals, such as schoolteachers, librarians, nurses, and lower management workers. These groups receive some privileges associated with the capitalist class, which they buy with relatively high income. But they receive higher income and status only if they produce, control, and disseminate knowledge and services supportive of the status quo. Professionals promote and maintain the existing class structure by holding positions in law, medicine, education, business, government, and the media, including television and the major journals and newspapers.[31]

On behalf of the owners of businesses and corporations, managers spend most of their time controlling the lower tiers of the working class, who produce the goods and services but receive little benefit from them. Professionals and semiprofessionals are supposed to sell the capitalist system to their class while providing the educational, health care, legal, business, and entertainment services to maintain the working class as a whole. Politicians rely on taxes that come disproportionately from the working class to subsidize the military, health, insurance, oil, and other capitalist industries, which provide the money to elect them to office.

Without primary ownership of the means of production, the upper tiers of the working class mainly derive income from salaries. These salaries are often significantly higher than the wages of workers below them. Living in separate neighborhoods, with distinctive lifestyles and expensive consumption habits, the upper echelons of the working class rarely identify with workers below them. This remains the case even though most professionals and semiprofessionals, like those below them, have only or primarily their productive abilities to sell in order to make a living. However, a real difference divides workers. Although the working class does not own the means of production or control finance, many in the upper tiers of this class exercise a relative degree of control over their labor process. This control is not true for the vast majority of those in the working class.

Dividing the Working Class by Gender, Race, and Income

The working class is also divided by gender. Gender divisions in the working class include the fact that in 2005 women earned about 77 cents an hour to every dollar earned by men, an increase from 59 cents in 1964.[32] But it is important to understand that this gap decrease is due in part to the fact that men's wages are falling faster than those of women, and women's earnings have still not kept pace with inflation. In fact, full-time, year-round earnings for both men and women fell between 2003 and 2006, and during 2005–6 annual median earnings fell by $2,353 below peak levels in 1999 for men and $1,335 for women.[33]

This closing of the gender wage gap also hides the fact that while (primarily) white women with advanced education have seen remarkable upward mobility in recent decades, accounting for half of all professional, managerial and related occupations in 2005, the majority of women endure low-wage, insecure jobs with no status and little if any benefits.[34]

But wages are only part of understanding the lives of working women. Studies continue to show that, while men have picked up some of the slack, married women still do the overwhelming majority of unpaid domestic labor and child care even if they have jobs outside the home. In 2006 it was estimated that a stay-at-home mother's work was worth $134,121 a year, with women's unpaid work collectively in the United States worth $14 billion a year.[35] In fact, women often reduce paid working hours to care for children. All of the above helps account for the findings of a study by the Institute for Women's Policy Research that, over a lifetime, the gender gap in pay is much more substantial. In their findings, men make 38 percent on average more than women over a lifetime and *one-third* of all U.S. women live at or below 200 percent of the federal poverty line.[36]

In addition to gender stratification, class is also deeply conditioned by racial stratification. A comparison of median household income, as well as percentage of populations in official poverty for all racial/ethnic groups, demonstrates this clearly. The median household income for whites in 2006 was $52,423, and the poverty rate for whites was 8.2 percent. All other racial/ethnic groups have a lower median household income (except for Asian-Americans), and a higher percentage of their populations at or below the official poverty line.

For example, the majority of professionals and semiprofessionals in the United States are white, but African-Americans have joined them in increasing numbers in the last three decades. Census data for 2005 shows that individual income for the upper third of African American workers is the following: 17.4 percent of African Americans earn above $75,000 annually, and another 16.3 percent earn between $50,000 and $75,000. However, at the lower end of the income scale, blacks have *lost significant ground* since 2000. After black poverty had fallen 10.6 percentage points from 1993 to 2000, and teen pregnancy among black teenagers was down 40 percent since 1990, the deteriorating economic situation after 2000 hit black lower-wage workers even harder than other groups.[37]

In short, upper-income black earners are in sharp contrast to the deteriorating conditions of lower-working-class African Americans since 2000. When we look at the situation of African Americans as a whole, we find that in 2006 this group had the lowest median household income of all racial/ethnic groups in the United States. African Americans earned 61 percent of the median for white households ($31,969 compared to $52,423 for whites). In 2006 African Americans had 24.3 percent of their population at or below the official poverty line, compared to 8.2 percent of whites. Latino households earn 72 percent of the median for white households ($37,781) and had 20.6 percent of their population at or below the official poverty line in 2006. With $64,238 for a median household income in 2006, Asian Americans had a higher median than whites. But Asian Americans have a larger proportion of their population in official poverty (10.3 percent compared to 8.2 percent for whites). We see how racism structures income and one's place in the working class when we consider that even though whites, at 43.9 percent of the total number of the officially poor, are the largest racial group of poor people, whites have the lowest proportion of their members in (official) poverty than any other racial/ethnic group (8.2 percent). Blacks and Latinos are almost *three times* (2.7) more likely to be impoverished than whites. In other words, while there are more white people who are officially poor than any other racial/ethnic group, because of racism, *one has less of a chance of being impoverished if one is white.* In addition, centuries of racism also guarantee that whites have a higher net worth or wealth, that is, all that can be personally owned beyond income, than people in communities of color. In 2004 the incomes of people of color were 56 percent that of whites, but their net worth was less than half, about 27 percent of whites.[38]

However, the working class is even more deeply divided by income than it is by race and gender. Differences in earnings between men and women and between whites and communities of color, while significant, are not as great as differences in income between the upper and lower sectors of the working class. In the past three decades the productivity of the U.S. workforce has doubled, and since 2000, the U.S. has seen productivity up 20 percent, with simultaneous growing wage inequality between the upper quintile of workers and everybody else. At the higher end of the wage scale, where virtually all income growth has gone, both male and female professionals, managers and related occupations (primarily white but of all racial/ethnic groups) realized significant gains. In 2007 this includes real hourly wages of the top 5 percent of workers up about 9 percent. Economists Jared Bernstein and Lawrence Mishel observe a *historically high gap between upper-income workers* and middle- and low-wage workers when they consider that the median hourly wage rose by only 3 percent. Bernstein and Mishel write, "Most American workers have not shared in the growth and prosperity they have been helping to create."[39] However, far more than upper-income workers, it is the capitalist class that has reaped the lion's share of the productivity of the U.S. workforce. Recall economist Larry Summers's observation (above, page 74) that the economy works as if every household in the bottom 80 percent is writing a check to the top 1 percent in the amount of $7,000 a year.

In more concrete terms, despite the doubling in worker productivity in the last three decades (and a 20 percent increase since 2000), *real household income for the typical U.S. family has declined* over the last seven years, and median household income for 2006 ($48,201) was $1,043 below what it was in 1999, reflecting a period at the end of the last century when there was a small rise in real wages. In 2008, the nation's median household income was the same. At this point it is important to observe that 50 percent of U.S. households have incomes below this median of $48,201, many far below. For example, more than 15 million Americans live in households that bring in $7,800 a year.[40]

Another way to examine the situation of workers in the bottom half of the population is to consider that almost *one-third of Americans* are currently at or below the official poverty line or have incomes that are 100–200 percent above the poverty line and are still poor. In 2006, about 36.5 million were at or below the official poverty line, nearly one in every eight people. In addition, the age group with the highest rate of official poverty in the United States is children under the age of eighteen, numbering 12.8 million. Children are about *one-third* of the U.S. officially poor.[41]

Many who study poverty agree that the federal poverty line is set too low. For example, in 2007 the federal poverty line was set at $20,650 a year for a family of four. That same year, the Family Economic Self-Sufficiency Standard, released by the nonprofit Crittenton Women's Union, claimed that just to cover bare bones costs, or just to get by without substituting one necessity for another (like food for heat), a Massachusetts family of four needed at least $53,760.[42]

This is why many argue that far more than 36.5 million Americans are living with real economic hardship. Sociologist Kathryn Newman claims that the "near poor" are people in households with incomes between $20,000 and $40,000 a year for a family of four, including households at 100 to 200 percent above the poverty line. They number at least 57 million, and although they are not officially destitute, they struggle to make ends meet and are vulnerable to becoming officially poor. When you add numbers of officially poor and the near officially poor together, you get about 94 million who struggle daily against formidable economic hardships. Given a U.S. population of just over 300 million, almost one-third of people in the United States are impoverished or are nearly impoverished.[43]

People are poor or rich in this country primarily because of their location in the class system. That is the basic truth, even though the class structure uses racism and sexism to justify the deep divisions in working-class income. Racism and sexism give a "commonsense" explanation for the stratification within the working class and hide the enormous polarization between the working class as a whole and the capitalist class.

Increasing Income Stratification in the Working Class

In recent decades, due to major shifts in the U.S. economy, many professionals and managers have seen their positions erode, in terms of losing control over their work, their salaries stagnating or declining, or their positions disappearing altogether.[44] Even before the economic crisis that began in 2007 (with the implosion of the mortgage-backed securities of Bear Stearns) many in the upper working class were experiencing increased powerlessness and economic vulnerability. Similar to low-paid workers, professionals and managers not subject to downsizing often keep their jobs at the price of overwork.[45] Increasingly, they manage large coteries of part-time and contingent workers while also doing clerical functions inherited from the decline in secretarial and other support staff.[46]

Because most people in the upper tiers of the working class identify with the capitalist class and not with other workers, they are often surprised when their education, their maleness, or their whiteness no longer protects them from the vulnerability familiar to the rest of the working class. Educator Carmen Vasquez observes that the so-called middle-class camouflage of working-class chemists, teachers, and managers is revealed, however, when they lose their paychecks and move closer to inhabiting the same rung on the class ladder as the hamburger flipper who has been there her whole life. Vasquez calls on all who do not control production to recognize and defend one another.[47]

Others in the upper working class have been doing exceptionally well. They have seen salaries, benefits, and other perks significantly increase in the past two decades. This is particularly true of the symbolic analysts who de-skill working-class labor and increase centralized control over the work site for all workers.[48] The wealthiest sector of the class system, including the capitalist class (the upper 10 percent), owned 84 percent of all stocks and mutual funds in 2001. Members of the professional/managerial working class who own a disproportionate share of the 16 percent of stock and mutual funds held by the bottom 90 percent in 2001 often wish to grow their assets so that they can own and control the means of production and finance and join the capitalist class.[49] In addition, their attitudes toward the lower members of their class are no different from those of capitalists: workers should provide labor at the lowest possible cost.

While some in the upper 20 percent of the working class are losing ground while others have had soaring incomes (especially the top 5 percent of workers, who had an increase of 9 percent in 2007), it is clear that the bottom 70 percent of workers, if they have not lost ground, have had stagnant wages over recent decades. These are primarily service and manufacturing workers. They include clerical workers, skilled manual workers, and workers who are unskilled or have been de-skilled. The economic status of this sector is deteriorating rapidly. Economist Zweig describes the lower working class as including "those who are employed by others, do not supervise others, and have little autonomy over their work."[50] A few may own stock, but it affords them no control over capitalists or their own labor process. Their role is to work for wages, and their *wages constitute significantly less wealth than they have actually created* so as to produce capitalist profits. They also are the clientele for the upper working class who charge them high prices for professional services. However, professionals expect services provided by the lower working class to remain plentiful and inexpensive.

The lower sectors of the working class, the vast majority of U.S. workers, are always trading off on necessities (like food for heat or health care for rent) given the ubiquity of low-wage work in a high-cost economy. They include the more than 47 million Americans who had no health insurance in 2007 and the additional 58 million Americans who were underinsured in 2008.[51]

Vulnerable workers and families also include the 44 percent of full-time U.S. workers who have no 401(k) plan. Many who do have pension plans are also economically vulnerable because the Federal Reserve found that the average 401(k) balance of the 66 percent of workers who do have pension plans was only $56,878 in 2006. This explains an extensive Vanguard survey which found that before the 2007 subprime mortgage crisis only one-third of U.S. workers were on track to receive a 70 percent retirement replacement rate.[52]

In addition, other measures of the economic vulnerability of the lower sectors of the U.S. working class include the facts that even before the 2007 meltdown about 45 million U.S. families earned too little to even pay income taxes, and 12 million families, including 28 percent of all U.S. adults (56 million people), did not have a bank account or any relationship with a mainstream financial institution. In recent decades, customers of check-cashing stores and rent-to-own outlets, which make profits off poor people, have been growing.[53]

Given increasing economic vulnerability for the majority of workers, over recent decades many households have attempted to hang on to a so-called "middle-class" lifestyle through three major practices. One is through working overtime in which multi-earner families have one or both partners working multiple jobs.[54] In 2001, the average two-earner U.S. household worked ten more weeks a year (or 388 hours) than it did in 1972.[55]

Other common practices by workers have included drawing on equity from their homes to meet expenses not covered by their wages. Compared with 21 percent in the late 1990s, about 45 percent of first-lien mortgage owners refinanced their homes from 2001 to 2004.[56]

As we will see below, this practice has become obsolete given the 2008 subprime mortgage market crisis. Strategies to make ends meet for increasing numbers of workers and families also have included living on credit card debt. As of 2005, two-thirds of all credit card holders carry balances and pay finance fees each month and the average balance per cardholder is almost $5,000. As of 2005, unpaid credit card balances totaled $838 billion.[57]

With the growth of lower-wage work in the U.S. economy, vast numbers of young working-class whites and people of color have been condemned to minimum wage, low-skill, and no-benefit work.[58] Beneath them are increasing numbers who cannot find work or can find only part-time, contingent work. Companies decrease costs by hiring people during peak periods or periods of expanding output, only to fire them when production slows down.

Moreover, the professional/managerial sector is designing computers that further de-skill work so that more work can be downsized and outsourced. Historically, this follows the logic of the capitalist class, which has always sought to control and divide workers and de-value work by de-skilling craftspersons and creating the fragmented assembly-line worker. This historical process has now accelerated to include not only manual work in automated factories but also mental work in automated offices.[59] In tandem with the clericalization of professional workers, we see the professionalization of some sectors of the lower working class. For example, like professionals, more and more people doing clerical work and other forms of administrative support are expected to learn increasing numbers of skills on their own time while their low-skill salaries remain the same or erode.[60] It is also true that more work is becoming unpaid as well as underpaid. Profits go up for companies when they can increasingly appropriate their customers' unpaid labor. In settings from airports to hotel lobbies to grocery stores, to name only a few, customers must now do work done previously by paid employees. Companies are always trying to shift work from the paid job-holder to the paying consumer.[61]

At the very bottom of the working class are adults who work for sub-minimum wages, such as workfare recipients and the 10 percent of prison laborers who now make profits for capitalists.[62] The bottom of the working class also includes unemployed impoverished people who serve the upper class as reserve labor, keeping wages down when they do not have work and standing ready to be absorbed when the economy needs more workers. These people are often forced to subsist on crime, in the underground economy, or on rapidly eroding state welfare programs. As noted above, Americans living below the official poverty line numbered 36.5 million in 2006, 43.9 percent of whom were white.

The flight of both high- and low-wage work to even lower-wage countries through globalization, technological changes that enable work places to function more profitably with a smaller core of full-time workers, and increasing U.S. unemployment among all demographic groups in 2008, have led researchers to talk about "disposable Americans" and the "disappearance of work."[63]

Certainly the U.S. economy is unable to provide living wage work for increasing numbers. Yet rather than examine the class structure and the dynamics of globalization, both conservatives and liberals have other solutions to the deteriorating quality of most people's lives. Many scapegoat immigrants, and nativism is on the rise as more people flee the devastated economies in their own countries due to globalization and neoliberal economics at work there. Most believe in the remedies of working harder and obtaining more education. For example, a 2002 Pew poll found that close to two-thirds of Americans believe that economic success depends on forces within their control, and a majority envy the wealthy and hope to become like them. They do not realize that *each decade since 1970 has seen increasingly less social mobility in the United States* and less mobility than in other industrialized countries like Canada, Finland, Sweden, and Germany.[64]

Economist William Tabb says that the propensity for people to experience the basic unfairness of the capitalist system, "and at the same time accept it and to believe that they can do well against the odds," is difficult for those who see the need for social change and lament the ideological divisions in the U.S. workforce.[65]

In spite of increasing evidence to the contrary, most working people have been optimistic with regard to capitalism, perhaps because market ideology makes people feel powerful. Many scapegoat the government and labor unions they do not find helping them, or they are convinced by the conservative sexual agenda that people who are pro-choice or gays and lesbians are the source of their problems. They by and large seek individual solutions to economic issues, often through religious fundamentalism, not the transformation of the capitalist system and the increasingly polarized class structure. William Tabb observes:

> Lower income people are more likely to live in a harsher world of social and personal insecurity, with greater prevalence of single motherhood, more abortions, and too commonly verbal and physical violence. The psychology of many wanting to escape such a life is to embrace...absolutist guidelines which come with being born again in hope of finding support and strength. The [fundamentalist churches] offer a heart in a heartless world of economic dislocation and deprivation.[66]

Indeed, forms of religion that encourage people to endure suffering now in order to reap rewards later in heaven have always supported social injustice.

While Mike Huckabee's run for the Republican presidential nomination in 2008 showed a shift in some sectors of the religious right toward economic populism, the conservative response to worker immiseration has by and large been to blame individuals for the deteriorating quality of people's lives. The response of liberals to economic deterioration (in addition to advocating social programs that address some of the negative fallout from capitalism) is increasing the amount of education. However, when we see how the lower working class provides exploitable labor and other functions (such as suffering unemployment to keep the general wage level down) that are essential to maintain profits for the capitalist class, it is difficult to believe the dominant ideology asserting that education is the answer to upward mobility for the lower working class. If everyone in the lower working class became educated and moved to the upper tiers of the working class, who would do the worst work in the society for the lowest wages? Who would provide the basis for the affluent lifestyles of the upper working class and the capitalist class? Only relatively few token persons are allowed to leave the lower working class. When a few move up, they do not offer significant competition for professional managerial jobs. They also help maintain the ideology of hard work and the unquestioned privileges of those above.

Increased education is also limited as a response to the loss of higher wage work. Even if people increase education levels, as long as more high paying jobs, like those of the "symbolic analysts" (identified by Robert Reich above) move overseas, what good will education do when people are overqualified for the jobs that remain? In addition, the presence of large numbers of more highly educated people in a labor market that is shrinking the high wage sector means high-wage workers will find their income stagnating due to an increased supply of workers chasing fewer upper-income jobs.

Finally it remains to be seen how the economic meltdown that surfaced in 2007 will affect the American people's analysis of the causes and cures of economic dislocation. Will Congressional bailouts of the corporate, financial, and domestic sectors with current and future taxpayers' money raise class awareness? Will people see that our political economy is one in which the *profits* from the labor of the entire working class are *privatized* and enjoyed by the few, while *losses are socialized and borne by everyone?* Only time will tell.

Using Race and Gender to Hide Class

Since 90 percent of Americans are in the working class, it is important for the capitalist class and the wealthy in the upper 10 percent to keep this overwhelming majority as divided as possible so they do not act together to challenge their common subordinate position in the class structure. This is primarily achieved through income polarization as we have discussed, as well as by race and gender and ideological divisions. The systems of race and gender are harnessed by capitalists to meet their need to not only exploit but to super-exploit large sectors of the working class. Political theorist David Harvey maintains that class is the material site where multiple forms of oppression coalesce.[67] He also contends that we must work to address the injustice of class power without using class to marginalize other unjust power relations.[68] We can appreciate, for example, that disproportionate numbers of people of color and white women occupy the sectors of the lower working class because people's subordinate status in the gender and race hierarchies renders them easy targets for exploitation in the economy. If all workers are essential to support profit-making and are subject to receiving less than they produce by the capitalist class, then race and gender subordination further isolate those who must specialize in doing the worst work for the least amount.

Race and gender subordination are useful to justify the poverty or lower-working-class status of people *without having to analyze the class system itself.* The dynamics of class remain invisible by burying the issue of monopolized class power under questions of gender and race. When people are able to blame poverty on supposedly inferior races and supposedly weaker, less-competent females, they are less likely to notice the class structure itself. Yet much (though certainly not all) of the pain of race and gender oppression is rooted in the class structure, which exploits these and other oppressions so thoroughly. When people struggle against class, they are really working against *the material basis of all subordination.* Since this is the case, we need to pursue economic justice in order to redress injustices of racism and sexism and also to seek justice for white working-class men.

The Ideology of Hard Work and Bad Luck

While class is invisible as a meaningful social category in the United States, it conditions our lives in the most fundamental ways. Class has life-shaping consequences in terms of our personal sense of entitlement (or lack thereof), our degree of access to the social, political, and economic benefits of the society, and our likelihood of having to do the worst and most dangerous jobs in the society. Class is essential to the construction of our identities as capitalist people, the interpretation of our experiences, and the things we learn to desire. Class is encoded into our speech, dress, and assumptions about ourselves and others. Socialization into the class system is done through multiple institutions, including the family, the state, education, and the media. If we are to take moral and personal responsibility for our lives, we must become self-aware about how our class position has taught us to think about the world and our place in it.

To maintain the class system, elites especially are socialized into an "I versus others" worldview that supports individualism and self-interest at the expense of others. This worldview would have us believe that the relations people have with one another through the market are socially just. It would have us believe that the monopolization of control over the economy by the wealthy should be celebrated as "democracy," "freedom," and "human rights."[69] It would have us believe that the benefits bestowed on us, the upper echelons of the working class who think of ourselves as the "middle class," are what we have received according to our individual merit. It would have professionals and managers believe that it is only right and just that lower-working-class people support our lifestyles with low-cost production and services. Perhaps most important, it would have professionals and managers believe that they are fundamentally distinct from the lower working class and have no commonality with them vis-à-vis a relationship to the capitalist class characterized by exploitation.

We learn that capitalist leaders know what is best for us, that they use science and technology to enhance our lives, and that under their tutelage we will have access to more and better jobs if we are prepared for them. And if we are not prepared for the future, we have only ourselves to blame. In order that we will not notice the enormous stratification in income and access to resources, we learn that we have a unified society with a level playing field in which most people are flourishing under social cooperation. This is generally true for everyone except inferior races and genders and other individuals who do not work hard enough or are subject to random bad luck. Professionals, semiprofessionals, and those preparing to enter their ranks learn that we have nothing in common with those who are not doing well in the economy. We think of them as relatively few since we believe that most people have access to the privileges and resources we do.

Thus, it becomes easy to justify our positions and the unearned privileges we enjoy, as well as the suffering of the lazy or unlucky "less fortunate" others. We learn that self-discipline and hard work usually pay off, and due to our own hard work and individual merit, we are entitled to things that other people do not have. Socialization into the class structure gives us permission to be good capitalist people, dedicated to pursuing private consumption and profits and living without accountability to others, especially without obligations to share with them. We continue to believe that "budget cuts" are protecting "our money" from those we have been taught to believe are unworthy, when in fact these cuts lower the general standard of living for most of us by slashing programs that provide the majority with some measure of economic security.[70] Indeed, we learn mostly to admire and identify with those above us in the class system and to blame those below us. In this way, the ideology protecting our privileges in the upper tiers of the working class conditions us to deny attention and feeling to those we have learned are unworthy. To maintain unearned entitlement for some, the professional/managerial sector must be carefully taught to deny not only the privileges of so-called middle-class background, education, and other unearned resources, but also our common class position with those below us, including their suffering and the claims they make on us.[71]

Critically examining how we have been tutored in the social relations of class helps us see that class is not a property of individuals and individual merit, but a way that groups consolidate social, political, and economic power. Contrary to what we are told, most privilege is not earned, and most poverty is not deserved. Poverty is not the lot of "unfortunate" people suffering from random bad luck, for "the poor do not cause their own poverty any more than the wealthy create their own wealth."[72] People largely get their poverty or their wealth depending on their location in the class system.

Being tutored in the social relations of class power also helps us see that many of the increasing problems in the upper working class, such as downsizing, wage stagnation, and overwork, are rooted in the capitalist class rather than in those unemployed or underemployed in the lower working class. For most people with privilege, possessions and status have been won on the shoulders of the lower working class. They provide the available goods and services but, except for a token few, are barred from competing with the professional/managerial sector at the higher levels of the capitalist race. In making moral evaluations about our relations to others, Christians should be speaking about *class power*, how we participate in it, how we benefit from it, who lacks it, and how we share common vulnerability with those below us. As Christian ethicist Beverly Harrison says, proper theological work involves exposing the dynamics, including the class dynamics, that prevent just relationship among human communities.[73]

To continue this theological work of unmasking how we benefit from aspects of class power even as we are excluded from it, we need to move beyond the U.S. class framework to consider class relations in an increasingly globalized economy. To deepen an ethical evaluation of class relations, we need to understand not only the basic structure of class, but also how class relations have evolved in twenty-first-century global corporate capitalism. Class dynamics are changing due to the increasing globalization of capitalism as it becomes a fully integrated and increasingly vulnerable world system.

The Recent History of Capitalism

Given the structure of class elucidated here, it is apparent that social relations under capitalism cannot accommodate accountability between groups or equitable relations among people. As I have argued, if the most powerful 2 percent in U.S. society owns and controls capital (including human labor) in order to make the highest possible profits for investors, then the following must happen for the system to work: the professional/managerial sector must indoctrinate everyone into the basic goodness and "efficiency" of the capitalist project; the lower working class must be pressured to accept the lowest possible wages with the harshest conditions and lowest pay going to the weakest members of society; and the earth and its resources must be available for the exploitation necessary for profit-making. Minimal standards of human decency and the sustainability of the ecosystem are irrelevant to this process. Political analyst William Greider argues that everyone's sense of virtue is degraded by the present reality even though, according to the conscience of capitalism and its supposedly inevitable economic laws, there is no crime.[74] The lack of moral accountability in the class system becomes even more apparent when we examine social relations under current capitalist conditions and how they have evolved in recent history.

The profit-making role of the capitalist class necessitates making the greatest amount of product with the least possible input or cost whether from capital, labor, or raw materials. But making goods and services as cheaply as possible is only half of it. The capitalist class also needs buyers, for it needs to match supply with demand in order to maintain profit levels. Since local markets may quickly dry up, especially if potential customers make low wages as workers, capitalists always need access to new markets. New markets are essential to absorb excess product supply and to provide opportunities to reinvest the profits so that even more profit can be made. In recent decades, as it has also become clear that profits have outgrown the decreasing investment opportunities in the production of goods and services, the financial sector has grown to provide investment opportunities to continue the process of capital accumulation.

Today the capitalist class, which possesses the technology to make business geographically mobile and highly mechanized, has access not only to a nearly inexhaustible global supply of poor people willing to work for the lowest wages, but also to mechanized labor, which can exponentially reduce cost and increase output. Consequently, the key problem of the global economy is a growing surplus of goods, labor, productive capacity, and surplus investment-seeking capital. The current ability of the capitalist classes, including the U.S. capitalist class as well as those of Europe and Asia, to increase supply intensifies the potential for oversupply and increases global competition. Competition from other firms increases the pressure on the capitalists to cut costs, including further exploiting (getting more out of us for even less) the entire working class and destroying the ecosystem.[75] But as we can see, the very remedy to the supply problem at the micro level (cut costs including wages to be more competitive with your supply) increases the problem of oversupply at the macro level as firms both increase their supplies and further impoverish working populations so as to diminish the number of people able to become their customers.

The professional/managerial sector, ever vigilant for capitalists, tells us not to worry; oversupplied markets will eventually shrink to match demand since the economy is basically self-regulating. Individual capitalists, however, keep shooting themselves in the foot, so to speak, as they exhaust both natural resources, essential to the means of producing wealth, and the buying power of workers, essential to maintain markets. Capitalists keep cutting costs that deepen the impoverishment of the working class and ecological destruction. Capitalists also do all they can in the meantime to get around these problems by designing ineffective environmental laws and increasing their access to world markets (through free trade agreements, military intervention in other countries, and neoliberal economic policies).

The historical record demonstrates the various ways the capitalist class has dealt with the problem of oversupply. In the United States, the Great

Depression of 1929 was a major illustration of the illusion that a situation of excess supply and inadequate demand would self-regulate. As Greider points out, stock prices were driven up right before the crash because investors assumed erroneously that all those new factories being built could sell the things they were producing.[76] After years of suffering for the working class, especially its lower sectors, World War II ended the Depression as factories worked at capacity to supply materials for war, virtually creating full employment.

After the war, the oversupply that generated the Great Depression (with too many goods chasing too few buyers) was addressed by strengthening demand through economic policy promoted by the economist John Maynard Keynes. When the government adopted Keynesian policy, the capitalist class forced itself to do what it needed to do in order to survive — accept the growth of unions and union-wage jobs and the role of the state in promoting demand and stabilizing the economy. This included vastly increased military spending (ostensibly fueled by the Cold War) to guarantee profitable military contracts for the largest corporations, government regulation of banking and monopolies, and implementation of labor laws to keep wages up. Keynesian economics also included the policies of the welfare state (including social security, unemployment insurance, food stamps), which put money into the hands of consumers.

In the 1970s, increased competition for U.S. business, due to the revival of European and Japanese capitalist classes from their weakened positions after World War II, meant an *exponential growth in excess capacity*. Given the new technological powers of capital to become mobile, global, and mechanized, the U.S. capitalist class has no longer been willing to support the U.S. working class by accepting unions and other policies of the welfare state of the previous era. David Loy notes that "the economic support system [including union-wage jobs and a state welfare system that was created in the 1930s] to correct the failures of capitalism is now blamed for the failures of capitalism."[77] To make this assessment stick, the capitalist class became superorganized during the 1970s and used its class power to defeat such measures as labor law reform, progressive taxes, consumer protection laws, and antitrust legislation.[78]

Since the 1980s, most of the rest of the 1930s legislation has been dismantled, including the welfare state, as the capitalist class maintains a tight grip on both major political parties. The only part of Keynesian economic policy that is in full swing is military spending, part of the New Deal legislation supporting demand that creates astronomical profits for the largest corporations. Proposed military spending for 2009 is over $515 billion. This is the eleventh year of continuous increases in the base military budget and does not include a supplemental package of $70 billion for war in the Middle East.[79]

The Iraq war alone costs 10 billion a month (or $720 million a day or $50,000 a minute) in taxpayers' money while the U.S. educational system deteriorates and increasing numbers lack access to health care.[80] Increased military spending, especially on top of tax cuts to the wealthy, is done at the expense of domestic spending and support of the common good. For example, in 2007 the federal budget eliminated or reduced 141 social programs and cut nonsecurity discretionary spending by over $2 billion, closely matching the priorities in recent years.[81]

In addition, the United States is the world's leading weapons dealer and is promoting militarism by zealously expanding weapons exports.[82] War benefits the current system, not only because it absorbs military products, but also because IMF and World Bank loans for rebuilding after war-making puts nations and their economies securely under the control of Western capital.[83]

As a result of increased capitalist power, the institutions of the lower working class have been greatly weakened. U.S. workers are no longer afforded a protected niche, including union-wage jobs, within the global working class. Robert Brusca, chief economist of Nikko Securities and spokesperson for the managerial sector, says, "U.S. workers will have to realize that they are now competing for jobs against people who ride to work every day on bicycles, own only one pair of shabby sandals and are prepared to live with their families crammed into tiny apartments."[84]

Obviously, an impoverished U.S. working class will not be able to consume enough to keep profits up for U.S. capitalists. Consequently, the most recent way of dealing with oversupply is not limited to cutting costs by a wage race-to-the-bottom and the mechanization of work. Perhaps even more important, dealing with oversupply includes the proliferation of "free trade agreements" that will give U.S.-based corporations, whose domestic markets are weakening, better access to global markets. The upper class now requires the state to promote not Keynesian policies to increase domestic demand, but what is called neoliberal economic policy, which claims that when governments limit access to global markets, they constrain growth, limit prosperity, and increase unemployment.

A new way of dealing with the problem of oversupply lies at the core of the capitalist system: promotion of such neoliberal economic policies as global export-oriented, highly diversified, and quick-turnover production (since mass markets are drying up, keep supplying the affluent with small batches of ever changing products); flexible labor markets (cut wages with no long-term commitment to the upper and lower tiers of the working class); fewer social services, so a country can pay back loans to rich lenders; and less environmental regulation, which cuts into profits.[85] Neoliberal policies are being implemented globally through governments that must comply with capitalist lending institutions such as the World Bank and the International Monetary Fund. In this way, world financial institutions continue to destroy the local and regional economies of impoverished countries, once ransacked and "overdeveloped" by colonialism and neocolonialism, now "overdeveloped" as playgrounds for the newest profit-making endeavors of the global economic elite.

It seems clear, however, that this geographical "fix" by the capitalist classes is limited by the size of the planet, which only increases the desperate edge to global competition. Each transnational corporation (TNC) hopes that surplus supply will be resolved "when the other guy closes his factory."[86] Every corporation counts on finding a niche to protect it from the larger capitalist system. Strategies for corporate survival are variations on get-rich-quick-and-run schemes. They include forming corporate alliances to divide up the global market, exerting short-term demands for profit through diversified quick-turnover forms of production, shifting production to many markets in many regions (they cannot all fail at once), engaging in casino-like speculation in buying and selling assets through takeovers and mergers, and instituting neoliberal government policies that dismantle the welfare state and redistribute wealth in favor of the rich. And when these are not sufficient, military intervention to prevent alternative experiments keeps regions hostage to capitalist profit-making.

Although China is the fastest growing industrial economy, 80 percent of world manufacturing is still done in the United States, Western Europe, and Japan. Consequently, scholars debate the extent of globalization.[87] Disputing the extent of global trade, however, is not as important as recognizing that the working class has been weakened by capital mobility and by the power of the capitalist class "to launch new and terrifying exit threats — by hiring contingent workers and strike replacements, by restructuring production, or by threatening to close plants or shift production elsewhere" — even if they don't.[88]

That said, it is also true that industrial workers, even though declining in numbers in the global North, have increased their productivity at a staggering rate (doubling it in the United States in the past three decades). While capital mobility may threaten their power, these workers manipulate a productive process far more prolific than workers of previous eras. Hence, scholar Adam Turl observes that in concrete ways, "the *potential* power of the [industrial working class] has been consolidated and strengthened." He points out, however, that workers have yet to organize, consolidate, and use this potential power. This increased productive power, unlike capital mobility, is not a structural weakness of the working class but a political strength that workers have yet to address. Economists and labor advocates observe the need for workers to target capital's most vulnerable points, especially workers in transportation, communication, food supply and high technology, in order to claim this power.[89]

The System of Finance

Since the industrial sector has been diminishing in size (if not in potential power), and since stagnation is threatened by oversupply of products and services, capitalists in recent years have become increasingly dependent on financial speculation, not production of goods and services, to create profit. Today there is an enormous amount of investment-seeking surplus capital circling the globe.[90] Economic inequality has increased in recent decades not only because the capitalist system exerts downward pressure on wages and is always trying to get everyone to do more work for less pay, but also because, in addition to military spending, the speculative financial sector has been one of the few places to make increasing profits. Only the few at the top can afford ownership of substantial financial assets, because only they can afford the risks they usually entail.[91]

However, investment in the financial sector is making the economy not only more polarized, but also increasingly unstable. A recent unstable area in the financial sector of the U.S. economy was the subprime mortgage market, where from 2002 to 2006, wealthy investors bought mortgage securities (bundles of loans widely varying in their risk potential) in a $1 trillion subprime mortgage market to hold and sell at a profit.[92]

This system generated lucrative fees for the housing sector and supporting financial institutions. It also enabled homeowners to borrow heavily against their mortgages to finance "middle-class" consumption patterns even through their wages were stagnant or eroding. Unfortunately, since the financial system — banks, brokerage houses, ratings agencies, bond insurers, and federal and state banking regulators assigned values to these securities that did not reflect their market value, billions have been lost to these investors.[93]

An economic system whose engine is to make profit without limit for relatively few investors is bent on making anything and everything into a commodity — something that can be sold for a profit — even if sophisticated institutions are unable to assign accurate values to them, or are willing to misrepresent risk because the immediate fees and high interest rates are so lucrative, or are willing to loan them to borrowers who probably will not be able to meet payments. In other words, the requirement of profits without limits for investors has led to lack of oversight and more complicated and opaque securities that signaled "fraud or misrepresentation" across the board.[94]

When in early 2008 about a quarter of subprime mortgage holders could not make their payments (after banks and mortgage companies paid brokers to steer lenders toward such risky loans to generate fees from continuous refinancing of the loans), the buyers of these mortgages, including pension funds, investment banks, and wealthy individuals, were losing billions of dollars.[95]

But in terms of the stability of the U.S. economy, the more than a million households foreclosed in 2008 are not the worst of it. Many middle-income households are at risk because they have borrowed and spent against home equity that may no longer exist. The collapse of a major part of the financial sector rendering the foreclosure of so many homes means that *all* home-owners might loose equity (more than $2 trillion in 2008) in their homes.[96] This steep decline in housing prices as a whole portends the inability to borrow on home equity, one of the major sources of middle-class status and consumer purchasing power, thus threatening the entire economy.

Economic Crisis

As noted above, the capitalist system is suffering not only from excess production capacity, but also from excess investment-seeking surplus capital that is often dumped in toxic financial instruments that have little value or whose value cannot be measured.

Also noted previously, such subprime mortgage securities along with other shaky financial instruments like complex bonds and other derivatives have been places where surplus capital sought investment-making opportunities when investment in production and services has not been able to absorb all the investment-seeking capital. (This is due to many reasons, which include the maturation of economies, saturated markets, and the growing inequality of wealth that limits consumption of the goods and services of the productive sector, while increasing unemployment and underemployment.)

In other words, as a result of the endless search for unlimited profits, investment in the financial sector (that is, the "money-making-money" sector that exists outside of the production of goods and services) has increasingly attracted ever-larger amounts of surplus capital, causing the *shift from investment in production to investment in finance* as the major source of profits. Consequently, the financial sector of the U.S. economy has attracted growing investment in shaky or worthless financial instruments, like subprime mortgage securities, the dot.com frenzy, and other "bubbles." The military-industrial complex, generating a permanent war economy, has also been a boon for surplus-capital-seeking investment opportunities.

But the crisis that began in 2007 (with the failure of the investment firm Bear Sterns) demonstrates that the function of military spending as a way to absorb surplus and get the economy moving (as did World War II for the Great Depression) is no longer an easy solution. Current gargantuan U.S. military spending (exceeding $1 trillion in 2008 and constituting half of global military spending) has not been enough to absorb surplus capital. Consequently, investors took refuge in massive unregulated instruments of financial speculation, like irresponsible mortgage lending, excessive leveraging of stocks, and derivative securities that are so complex their value is unknown.[97]

The toxic holdings of the largest U.S. financial institutions created virtual economic standstill and a failed global banking system. This initiated massive Congressional bailouts of the financial and corporate sectors in 2008–9. In addition, a (much smaller) domestic economic stimulus package creating jobs in education, health care, clean energy, and infrastructure needs (as well as tax cuts for individuals at the bottom and the middle of the economy) was also passed to address the largest economic meltdown since the Great Depression. How effective these measures will be remains to be seen. From the perspective of critical economic theory, a question facing U.S. society is this: Has the three decades' shift in the current stage of capitalism from production to finance made capitalism less amenable to a reinstatement of growth by traditional liberal public policy remedies? Or in other words, could the meltdown be bigger than the government's capacity to respond (if not now then sooner or later)?[98]

More specifically the question is: Will public policy that regulates and stabilizes banks, that mandates investments in infrastructure, clean energy, and other green jobs, and that professionalizes low-wage service sector jobs (as called for by Robert Kuttner and other economists) sufficiently address this economic meltdown let alone ongoing ecological destruction?[99]

Critical theorists John Bellamy Foster and Robert McChesney argue *probably not* because, whatever may happen in the financial sector itself, they believe that domestic (civilian) government spending of necessity must be limited and *will not be enough* to respond to what ails us. They argue that the United States has maintained a ceiling on civilian government spending of 12–15 percent of GDP that has held fast for seven decades.[100]

Government spending, they argue, must be limited so that it does not encroach on the profit-making potential of private capitalist interests. John Bellamy Foster and Robert McChesney write that a ceiling on government civilian expenditures must be kept because beyond some minimal level, real estate interests oppose public housing; private health care interests and medical professionals oppose public health care; insurance companies oppose public insurance programs; private education interests oppose public education; and so on.[101]

In other words, will the structural problems of the core economy, especially its tendency to generate overproduction (excess capacity and rising investment-seeking surplus) and stagnation (unemployment and underemployment) and the growth in financial bubbles in response, be sufficiently addressed by liberal policy change that stimulates limited civilian spending? The definitive answer to these questions is not yet clear. But even though it *is clear* that capitalism has always been extremely creative in reinventing itself, the arguments in this book, informed by critical class theory, point to the limitations in liberal public policy measures to address the many crises of the imploding economy. These include the exploitation of a majority of workers (and their increasing inability to participate with dignity in the economy), the limited ceiling on government civilian spending to protect capitalists' interests, the destruction of the ecosphere, and the overaccumulation of surplus capital controlled by the few that is increasingly hard pressed to find sufficient (and workable) investment outlets to continue the process of capital accumulation.

Is widening inequality as a result of unjust class-based production, and the excesses of the financial sector as a response to capitalist stagnation, capable of remediation outside of fundamental structural change? Can we get the economy to serve ordinary people's needs without a groundswell from below to raise the ceiling on civilian government spending, thus encroaching on the power of private capital? And equally important is the question: If "getting the economy moving again" requires individual and military consumerism and the creation of endless needs, endless war, and endless waste (especially toxic heavy metals), can the economy ever have green priorities and still serve profits without limit for relatively few investors (that is, remain capitalism)?[102]

Liberal economic policies will hopefully manage to eliminate the worst aspects of neoliberalism, and slow down the economic and ecological crises. Yet it is also probable that such policies like regulating finance and protecting labor and the environment, however crucial, will not eliminate the *primary causes* of the economic emergency which are the *core dynamics* (overproduction, stagnation, and ecological destruction) required to continue capital accumulation and reproduce the capitalist system. Rather the arguments here support the suspicion by economists working out of critical class theory that liberal policy and other government rescue measures will *not* inaugurate "a sustainable structural change in the business model" and "a new era of financial market innovation," but will more likely "lay the groundwork for still more layers of debt and additional strains during the next economic advance."[103]

There may be no way around *fundamental shifts in all social relations* that would meet genuine needs through democratic control of the political economy with the necessary accountability to the ecosphere. This, of course, would require a cultural (including religious) transformation of what are considered to be the components of a good life.

Managerial Control

As capitalism creates increasing instability through segmented and authoritarian work, union busting, lower wages, de-skilling, the threat of exit, and the promotion of unregulated finance, it becomes evident that the capitalist class is as interested in control as it is in profit-making. The capitalist work process is characterized by hierarchy and the use of technology to de-skill and control people. In the design of the workplace, value is placed on a few elites who dictate goals and the means to get there ("efficiency"), many goods that are delivered quickly regardless of quality ("calculability"), products and services — and people — that are scripted similarly ("predictability"), and bureaucracies that decide what people need and who gets access to information, and utilize continuously innovative technology to control workers ("control").[104] As the capitalist class implements "flexible accumulation" and shifts work from one region of the world to another and from one product line to another while employing continuously changing technology, it functions as a permanently disruptive force.

This process has traditionally created massive insecurity and instability for the lower working class. Once largely protected from these dynamics, the professional/managerial sector is now vulnerable to them as well.[105] Indeed, the front office and the back offices have suffered as enterprise moves industrial jobs to regions of the world without a tradition of industrial organizing, mechanizes work, or revives patriarchal subcontracting and family labor systems (sweatshops) in the United States. With the collapse of the material conditions for working-class politics, such as business dependence on a region's workforce, capitalists feel less pressure to make concessions to popular social needs.[106] At the same time that the state has given a freer hand to industry through deregulation, the structure of the global financial system is becoming more centralized. David Harvey concludes, "What is most interesting...is the way in which capitalism is becoming ever more tightly organized through dispersal, geographic mobility and flexible responses."[107]

Ironically, these innovative, disruptive work processes create a bland and homogenized society. One can jet travel for hours and still be in the same boring commercial landscapes, monolithic urban areas, and predictable suburbs. One can search the mainstream media in vain for variety in political perspectives. Perhaps even more to our peril, the homogenizing of capitalist culture is built on the homogenizing of nature. As the economic system destroys diversity in human societies, so also it destroys diversity in the ecosphere. "As hundreds of species life disappear each year and at an accelerating rate," Ynestra King argues that "nonhuman nature is being rapidly simplified, undoing the work of organic evolution."[108]

Capitalist work creates a society that emphasizes quantity with a corresponding lack of interest in quality or real variety. What is supposedly best is more of the same (whatever superficial camouflage tries to convince us otherwise) delivered quickly. This is as true of McDonald's and Pizza Hut as it is of the Internet. Native talent is replaced by machines, and people adopt corporate-designed scripts for personal emotional expression. Work and the pace of life are subject to speedup in order to shorten product turnover time and increase profits.[109] While the capitalist class struggles to win a game in which some must lose, work is grim.

Not valued in work or society are democracy, variety, continuity, production of a quality item, environmental well-being, emotional labor, including caring for children and helping people, and enjoyment of a good time.[110] In capitalist work people remain isolated, anxious, and insecure, feeling extraordinarily vulnerable to the universalizing power of the economy over their lives. One must search hard for a piece of life that is not up for sale as more areas get pulled into the profit-making system, from vacation packages to dating services to exercise clubs. Harvey maintains that the accelerating turnover in goods and services provides the material base for the accelerating turnover in values. Notions of accountability, responsibility, and commitment seem almost quaint. We have flexible, disposable workers, products, and values, as well as a master narrative shaped around the individual pursuit of an isolated self-interest.[111]

Feelings of insecurity and a lack of alternative values condition people to self-police, a dynamic fundamental to the maintenance of the class system. However much bureaucracy and technology can control us, capitalist profits are absolutely dependent on self-disciplined workers who have internalized capitalist values and the corporate worldview.[112] Without alternative values, good capitalist people have coped with their insecurity by escaping into consumerism and the "shop till you drop" ethos, fueled by the $147 billion spent in advertising in the mid-1990s. Our desires are as socially constructed and manufactured as the goods that satisfy them.[113]

The need to manage and control is so essential to the capitalist ethos that it increasingly takes on a life of its own. The capitalist search for security in a basically insecure system means that managerial domination supersedes classical market forces. When the technology is available, *business is coordinated by manager manipulations more than by market mechanisms.* (As the previous sections discussed, this seems even truer in the financial sector of the economy.) For example, Stanley Deetz observes that the coordinated capacity of managers using sophisticated telecommunications far exceeds the market in business transactions. Deetz notes that "companies such as General Electric primarily escape classical market forces by quickly entering and exiting different markets," according to the get-rich-quick-and-run strategy of contemporary capitalism.[114] Deetz claims that with nearly all fundamental economic decision-making in the hands of managers whose boards consist of managers of other corporations, "the pursuit of profit often becomes subordinated to the attainment of efficiency in bureaucratic organization."[115] Capitalism is evolving into a system that seeks control first and profits second. Like the student who seeks grades with learning as a by-product, capitalism seeks control with profits as a by-product.[116] Ethicist Beverly Harrison agrees when she recognizes the laissez-faire market of neoclassical economics as the "deism of modernity." Harrison says that the "free market" has never existed since "the whole point of capitalism is to *control* markets."[117]

Drawing upon psychoanalytic descriptions of the "Authoritarian Personality," Marc Estrin argues that the weak egos and sexually repressed personalities of many corporate and political bureaucrats drive them to a "rage for order" in which fear of social chaos, including unpredictable sexuality, may be more important than the need to maximize profits or save money.[118] Spending on impoverished people, who are often stigmatized for their sexual practices, is a particularly good example where authoritarianism is promoted despite financial loss. Women who have received welfare note that as government dismantles the welfare state, it is evident that the logic of spending money on poor infants and children in order to avoid much bigger health, education, and prison costs down the road is lost on those who need to control and punish poor single mothers.[119] Similarly, political theorist Carole Pateman states that capitalist owners will not fully automate the work process, however much it reduces their cost, because employers cannot exercise managerial control over machines.[120]

When it becomes clear that the need to control is even stronger than the need to cut costs, it seems that what is going on in our collective situation is more than desire for profits benefiting the top group. To characterize such corporate and political leaders as simply greedy or mean-spirited misunderstands the origins of managerialism in the authoritarian personality and limits effective response.[121] Managerialism as a set of routine practices seeks control over workers, nature, and all subordinate populations associated with nature, even at the expense of profit. The managerial impulse of the authoritarian personality will remain a critical issue for society even if the economy is democratized. The violence involved in controlling and manipulating others has always been essential to a polarized class structure. However, this violence from above is increasing in intensity as economic vulnerability climbs up the class ladder and as crisis becomes ever more ubiquitous. Our social ideology, however, warns us against violence from below and only further mystifies our economic and other social relations.

Who Benefits and Who Suffers?

Who lives and suffers behind the money and goods amassed and enjoyed by elites in the system of managerial corporate capitalism? The question for an ethical economics is this: If people and the earth give of themselves to sustain me, do I have moral obligations to them? When we consume something or when we count our money, do we know what went into making the money we have or what went into making what we consume? Do we know what was destroyed, or if the workers or the ecosystem itself was justly compensated for it? In Catholic social teaching's terms, was the social mortgage paid? What do we need to know in order to develop an economic ethics of right relationship? These questions are crucial to moral agency but are not allowed to surface in capitalist culture.

Since the rise of industrialism in the eighteenth century, capitalism has meant lack of scarcity and increasing ease of life for relatively few on the planet while it chains greater numbers to brutal forms of domination. This economic system erodes moral accountability until people become organized to make it so, as they have during certain periods. The long, hard struggles for labor, civil, and women's rights are part of the history of protest of the profit-making system. People who gave their lives in these struggles are part of the enormous costs of prosperity. They are often little known or forgotten because elites do not wish to acknowledge that the basis of "the good life" is built on the abuse of others. An indicator of the abusive relationship between the global elite and the impoverished or economically vulnerable world majority is that of "gush up" (as opposed to so-called "trickle down") as noted in the Introduction. The phenomenon of "gush up" is being intensified through the process of "globalization," which is the internationalization of state intervention on behalf of the wealthy, whether the country is in the global South *or* North. Professor of public policy Vincent Navarro of Johns Hopkins University cites the work of economist Branco Milanovic, who documents that inequalities have increased dramatically not only between affluent and impoverished countries but also *within* them. Milanovic shows how the top 1 percent of the world's population received 57 percent of world income in the opening years of the twenty-first century, and that the income difference between those at the top and those at the bottom of the global economy increased from 78 times in 1960 to 114 times in 1998. Because global capitalism harnesses all nation states to serve the global elite at the expense of the global middle and impoverished sectors, 20 percent of the richest people in the world live in impoverished countries and the U.S. working class in one of the first victims of the policies of the U.S. political economy.[122] Navarro writes:

> Cutting social public expenditures [as well as wages and taxes on the wealthy] advocated by the IMF and World Bank [as well as U.S. domestic policies] is part of neoliberal public policies pushed by the dominant classes of both the North and the South at the expense of the well-being and quality of life of the dominated classes throughout the world.[123]

Through the market system, these relationships remain invisible. Elites are fed, clothed, and entertained by children, women, and men whose situation as producers of the good life for us is all too often little better than slavery. The following examples uncover only the tip of the iceberg of how this is so. For a start, capitalists can contract work to thousands of small sweatshops throughout the globe that distance the owners as well as the consumers from the women, children, and men whose labor provides the base of the profit-making system. They include, for example, the twenty-five thousand mostly women and girls in Indonesia who make Nike, Reebok, Adidas, and other famous-brand shoes while living in bamboo huts and sharing a tiny living space with five or six other workers. They include the millions of Chinese who labor long hours for little pay to make the toys, leather, shirts, television sets, and other goods whose low prices benefit American consumers and whose wildcat strikes rose dramatically in the 1990s.[124] They include the millions of women, female adolescents, and children who provide sexual service stations for affluent men in Manila, Bangkok, Rio de Janeiro, and Brussels.[125]

Closer to home, they include farm workers who pick our tomatoes in Immokalee, Florida, for about 45 cents for every 32-pound container, a subpoverty wage of about $9,000 a year that has remained stagnant for almost thirty years. When they received a one penny raise for each container from the franchise Taco Bell in 2006, their wages went up by 75 percent.[126] Workers at the bottom also include California strawberry pickers who endure intense back pain, sleep on dirt floors, and make $5,000 laboring seven to nine months a year without benefits.[127] They include Mexican, Central American, and Laotian immigrants who, as mentioned in the previous chapter, cut and pack meat for low pay in the Midwest. These immigrants endure grueling work that can often be sustained for only a year or less. The Immigration and Naturalization Service, working in conjunction with taxpayer-subsidized meatpacking giants, initially looks the other way, but then deports these workers before the industry has to start paying health insurance. Thus, the government supports the capitalist class to keep labor transitory and invisible so that industry is assured an inexhaustible supply of low-wage workers.[128]

As we in the upper echelons of the working class feed, clothe, and entertain ourselves, we are intimately connected to the lives of the women, children, and men who are exploited by terrible conditions of overwork, underpayment, deplorable living environments, and sometimes death in order to provide what we consume and what we have been taught to desire. The blood, sweat, tears, and suffering behind what we consume are carefully hidden from us. We are told instead that CEOs, mutual fund managers, investment speculators, and other members of the business hierarchy are the economic heroes who create the wealth and are benefactors of the general welfare. We are told that foreign workers get low wages because of their low productivity and that they prefer low pay to the company's pulling out. Never mind the centuries of colonial and neocolonial impoverishment by the West, which robbed them of control over their land, labor, and resources. Never mind the escalating wildcat strikes by these "contented" workers. Never mind that so much labor is done under U.S.-sponsored dictatorships notorious for human rights abuses and sustained by bloated military budgets. In the United States, we are told that low-wage workers are independent, responsible achievers, no matter how impoverished they are.

Popular ideology promulgated from academia and the media tells the rest of the working class that when we pay what the market will bear, we pay a just price for our goods. Never mind that the market bears not only unjust social relations, but the vast destruction wrought to other resources, animals, and the earth itself. Most of what we buy seems rootless and pristine. It comes in antiseptic containers, often neatly shrink-wrapped, from which all traces of connection to human, animal, and plant life, all traces of human suffering and oppressive social relations, have been expunged.[129] We are distanced from the environmental destruction and social labor that went into the goods. Resources used for the product may become extinct, or pollution from its manufacture may be more than the ecosystem can absorb. Whole human beings, often adolescents and children, are reduced to hired hands, and their blood, sweat, and tears along with the earth and its creatures are treated as if a storehouse to be plundered for our consumption. The upper working class buys in charming boutiques, designer malls, and overstuffed supermarkets in which the macabre nature of the commercial project is thoroughly masked and the origin of capitalist goods is never questioned. Like the Nazi selling of Jewish children's clothing, only the condition of the goods counts — not too many bullet holes or bloodstains.[130]

In addition, the macabre nature of capitalist commercialism is rising up to threaten more and more of us physically as well as morally. Under conditions of deepening poverty, bacteria are evolving into more virulent forms. We have seen the reemergence of diseases long thought banished, such as leprosy and tuberculosis. The majority of people with AIDS, both in the United States and in the rest of the world, are people for whom poverty is the primary and determining condition of their lives.[131]

Poverty and the system of profit-making also lie at the root of the increasing contamination of the world's food supply. Here especially, the capitalist class and the working class are becoming equally susceptible. The globalization of the food system means that it is increasingly difficult to safeguard what anyone eats. U.S. supermarkets contain raw fruit, vegetables, meat, and eggs that have been saturated with pesticides banned in the United States (but sold for profits elsewhere) and/or laden with increasingly virulent foodborne infection not typically (but increasingly) found in the United States. Elites who refuse to eat fresh produce in Two-Thirds World countries return home and buy it in their local supermarkets. In addition, privileged Americans have been spending half their food dollar in restaurants where food-service workers, among the lowest paid in the labor market, have no health insurance, may have infectious diseases, and may not wash their hands.[132] The food system connects us all intimately, including directly exposing elites to some of the harmful effects of poverty. The contamination of the world's food system is a sobering example of how the chickens have come home to roost.

If the origin of capitalist goods is not questioned or monitored in the global economic system, neither is the origin of our money. Like market exchange, money draws a veil over the social relationships that provide the context for our money. When we analyze the historical geography of our money, for example, or our family's money, we see how it has been amassed on the backs of other groups, especially groups who suffer multiple oppressions. Minnie Bruce Pratt, a white university professor, says she cannot evaluate the money she earns without acknowledging that her family's class position, essential background for her ability to receive a Ph.D., was built on "the pain and blood of people in the past and the present." This includes a great-grandfather who took land from Creek Indians and farmed it with slave labor, a grandfather who worked as a security guard for a coal company's plunder, and a mother whose earnings came from teaching in a segregated white school while leaving her daughter, Minnie, in the care of a black woman who was paid low wages.[133]

Like Pratt, I experience the difficulty of finding out about my family's economic history. It is a history that, as Pratt says, is "hidden with a veneer of respectability and has to be pieced together through bits of conversation and my own knowledge of class theory." Most of us know more about the pedigree of our animals than of our own family class histories. The history of my "grimly held class position" includes Dutch tobacco farmers in North Carolina who made their profits off slave labor and the labor of their Cherokee wives. These native women, like my great-great-grandmother, lost their ancestral homes, were reduced to their wifely roles, and were passed off to their progeny, including my father, as "white" women who "drank too much coffee." Pratt encourages us to rethink the idea of "my money," to "rethink the idea that what we make or acquire is exclusively ours to control, to rethink the idea of *mine*."[134] The social labor our money represents is not ours alone but includes the labor of all those who have contributed to our class position, including our families. We need to learn more about the others whose years of heartbreaking work supported the status of our families. They are part of the reason that we occupy this particular section within our country's class structure. They are the ones to whom we are indebted.

How Elites Are Vulnerable and Damaged

It is a myth that only those in subordinate groups are hurt by the status quo. However many unearned advantages that people in the professional/

managerial sector enjoy in the capitalist system, they, too, experience class vulnerability. They are hurt economically and damaged morally as the following discussion illuminates.

Like that of other workers in our class, the labor of the professional sector is made into a commodity, "thingafied," or made into a means for another's end. Fueled not only by the need to make a profit but also by the need to control, the de-skilling and the overall degradation of work are an ongoing process occurring across all occupational lines.[135] Like the lower tiers of the working class, many managers and professionals have been let go as the upper-class owners of unregulated technology and capital mobility make more profits without their hired hands. The corporate downsizings of the 1990s turned against blue-collar workers and people in the front office as well. Corporations such as GE, GM, Boeing, and IBM destroyed millions of high-wage jobs in the 1990s by exporting work to low-wage countries.[136] For example, corporations can get people with Ph.D.'s in computer engineering in China, India, Russia, or the Czech Republic at a fraction of the cost of U.S. professionals.[137] Given the increasing vulnerability of the majority of workers, managers are in less demand because fewer workers need direct supervision in order to produce more.[138] Other signs of erosion in the upper working class include the fact that, while only 30 percent of the U.S. population had a college degree in 2004, the earnings of college graduates fell 5.2 percent between 2000 and 2004.[139]

Another indication of the vulnerability of the college-educated is that, while long-term unemployment increased between 2000 and 2003 for the entire workforce by 198 percent, for those with a college degree or more, the increase was 299 percent.[140] These statistics are important to remember when economists, educators, business executives, and political leaders, both Democrats and Republicans alike, promote the almost universally accepted claim that good work at good pay is available for all hard-working, educated Americans. Those who are educated about the labor market know better. We know that almost half, more than 45 percent, of the nation's workers, no matter their education or skill level, earned less that $13.25 an hour in 2004, or $26,700 a year for a full time worker. As economist Louis Uchitelle writes, "Rather than having a shortage of skills, millions of American workers have more skills than their jobs require. That is particularly true of college educated people who make up 30 percent of the population today."[141] Even before the economic meltdown of 2008 Uchitelle wrote that low-wage work will only increase in the future. He predicted that seven out of ten occupations expected to grow the fastest from now until 2012 are those that pay less than $13.25 an hour on average, many under $10 an hour. They include, "retail salesclerks, customer service representatives, food service workers, business service workers, cashiers, janitors, nurses' aids and hospital orderlies."[142]

While upper-income jobs (whose wages have been falling) are predicted to continue being generated in health care, high-tech services, biotechnology, accounting, technical research, and education, the amounts generated may not keep up with the college educated. While about 30 percent of Americans are college educated, it is predicted that the occupational composition of jobs requiring a college degree will require only 27.9 percent of the workforce by 2012.[143]

Professional/managerial elites, and those aspiring to this sector, do well to be critical of our training to admire above, scapegoat below, and blame ourselves. We need to take a thoughtful look at the commonalities of our position with those in the lower working class. Analysis of class makes it evident that those on top are supported by a pyramid below. Moreover, far more people have a stake in securing good jobs than in maximizing profits. Along with people in the lower working class, we also create social wealth, although capitalist discourse acknowledges our role only as consumers. We need to better connect our contributions as well as our economic vulnerability to the same capitalist dynamics that are exploiting other working-class people, albeit with greater intensity than they are exploiting us.[144]

Professional elites are not only vulnerable economically, but also damaged as moral and spiritual persons by this class structure. When people are "thingafied," when they are bought for their labor as if they were machines, and when they are thrown away whenever their labor no longer yields the highest possible profits, they do not enjoy full personhood. However, there is little outrage over the way most workers are treated because capitalist society is saturated by behaviors (including racist and sexist behaviors) that reflect the belief that persons are things to be manipulated for others' purposes.[145] Capitalism naturalizes injustice as "the way things are."

While some recognition exists that slavery and rape are denials of personhood, escalating patterns of child abuse, sexual violence, and poverty show that a fundamental lack of respect for the rights of people to direct their own lives is widespread in capitalist culture. Indeed, capitalist profits and the needs of the authoritarian personality depend on "thingafying" and controlling people. In addition to more gross abuses, even the most everyday relationships are being divested of their ethical and spiritual dimensions as they are subsumed under the producer/provider and consumer/client relations of capitalism. Sociologist Robert Bellah explains, "All the primary relationships in our society, those between employers and employees, between lawyers and clients, between doctors and patients, between universities and students are being stripped of any moral understanding other than market exchange."[146] In competitive consumer capitalism, as Catholic monk Thomas Merton once said, even love becomes a business deal.[147]

What is immoral about treating persons as things? Whether workers or consumers, persons treated as objects lose (or are denied) their fundamental bodyright, or right to control their own bodies. Also at stake is their capacity to trust others, a capacity fundamental to human well-being and to moral social relations. Social environments are able to develop trust between persons when persons feel valued primarily for who they are, not for how they meet other people's needs. Trusting relationships are essential for human survival since no one can live apart from interdependence on others. In addition to basic survival needs, the capacity to trust is essential for human flourishing and the development of empathy, cognition, and creativity.[148]

Violation of Trust—Destruction of Community

Philosopher Lawrence Mordekhai Thomas contends that "evil occurs when the moral affirmation of trust is put to the service of immorality."[149] Trust is violated, for example, when notions of equality, fairness, and labor contracts are used to mystify immoral social relations in the workplace. In the capitalist workplace, the moral affirmation of trust by workers in their employers is put in the service of oppression and violence. Given the class structure in the U.S. economy, all persons are damaged by capitalist work relations that are unequal and exploitative but are promulgated as just and generally believed to be so. These work relations involve a violation of trust perpetrated by those who have the social, political, and economic power to name reality (i.e., labor contracts) in service to their immoral purposes of profit without limit and the need to control people.

As Thomas explains, what is so painful about oppressive relations is that they depend on the trust and cooperation of subordinate groups whose moral capacity to trust other human beings is then used by dominants to abuse them. Evil and the corruption of human character occur when human beings, who fundamentally need to trust others, live within exploitative social relations that violate trustworthiness *while everyone pretends otherwise.*[150] The corruption of character may be even more true for dominants because subordinates have often maintained their integrity by active resistance to these arrangements.

Such violations of trust, including naming unjust relations as fair, equal, or loving, separate people and place groups in opposition to one another. This situation negates spiritual needs for friendship and solidarity by destroying the basis for community. The affluent minority damage their common human decency when they make super profits off others under the guise of market exchange, the supposed engine of justice. Everyone, including elites, suffers when *amassing and consuming profits substitute for community.* The human spirit needs sensuous connection with others. When we live off relations that violate trust and isolate people, we become dependent not on them but on our money.

When a culture becomes obsessed with controlling others and making profits off them, we try to fill up our lack of meaningful human relationships with consumer goods. Indeed, market societies must frustrate spiritual needs for friendship and solidarity so that people will consume in an effort to compensate for their loss. However, money and possessions are poor substitutes for the fulfillment of spiritual needs. Repeated studies have shown that beyond a basic and very important level of consumption, there is little difference in people's self-reported happiness with rising amounts of income.[151] Maintaining a class elitist society necessitates "a collective failure to acknowledge the needs of the spirit."[152]

Sociologist Kenneth Westhuis agrees with this assessment, arguing that we are "not only what Herbert Spencer [said we are], a collection of acquisitive, competitive selves craving satisfaction of individual needs." We are "also...cooperative species-beings, *craving the chance to serve.*"[153] Species-beings thrive only within an intricate web of just social relations. The ultimate interest of each lies in promoting the interest of all. British psychiatrist Adam Phillips agrees. He writes that the desire for money and possessions is a substitute for fundamental needs for affection, respect, and self-determination. These needs can be truly satisfied only in flourishing human communities. If this is the case, as I believe it is, then we are bound to be bitterly disappointed in our capitalist quest for happiness since, as Phillips says, "money is only worth what it can actually buy."[154]

Human beings, including the professional sector, long for community as a place to experience mutual respect and to create identity as we serve and are served in caring, reciprocal relations. Our humanity is wounded and our happiness is diminished by impoverished, parasitical relations. Such relations betray friendship. They keep us in the daily grind of the individualistic, competitive rat race in which some groups live off others and economic insecurity is increasing, even for professionals at the top of the working class.

The happiness of the affluent minority is also diminished when we learn about what is really going on in capitalist relations. It is difficult to fully enjoy what we have when we realize that so many others have much less, and further that what we have is related to their impoverishment. When asked what stood in the way of her pleasure, novelist Lisa Alther responded, "A knowledge of the violence and misery many other people and animals are undergoing as I sit enjoying my petty pleasures." To the same question writer Nancy Mairs replied, "My pleasure is marred by my awareness of all the people whose circumstances...prevent them from enjoying the tranquillity I treasure....I worry that I derive much of my pleasure, in one way or another, at their expense."[155] Writer Alice Walker lives with the knowledge that "we are wearing clothing that cost somebody's life," and she grieves "being accomplices to evil acts done in our name and with our hard-earned cash."[156] As for me, shopping, dressing, eating, and doing work I might wish to do are no longer the easy pleasures they once were.

Discovering how the class system works and how it is deeply intertwined with racism, sexism, and ecological destruction is disconcerting to elites. For one thing, we can no longer thank God for "blessings" we have actually stolen from others. Yet if to be human is to create a moral world, then perhaps we are better off living with the discomfort. It is more human to be challenged by it than to live out our days in ignorance of the grossly immoral relations and enormous human suffering that undergird most aspects of our affluent lives. It is better to know than not to know others' suffering and our own increasing vulnerability.

Solidarity Is the Solution

The solution is solidarity. Solidarity means working together to claim a fair share of power in a class structure that impoverishes some, privileges others, and damages everyone. Solidarity from a religious perspective offers a different path to happiness than the dominant religion, that is, the worship of market consumerism and stock market profits. Solidarity affirms the spiritual need of human beings for sensuous human connection, including friendships, trusting relations, and places where no one is excluded. Solidarity expresses the communitarian ethic of biblical faith and embodies the social justice principles of church teaching. Jesus lived in solidarity, and that made subordinate groups eager to follow him.

Emanating from the bottom 90 percent, solidarity can generate a mass movement (most likely triggered by a border-crossing minority) to expand democratic struggle. For solidarity to happen, it is necessary (though not sufficient) that large sectors gain rational *understanding of how the political economy works to benefit the few* and keeps the majority, across diverse income, racial/ethnic, gender, and sexual orientation identities, hostage to profits without limit.

This solidarity movement needs professional persons to be clear on how we are economically vulnerable to and morally damaged by present arrangements. It needs people able to connect our private economic pain not to personal failings or scapegoated others, but to larger public structures. It needs people who are not compliant with the capitalist construction of our identities as individual consumers, but think instead in terms of our common class interests with those below. It needs affluent people who know that the success of our individual efforts is based on privileged access to resources that are becoming increasingly scarce and may disappear altogether. It needs people who understand how solidarity with the lower working class will benefit all persons across race and gender lines.[157] This kind of solidarity will be built only when fragmented sectors of the working class conceive of our interests in common class terms and become sufficiently organized to change the roles we play that promote the status quo. When we understand how systems and institutions violate religious norms and our own humanity, we seek further discernment about what actions and practices appropriately resist these systems. Furthermore, it is likely that such solidarity will depend disproportionately on white women and on men and women of color who, studies show, are most likely to support the interests of poor and lower-working-class people.[158] My guess is that solidarity will also be built disproportionately by Jews, who have always been overrepresented in movements for justice, such as the civil rights, labor, and feminist movements of recent U.S. history. Because such solidarity necessitates a vision of alternative institutions and policies, it will gain momentum only by the increasing hard work of intellectuals and activists who join community struggles with those at the work site.

It is also true that rational understanding will have to be supplemented by political work addressing the human unconscious. As will be discussed in chapter 4, feminism and gay liberation help us understand how sexual repression and the patriarchal coding of desire support the authoritarian personality and interfere with greater democracy.[159] Since morality is a cognitive-affective process, rational understanding must also draw on emotions like empathy to convey the deep connections between the self and others. Religion also is a powerful resource for moral emotions. Since feeling fundamentally alone in the world fosters belief in the rationality of greed rather than sharing, a solution to the class structure will be fueled by feelings of sensuous connection with others that promote compassion for oneself and for them.

In order that more just social relations become normative, the hierarchies of male dominance and the sex/gender system, as well as the class structure, must be transformed. But most important of all, we create a more just society not primarily by making moral arguments or by activating moral emotions (though these are essential parts of the process), but by *concrete forms of resisting injustice together.* The solidarity emanating from the bottom 90 percent can transform society through initial strategies that wrest power from publicly subsidized "private" markets and make the capitalist class start paying its way. Changes include ways of more justly compensating workers while reducing hours and improving working conditions, building a social infrastructure for everyone's security and the better integration of work, family life, and environmental well-being, initiating reparations for groups who historically have given excessively for the well-being of the affluent few, and electing governments that implement this agenda for an ever vigilant constituency.

Although we seem a long way from this vision at the moment, the moral emotions that ground common human decency have not yet been thoroughly quelled. Repeated studies have shown that most people favor deep cuts in military spending, the public funding of elections, higher consumer prices to get rid of sweatshops, and other social justice measures.[160] We deserve an economy that provides our food, clothing, and other consumer items without incurring the suffering and impoverishment of children, women, and poor men. We deserve jobs that do not entail the violation of trustworthiness, the violence of poverty and environmental destruction, and the abuse of our labor and dignity as human beings. Given the situation of decreasing global demand due to the proliferation of low-wage and mechanized work, we are naive if we believe our professional jobs, which cushion some of us from the worst labor abuses, are stable and long term. Nevertheless, we deserve an economy that creates and sustains dignified work and economic security without violating the ecosphere. We deserve an economy in which workers decide what to produce, how to produce it, and how the surplus is to be reinvested. We deserve meaningful work that is well compensated, stable, long term, and respects the environment. We need to build institutions that reproduce this justice.

Christians especially, who have a strong ethical tradition regarding the immorality of a polarized class structure, need to find ways to help people implement their best moral convictions. Christian teaching promotes solidarity that encourages experiments with new social structures and new forms of economic organization "that are increasingly in line with . . . the needs of the weakest."[161] Biblical and church resources are important in informing practices of solidarity and resistance as Christians and other moral agents decide where to stand and what to do.

FOUR

Constructing a Compassionate Sexuality

Among the most effective ways of oppressing a people is through the colonization of their bodies, the stigmatizing of their desires, and the repression of their erotic energies. — ERIC ROFES

THE STRUCTURES OF GENDER and the sexual system are sites of unjust social relations that are intimately connected to other structures of oppression. This chapter examines how the cultural construction of gender and the sexual system grounding it are essential to maintaining class exploitation, racism, and the destruction of the natural world. When we understand the dynamics of gender and sexuality or, as Gail Rubin coined it, "the sex/gender system,"[1] we can see better how sexual liberation for all persons is essential to a broader progressive agenda that includes economic, racial, and ecological justice. Understanding the sex/gender system helps elites see how everyone's potential for communication and justice-making is distorted by this unjust social structure.

The Dynamics of Gender

In our culture, gender is polarized to serve many purposes: a sexual division of labor; the selective allocation of material, emotional, and political resources; and a popular mind-set that is comfortable with relations of domination and subordination. As we shall see, gender creates the peculiar class position of women that has yet to be adequately analyzed. The basis for maintaining the differential access to class privilege experienced by most men and women is found in the *patriarchal coding of erotic desire,* essential to gender formation. Erotic desire, the capacity to name and affect the world, is the basis for one's sense of entitlement (or lack thereof) to social and political power. Thus, gender formation, in conjunction with class and race structures, becomes a site for repressing people's erotic energies so that a few may monopolize power in the society.

The polarization of gender is based first on a polarized notion of biological sex. Human beings are socially constructed, not necessarily biologically

111

constructed, as either male or female. Persons born with both genitalia are considered to be at best "hormonally imbalanced," and through surgery and medication they are forced to choose one or the other genital/hormonal system. Even though male and female do not adequately account for human sex variation, sex polarization is essential for the construction of a polarized gender system.[2]

Gender polarization both reinforces and is sustained by a sexual relationship system that requires heteronormativity and monogamy. Such a sexual system, in turn, reproduces males and females into "properly gendered" (heterogendered) men and women. Such men and women, especially if they are white and affluent, tend to view dominant/subordinate relations as commonsense, including the exploitation of most white women and people of color as well as the domination by affluent white males in economic, political, and cultural life.

The process of gender polarization is based on the division of human attributes into binary opposites. This process assigns one set of attributes (especially ability to do child care, emotional work, and exploited labor) to most women, and another set of attributes (especially propensity for intellectual work, leadership roles in society, and better-paid work) to some men. The purpose of gender, as well as the other major social distinctions, is to allocate privilege and power to some groups at the expense of others. Persons identified as the female sex are socially constructed as women so that they will provide free and unlimited child care, domestic work, and other emotional labor, and provide with other subordinate groups the exploited wage labor in the society. Persons identified as biologically male are socially constructed as men so that some men can have dominance over other men in economic, political, familial, and reproductive matters, and all men, to greater or lesser degrees, can have dominance over at least some women. It is also true that race and class privilege may override the typical gender dynamics so that some women exercise social, political, and economic dominance over other women and some men.

The experiences of gender are multiple because gender is further stratified by structures of class and race and other intersecting differences that have evolved historically. The gender oppression experienced by poor women of color who are lesbian is qualitatively different from the gender oppression experienced by white affluent heterosexual women. Otherwise said, privilege in the class and race systems softens the impact of gender subordination for some women, while subordination in these systems intensifies gender oppression. Similarly, gender privilege is intensified for some men and diminished for others, depending on their class and race positions.

Women of color have reminded white feminists that isolating gender allows some women to ignore their class and race privilege. They have challenged white feminists by developing theory that shows how class, race, sexual orientation, and able-bodiedness or disability can deeply qualify the experience of gender identity.[3] Philosopher Ann Ferguson observes that at least ten race- and class-stratified genders have been identified, and these different racial and class genders do not agree on what counts as primary sources of oppression.[4] For example, even though African American women suffer race and gender subordination, these are not equal forms of oppression in a white racist society. Given the harsh realities experienced by African American men, including the fact that only about half of African American men are now in the labor force, African American women gain more economically by changing their race rather than their sex/gender.[5]

While there is no common experience of gender for women as a group, gender does have meaning. For example, all women, regardless of their class or race privilege, have to struggle for civil rights. Furthermore, the patriarchal sex/gender system, as well as the race system, has been thoroughly harnessed by the class system to serve its purposes. In fact, this has been so completely accomplished that class is now the material basis for all people's oppression.

Gender and Economic Power

Given that most women work unpaid in the home and do disproportionate amounts of exploited labor outside the home, a major function of gender polarization is to make most women work harder than the men in their class and race group. Through gender formation, women and men contribute in different ways to the reproduction of class society. At the same time, as we have said, since gender subordination is intensified by race and class subordination, and diminished by class and race privilege, different constructions of gender also divide women.

Most women are constructed not only to work at low-wage labor but also to monopolize domestic labor. Domestic labor is the cooking, cleaning, and nurturing work required to reproduce class society, that is, exploited labor power and the capitalist class itself. For most women, unshared domestic labor is work they must do in addition to wage labor. Their work provides unpaid and unlimited care and maintenance for current workers (usually male partners) and also reproduces and maintains new workers (children).

In addition, some women are situated outside the industrial wage relation. Their labor reproduces exploitable lower-working-class workers in their own domestic spheres as well as upper-working-class exploitable labor in the professional households where they work.[6] A relatively few women and the women they hire through their class and race privilege work to reproduce and maintain the capitalist class itself. Consequently, through various race- and class-stratified ways of subordinating women, the capitalist class keeps the maintenance and replacement of exploitable labor power, as well as the reproduction of the capitalist class itself, as cost effective as possible. Polarized gender formation reproduces and maintains workers and capitalists for free for the capitalist class.

Clearly, the more privileged a woman is, the less she endures gender subordination. The more class and race privilege she has, the less she contributes to the material labor of reproducing class society. Through her position of privilege, she can exploit the labor of more subordinate women (and men) to do this gender work for her. The most privileged women do not do domestic labor or wage labor. Their class and race dominance eliminates most, not all, of the subordination that comes with gender. However, while the most privileged women can more or less divest themselves of gender subordination, they do this at the expense of the intensified gender subordination of other women.

Most women participate with greater or lesser degree of severity in gender subordination. The majority of women of all races do all or most of domestic labor and engage in disproportionate amounts of exploited wage labor as well. Although all workers are exploited in the class system, women's free and unlimited domestic labor serves as the basis for women's disproportionate representation in the super-exploited tiers of the working class. Here the majority of women labor in low-paying, stressful jobs, which are public extensions of unpaid housework.

Thus, gender polarization requires most women to work a double day: the first day for patriarchy and capitalism, and the second for capitalism. Some women use their class and race privilege to exploit other women to do one or both days for them. Properly gendered women work the first shift for patriarchy when they provide men with more leisure, more nurturance, more sex, and more domestic services at home than women themselves usually receive. They also work the first shift for capitalism by reproducing and maintaining the workforce for free. Women work the second shift for capitalism by doing wage work and keeping wages low, due to their unpaid labor at home. One could argue that women support patriarchy on the second shift, as well, by giving men more opportunity for the better-paying jobs.

In terms of women's peculiar class status, working a double day means that most women support capitalism in the home as well as at work in ways that do not apply to most men. Consequently, no matter what class position women may share with men in the public sphere, women's additional position as a domestic laboring class gives them a different position from men in the overall class structure. No successful formula has yet been found that analyzes the class position of women in relation to that of men.[7]

Women's position as a domestic laboring class has enormous ramifications for their access to economic and political power. As I have said, this double shift for most women is the basis for women's disproportionate presence in the lower rungs of the labor market, including jobs that are public extensions of housework. In the United States in 2005, women as a group earned 77 cents to every dollar earned by men, an increase from 59 cents in 1964. As discussed in chapter 3, the increase was primarily due to a decline in men's earnings as the labor market lost better-paying jobs to foreign investment, downsizing, mechanization, and proliferating low-wage work. Even so, remember that U.S. men make 38 percent on average more than women over a lifetime and *one-third* of all women live at or below 200 percent of the federal poverty line.[8]

In addition racism affects women's labor as shown by the median earnings for different groups of racial/ethnic women. The Feminist Majority Foundation estimated that in 2003 the median annual earnings for white women were $31,169 (75.6 percent of white men whose median was $41,211); the median annual earnings for African American women was $26,965 (65.4 percent of white men); the median annual earnings for Latinas was $22,363 (54.3 percent of white men). A study by the Institute for Women's Policy Research, with similar findings to those previously mentioned, also found that the median for Asian American women was $33,100. The median for Asian American women is higher than white women, but these higher earnings are offset by higher poverty rates in the larger category of Asian American women.[9]

Racism affects the potential for women to be higher earners in that in 2005, 27 percent of all women aged twenty-five or older had a college degree, but only 19 percent of black women and 12 percent of Latinas in this age group had a college degree. This may explain the additional fact that, in 2005, 39 percent of all white women and 45 percent of all Asian women held upper-income jobs in professional/managerial and related occupations, but only 30 percent of black women and 22 percent of Latinas did.[10]

The deeply gendered and racialized nature of the political economy is seen not only in the racially stratified and gendered division of unpaid labor and sex-segmented labor markets, but also in gender-structured social welfare policy.[11] Here men receive "entitlements" such as veterans' benefits and unemployment insurance, whereas women receive "handouts" such as welfare. The need for welfare policy, or "public patriarchy" as it has also been called, has deepened in recent decades as men have lost economic ground in late capitalism and, therefore, their "marriageability." As familial patriarchy has declined and families have grown more dependent on women's lower-wage work, public patriarchy in the form of state intervention in the family has increased. Sexism also increases as women are targeted as the problem for family instability and social deterioration created by advanced capitalism. Public patriarchy enlists professional-sector women among the doctors, welfare workers, public health nurses, child psychologists, and social workers who often infantilize women from the lower tiers of the working class and remind them of their intellectual, emotional, and physical inferiority.[12]

While capitalism largely harnesses male dominance for its purposes, it is true that capitalism also works to erode patriarchy. Women's increasing representation in the labor market means that some women are able to have real choices about marriage. Due to the inroads of wage labor, people's greater opportunity to live outside the traditional family has been a major impetus for the recognition of lesbian and gay sexual orientation and the gay liberation movement.[13] Nevertheless, the class system also "softens women up" for men. Given that the median income for women workers (meaning that 50 percent of all women workers make this amount or less) was $30,724 in 2003, most women with children do not have the financial resources to live independently from men.[14] Laws and other public policies intensify this heterosexist situation when marriage, rather than citizenship, is used to distribute such resources as tax, health, and housing benefits.[15]

In global terms, the class gap between women and men is even greater than in the United States. Ethicist Daniel Maguire quotes a United Nations report, which states that "women constitute 70 percent of the world's 1.3 billion absolute poor, own less than 1 percent of the world's property, but work two-thirds of the world's working hours."[16] Drawing on the work of philosopher-economist Amartya Sen, Meera Nanda says that "women are poorer than their male counterparts in all socioeconomic groups...because of culturally determined consensus about their 'worth' that determines their relative access to the available goods and resources, both material...and cultural." Nanda reminds us that "all members of even the poorest families are not equally poor."[17]

Despite these enormous constraints, women have been active around the globe in resistance to exploitation and oppression. Hazel Carby studied the diversity of twentieth-century women's struggles, including the Igbo women in Nigeria against British colonialism; black women's leadership against land seizures in Africa, Latin America, and the Caribbean; the long history of fighting against unpaid and wage labor by women in India; and the organized struggles of Asian women in Britain, not only against male-dominated capitalism but against white women employers as well.[18] Women of color in the United States have relied on female networks and the extended family in their daily struggles for survival, revealing that family, though often oppressive, can be a powerful resource for some women. Class- and race-stratified gender creates not only victims but also creative resisters.

The political economy in both its privatized and its public spheres uses gender polarization to give some men numerous privileges and power not available to most women. Because women also constitute a domestic laboring class that serves both patriarchy and capitalism, women belong to a different class group than can be accounted for in traditional class theory. However, given that women disproportionately share the worst wage-labor exploitation with some men, women's poverty is deeply rooted in the class structure as well as the structures of gender and race.

Although there is no common experience of gender oppression since gender is so deeply stratified by race and class, gender oppression does have meaning. However much the experience of gender is mediated through the exploitation of women in public work, for example, it is also true that male supremacist relations in family nurture, domestic work, and sex have persisted through different modes of production such as those in the former Soviet Union, China, and Cuba. However much the experience of gender is mediated through race or class, in all male-dominant societies women, because they are women, are expected to serve and care for the men and children in their race, class, and kinship group.[19]

Gender, Eros, and Cultural Power

As the basis for the exploitation and oppression of women in domestic labor and wage work, a polarized gender structure constructs women differently from men through the patriarchal and capitalist shaping of erotic desire. Christian ethicist Beverly Harrison defines the erotic as our power to identify, name, sensuously connect with, and affect, our world. The erotic is the source of our energy and all our doing. It is the opposite of numbness and passivity. Harrison explains that erotic energy emanates from living deeply in our bodies and being able to discern what we feel. Erotic energy empowers us to become subjects of our own lives, to be moral agents as we create mutual relationship in sensuous connection with one another and the natural world.[20]

I agree with Harrison and would like to name my experience of the erotic. This is a difficult task since words always fall short of the experience. Being pressed, I would say that the erotic has to do with intensity of engagement, a heightened sense of excitement, awareness of one's ability to affect others, a deepened sense of vulnerability, and the need to express joy and gratitude. Erotic experiences with my and others' children, with women and men I love, with the ocean or the forest, while writing or running or teaching, are whole-body, whole-heart, and whole-soul experiences. Erotically empowered, I am as aware of the other as I am intensely aware of myself. I live completely in the present moment and am totally absorbed in the sensuousness of the person, environment, or activity that commands my attention and resources. I wish to touch, move with, feel with, be forever with the other. In the erotic moment, consciousness of all else is gone. The present is all there is in this world and all I want ever to be. The fact that some would call my experience of the sensuous erotic a "mystical experience" demonstrates the inadequacy of a dualistic worldview that separates the material world from spiritual reality.

The erotic experience makes me feel power intensely shared with others. I am deeply assured that I have power to make a difference in others' lives, even as my sense of vulnerability to their power is heightened. I need others to care for and about me. And I sense that I am as vital to their well-being as they are to mine. I find such mutuality exhilarating. Because the erotic mediates to me the fullness of being alive, both in my ability to impact others and in my joy in being treasured by them, I feel gratitude and joy. Fully empowered, I wish to pass on my power and fullness of being to others. Marvin Ellison sums it up: "Erotic power [is] a significant moral power, making intimacy possible between people and their world."[21] Erotic power, then, has to do with shared power, with heightened awareness of self and others, with cherishing vulnerability even as we increase energy for doing. In this, the erotic is our power for justice-making, our power for creating right relations with ourselves, others, and the world that sustains us.

Under the system of patriarchal domination, however, eros must be considerably distorted for purposes of social control, exploitation, and oppression. Dominants especially target women and other groups who, like women, are overassociated with their bodies and their supposed inferiority. If these groups are socialized to repress eros, they are disempowered for purposes of maintaining the unjust relations of the status quo. Drawing on the work of Patricia Hill Collins, Ellison contends that our social system has a fear of deep feeling and of our tendency as species-beings to connect with one another. Our capacity to identify across diversity and engage in an expansive "big love" must be denied. For monopolized power to be sustained, power-sharing erotic energy must be distorted, that is, we must be disempowered and disconnected from ourselves and others.[22]

In patriarchy, eros has been harnessed to the need of producing heirs and narrowed to a focus on male-dominant genital sex and reproduction. Under systems of male dominance, women have had to give up the control of their bodies to fathers, husbands, and other male authorities who monopolized power in other areas of life as well. Patriarchy seeks to divest women (and men of subordinate class and racial/ethnic groups) not only of their economic power, but of their sexual and political power as well.

Part of regulating sexuality is to racialize it. In opposition to sexualized racism, discussed below, "good women" have been constructed as "white." To be white means to be without sexual desire or to have sexual desire only for husbands who require their monogamy. This exclusive ownership has been necessary so that propertied men could control women and their reproductive powers, for purposes of inheritance. Patriarchal men have traditionally not been bound by monogamy. While Christian and other forms of religious marriage, as well as secular marriage in contemporary liberal societies, have supported monogamy for men, men have usually operated under the cultural permission of the double standard and the widespread belief that "boys will (and should) be boys."

Men have reinforced women's lack of bodyright, including the absence of cultural permission to exercise sexual desire or be in touch with a sense of political, economic, or social entitlement by escalating rates of physical, emotional, and sexual abuse. Rape, sexual harassment, and other forms of violence against women are on the rise everywhere. The domestic sphere where most women labor for numerous unpaid hours is often the most dangerous place for women. In the United States, a woman is beaten in her home every fifteen seconds, and at least one in every ten perpetrators is a man from the professional sector.[23] In addition, between one in five and one in seven U.S. women will be the victims of a completed rape.[24]

One-quarter to more than half of women in many countries of the world have been physically abused by a present or former partner.[25] Given the prevalence of violence in women's lives, the threat of which affects all women, there is a remarkable lack of attention to how this violence damages women's sexuality and self-esteem, including women's sense of entitlement to bodyright and social power. If eros is the site of our personal power and passionate connection to the world, the patriarchal narrowing of eros to genital sex and the distorting of sexuality into a site of danger rather than pleasure do not bode well for the empowerment and well-being of women.

In addition to the patriarchal coding of sexual desire, the capitalist coding of desire further narrows the erotic for men as well as women. The implications of capitalist eros are also significant for race privilege. As discussed earlier, the disciplined capitalist workplace requires an industrial morality that represses the human capacity for sensuous connection with oneself, one's labor, other people, and the natural world. Playful people who enjoy leisure and a more spontaneous sexuality are not good for business. They threaten those whose need is to exercise managerial control at the work site. As a result of the capitalist manipulation of human eroticism, the patriarchal focus on a regulated marriage ethic and male genital sexuality has only intensified in the service of capitalist interests. The erotic has been harnessed to the service of the work ethic, reproduction, and the selling of products.[26]

People who enjoy socially useful and self-gratifying sensuous work do not flourish under the strict routines, repetitive nature, and antiseptic (or dangerous) environments of capitalist work. For example, in their efforts to get the most out of exploited labor power, capitalists in the early twentieth century developed the "science of work." In this process they "investigated and redefined the relationship between machine and human being to allow for the 'calibration' of workers — the 'mechanical' fine-tuning of their bodies — to fit them to machinery."[27] The erotic as genital supremacy confined to the home becomes even more necessary as bodies are transformed into desexualized machines of public labor and means to profits in the marketplace.

Historically, the patriarchal focus on male genital sex became harnessed to the service of reproducing class society as it kept upper-working-class women in the home to bear and raise the next generation of workers. Even today, highly regulated and narrowed eros, in which people have cultural permission for sex only within heterosexual monogamous marriage, serves capitalism by generating surplus eros that can be mobilized for profit-making. Unmet erotic desire is used to sell products as well as to create new commodities that can be sold for profit. These include the enormously lucrative global corporate businesses of prostitution and pornography. The sex industries function as safety valves for repressed and distorted eros. In addition, because of anti-sex taboo, these industries involve a lower-paid, more vulnerable labor force, which guarantees a higher profit margin.[28]

Capitalist culture deals with unmet erotic desire in ways that also promote racism. As discussed in chapter 2, at root racism is a cultural construct tied to attitudes, behaviors, and social patterns that are anti-poor and erotophobic. Given highly regulated (white) sexuality, unmet erotic desire is channeled not only into consumption but also into scapegoating. The racial identities of men and women of color, as well as Jewish people and even white working-class people, have been constructed, in varying degrees, to carry the negative body and the rejected sexuality of whites. White religious prohibitions against sensuality, along with the rigid sexual regulation in (white) industrial morality, have turned people of color, their bodies, music, and other cultural elements into dangerous carriers of the erotic as forbidden sensuality.[29] Whites project their fascination about forbidden sexuality onto people of color who become "exotic." They also project loathing about sexuality, carefully learned, onto scapegoated others, who become dangerous and in need of white social control.

Those who carry the negative body, especially communities of color, white Jews, and gay people, are caricatured as sexual predators. Jewish people become "carnal," lesbians and gay men become "pedophiles," black men become "rapists," black women and working-class white women become "whores," always ready for sex, and poor women of color become "promiscuous welfare cheats." White women, or more accurately, those wishing to achieve white normative status, must present themselves as devoid of sexual desire, except for their "marital duty." Thus, the gendered, racist construction of sexual desire divides "good" (white) women from most "promiscuous" women of color since "good" women do not have sexual desire, but enjoy being submissive and compliant to men. Historian Evelyn Brooks Higginbotham suggests, "Gender identity is inextricably linked to and even determined by racial identity."[30] And, we might add, racism is inextricably tied to those who carry the disrespected sexual body.

On the other hand, properly gendered men with class and race privilege have cultural permission for sexual desire and are socialized to feel entitled to sex with women. They feel especially justified in sexual entitlement to women of color, and to a lesser extent poor white women, because such women are viewed as not properly gendered and therefore always "ready for sale."[31] Since men of color and white Jewish men are often viewed as oversexed rivals, white men must protect "their" women from them. Sexualized racism is used to justify eroticized violence, including the rape of women of color, and such practices as lynching African Americans in order to control subordinates who might be tempted to resist.

As more women live outside marriage, as lesbians and gay men become more visible in their demands, and as more men lose marriageability in the radically restructured economy, patriarchy is waging a war against these capitalist inroads to its traditional forms of gender privilege. This conflict is especially seen in the obsession with family values and increasing emphasis on both gender polarization and heterosexual monogamy. In this climate, gender privilege in sexuality can be overruled by the racist coding of sexuality. As legal scholar Patricia Williams explains, "Race is less about biology than cultural imagination." Williams agrees with novelist Toni Morrison's assessment that Bill Clinton, a saxophone player who engaged in adult consensual sex outside marriage, has failed to fully achieve "white" racial status in the society. Williams describes Clinton as "skewered with all the tropes of blackness" because, in Morrison's words, he is the product of a "single parent household, born poor, working-class," whose body, whose privacy, and whose "unpoliced sexuality became the focus of persecution."[32] A U.S. president can sign a 1996 welfare bill that cuts billions of dollars to poor legal immigrants, low-income disabled children, working-poor families, and the elderly poor, and dismantle a sixty-year legacy of federal responsibility for other poor families, and people yawn. However, when nonmarital sex occurs in the White House, we have the second impeachment trial in U.S. history.

The gendered and racist coding of sexual desire has enormous ramifications for people's sense of personal power and entitlement in society. Those who endure the weight of a deviant sexuality as well as those who are not supposed to have sexual desire at all are regulated at the central site of their personal power. Their desires as moral agents are not only discounted; they are seen as dangerous and in need of control for purposes of social order. Their capacities for sensuous labor, for naming reality from their point of view, and for deep connections to others threaten the status quo. Therefore, the patriarchal and racist coding of desire must eroticize inequality as it increases fear and enforces conformity to all the systems of oppression. White class-elitist men have been allowed, even encouraged, to have privileged access to the labor and sexuality of subordinate others who are the majority of the population. For everyone else sexual expression, and personal power, is highly regulated. It is centered on the expectation of heterosexuality and monogamy, or highly restricted sexual entitlement, especially for those who wish to achieve properly gendered female and normative "white" racial status in the society. Theologian Mary Pellauer asks, "What stirs in our orgasms, that there should be so many obstacles around them?"[33]

Heterosexual monogamy, and the gender polarization necessary to reproduce it, is so invested in patriarchal, capitalist, and racist interests that our sexual system cannot sustain clear boundaries between sexual intimacy and sexual violence. For example, many don't know how to separate flirting from behavior that escalates into harassment and humiliation. Neither can the sexual system sustain boundaries between fidelity in relationship and monopoly ownership of a partner's body and sexual, emotional, and physical resources. In recent times, there has been less cultural permission for the double standard for men as intimacy relations become even more tightly bound to the system of property relations.[34]

Even though women's experiences of sexual disempowerment vary according to class and race, gender oppression in this area as well as in the class system does have meaning. In all male-dominant societies women have struggled relentlessly for control over their sexual and reproductive functions, and most women have had little or no control. Men within the dominant class and race groups have been socialized to expect entitlement to women's bodies, including legal control over them. Catholic ethicist Christine Gudorf characterizes women's relative lack of sexual and reproductive choice as a violation of bodyright, which is foundational to the full personhood and moral agency of all human beings.[35] Former psychoanalyst Alice Miller likens the enforced divorce between the self and one's inner desires to "soul murder."[36]

Gender has meaning because in all male-dominant societies, cultural permission is granted for sex only if it is between a man and a woman within the institution of marriage or a similar form of ownership pattern. In male-dominant societies, men are socialized to demand entitlement over (at least some) women's physical and emotional labor as well as their sexual services.[37] Women do not have cultural permission for sexual desire or sexual agency. In capitalist, racist, male-dominant societies men have cultural permission to punish the women — and men — whose sexual desire is deviant by virtue of not having achieved female or "white" normative status, or by virtue of being gay, or even by virtue of having been raped.

While women suffer gender subordination differently (and men wage gender dominance differently) according to race and class, all women suffer from a lack of equality with the men in their group. While women participate differently in the unpaid and wage labor aspects of gender subordination, as well as in permission or persecution for sexual desire, "all women suffer disadvantage in the political sphere."[38] All women, even capitalist class women, must struggle for equal rights in the society.

It Has Not Always and Everywhere Been So

Leslie Feinberg argues that most people subscribe to the "Flintstone" school of anthropology. They believe that social change is not really possible because the way we are now is the way things have always been.[39] Despite popular belief, it simply is not true that gender-polarized men and women are what being human is always about. It simply is not true that heterosexuality and monogamy have always had normative status in every culture's sexual ethics. Anthropological study provides evidence that our notions of biological sex, gender, and heterosexuality are socially produced. Historically and culturally, gender is much larger in human experience than the "heterogender" that supports heteronormativity. "Properly gendered" (heterogendered) males and females, heterosexuality, monogamy, or even biological maleness or femaleness is not a natural or universal human condition.

As mentioned previously, persons in Western culture born without clear differentiation into one of the two socially defined biological sexes have been forced to choose whether they wished to live as socially constructed (heterogendered) men or women. However, this has not been the view of all societies. For example, the Dine (Navajo) nation in North America viewed persons born with both male and female genitalia not as imbalanced and in need of correction, but as examples of human completeness.[40]

We see especially how biological sex, maleness and femaleness, is socially constructed to support heterogender when we consider the struggle of transgendered people. Transgendered people wish to express themselves as a gender different from the gender the culture has attached to their biological sex. Called such names as transvestites, transsexuals, drag queens, and cross-dressers, they are considered gender outlaws. In male-dominant, racist, capitalist societies, biological females whose self-expression is "masculine" or males whose self-expression is "feminine" are mistakenly assumed to *always* be stereotyped lesbian or gay, and they are subject to everything from harassment to violence to murder. Yet there is a whole range of ways for biological males and females to express themselves.[41] Many possible configurations exist between biological sex, gender expression, and sexual practice.

In societies that do not need a polarized gender structure to support heteronormativity and its vested economic and political interests, transgendered people have expressed their gender without derision and violence, and they have been honored. The colonial invaders named transgendered people, thought to have flourished in more than 135 North American Indian nations, *berdache*. Honored as shamans, great warriors, or the highest-ranking members of governing councils, the *berdache* were tortured and burned at the stake by Christian invaders. The economic, social, and political values of European Christians made incomprehensible these powerful leaders of their societies — male women, female men, and bisexed, bigendered, and bisexual individuals.[42]

Moreover, societies that do not need a polarized gender structure and heteronormativity do not enforce monogamy. Caribbean slaves ridiculed the new slave codes of the 1780s, which promulgated European marriage to encourage the local breeding of slaves. They wished, to the contrary, to continue their practice of each man and woman living together for as long or as short a period as they pleased. Alfred Caldecott, a nineteenth-century church historian, said of this situation, "There is in the Negro race a nearer approach to equality between the sexes than is found in the European races."[43] However, Europeans perceived equality between the sexes, the independence of women, and men's lack of interest in sexual control (and militarism) as signs of primitive backwardness and racial inferiority that needed to be eradicated.

The work of anthropologists Peggy Reeves Sanday, David Levinson, and H. P. Phillips shows that societies that do not enforce regulated sexual desire have egalitarian relations between the sexes and little violence.[44] Sanday found that in 47 percent of 156 tribal societies violence, including rape, is rare when gender polarization, racism, and other hierarchical differences are not present in the society.[45] David Levinson found that gender-based violence was virtually absent in 16 out of 90 peasant and small-scale societies. In the work of H. P. Phillips, the Central Thai were especially noteworthy for their disdain of aggression and their highly developed methods of conflict resolution. Among the Central Thai, divorce was common, men were as likely as women to engage in domestic labor and child care, and women were as likely as men to manage the family business.[46] Cross-cultural studies provide ample evidence that domineering males are as socially constructed as submissive females. Male conditioning, not the condition of being male, is at the heart of male dominance.

Multiple studies provide evidence that lack of erotic regulation and freedom in gender and sexual expression are important for social peace. Using the massive cross-cultural research of neurophysiologist James W. Prescott, ethicist James Nelson points out that sex-positive and body-positive societies that allow a great deal of touching and physical nurturance are predictably cooperative, peaceful societies. It is no wonder that male violence is so prevalent in gender-polarized, racist, capitalist societies where sexuality is highly regulated and presumed sinful until proven innocent. Nelson says,

"Body-selves deprived of pleasure become both angry and deadened. They search for violent ways of making themselves feel alive."[47]

Gender fluidity and fluidity in sexual practice threaten an economy that depends on the heterosexual monogamous family as the linchpin of other oppressive structures. These include the sexual division of labor, the oppression of people of color, and the monopolization of economic and political power by the privileged few. Indeed, many scholars have argued that the origin of the monogamous, heteronormative family lies in the evolution of society into polarized classes based on the private ownership of property. Kinship systems based on the property rights of a relatively few privileged men necessitated the subordination of women, children, slaves, and other men without property.[48] Leslie Feinberg concludes, "In reality it was the rise of private property, the male-dominant family and class divisions that led to narrowing what was considered acceptable self-expression."[49]

To understand the particular sex/gender system that so deeply shapes our humanity, we must see how heteronormativity and compulsory heterosexual monogamy (marriage) serve specific interests. Since sexual expression must be highly regulated for the purpose of maldistributing economic benefits and political power, it stands to reason, as studies confirm, that heteronormativity and monogamy are neither natural nor universal. As we have seen, heteronormativity is, in fact, the organizing institution for achieving two unequal genders conceived as "opposite." Heteronormativity includes the material deprivation and political disempowering of women as a group, lesbians and gay people, people of color, working-class and working-poor people, and others who as groups are not properly heterogendered and are overidentified with their (supposedly deviant) sexuality.

Outside a sex/gender system constructed to serve male-dominant, class-stratified, racist interests, compulsory heterosexual monogamy is not needed. Heterogender, heteronormativity, and monogamy exist not because they are natural to the human condition, but because they are needed to support the one interlocking system of patriarchal, racist capitalism. Chrys Ingraham asks, "Without institutionalized heterosexuality — that is, the ideological and organizational regulation of relations between men and women — would gender even exist?"[50]

I think fluid and evolving gender expression will always exist for purposes of varied self-expression. But certainly without a race-stratified class society, severe gender polarization would have considerably less social support. When we understand how essential gender polarization is, not only to the reproduction of male dominance, but to other forms of hierarchy and social stratification, we will understand the inability of most people to imagine an alternative sex/gender system.

The gender system is the first and most powerful experience people have of unshared power. Deeply ingrained into the social world of children, the gender-polarized heterosexual family teaches them that dominant/subordinate relations are normal and natural. People raised in sexist environments believe that men's entitlement and women's self-sacrifice are necessary expressions of human love and essential to the right ordering of society. People raised in gender-polarized families are conditioned to accept race hierarchies, abject poverty, and arrogant affluence as the way the world naturally is. People conditioned to accept gender hierarchy have little trouble with white supremacy and with the reality that some groups suffer economic exploitation and cultural marginalization to the benefit of others. People raised in heterogendered, monogamous families understand intimate relations as property relations. They believe it is only right and just that parents exercise ownership rights over children for whom the community is not responsible, and that a partner is the source of their personal supply of emotional and sexual resources over which they should have monopoly control.

With the sex/gender system serving so many functions, it is no wonder that people with more fluid gender expressions or sexual practices attract fear, loathing, and social ire. They threaten the foundations of the whole social (dis)order. Liberation efforts waged by some heterosexual women, gays, lesbians, transgendered people, and their allies to interfere with the polarized gender structure and reconstruct the traditional family threaten to destabilize society when they challenge this foundational system.

The problem, however, is not the breakdown of the family; the problem is *the traditional family itself.* The reason the nuclear family is breaking down — or exists as one of the most dangerous sites in North America for women and children — is because people in it are often isolated emotionally and stressed economically. The real problem is the capitalist family structure, which is based on ownership patterns and is in service to the system of profit-making.

As we have seen, there are many societies, primarily societies of color, with different sex/gender systems and different constructions of family. British social theorist Hazel Carby cautions, however, that better-looking social relations in alternative systems may not mean that women and others are not oppressed. Assessments from outsiders cannot determine what is important to the people themselves in these societies.[51] U.S. historian Howard Zinn is also aware of the dangers of romanticizing. Nevertheless, his reading of the historical record is that Europeans "were not coming into an empty wilderness but into a world which in some places was as deeply populated as Europe itself, where the culture was complex, where human relations were more egalitarian than in Europe, and where the relations among men, women, children and nature were more beautifully worked out than perhaps any place in the world."[52] Despite our "Flintstone" perceptions of gender and sexual ethics, it seems clear that patriarchal and capitalist systems have created a historically bounded sexual morality and system of family relations that would hardly be credited with much moral wisdom by many societies.

How Elites Are Hurt

All women, at least to some degree, suffer from our sex/gender system. This system makes women responsible for more work than the men in their group. Many women are forced to work harder than other women and most men. Apart from their actual sexual practice, the sex/gender system punishes women for sexual deviance because of their race or ethnicity, social class, or sexual orientation. It also gives cultural permission to punish even women with class and race privilege who claim sexual desire outside monogamous patterns. And it makes the denial of equal political rights to all women seem commonsense.

Our sex/gender system also gives cultural permission to discriminate against or punish the men who, like women, are overidentified with their bodies and a presumed deviant sexuality. These include white Jewish men, men of color, gay men, working-class and working-poor men, whites who have not achieved "white" normative status, and disabled men. However, dominants also suffer, including race- and class-privileged heterosexual males. Their children suffer, too, because the family care system is collapsing across the socioeconomic spectrum.

It is a mistake to think that our sex/gender system does not hurt class- and race-privileged men. Like most men, privileged men are socially constructed by the ideology of masculine dominance to repress many of their human capacities. This repression is necessary for such men to become aggressive and seek control over women and as many men as possible. Privileged men rely less on personal forms of aggression, such as harassment, battering, and rape, because they have more deadly forms of violence at their disposal, such as unshared economic and political power.

Privileged men, like most men, are socialized to deny certain emotions, especially the pain and humiliation they feel from men who have authority over them. Most males at some point in their lives are harassed, intimidated, humiliated, and abused into being properly gendered men. They are pressured to conform to certain stereotypes and play certain roles or else stand in danger of losing their manhood. These roles include making fun of women and the emotional work required to bring about relationships of mutuality and reciprocity. They include aspiring to (uncritical) leadership in a violent society that promotes war and readiness for war, makes "killings" in the market the highest expression of human achievement, prevents people from meeting basic needs, and destroys the environment.

Male gender formation carefully sets up privileged men for this work as it deprives them of the human skills for relationship and nurturance. Educator

Paul Kivel observes that "it takes years and years of training to make boys into violent men."[53] In short, privileged men are hurt because, like most men, they are truncated people without access to their full human capacities. One could argue that many privileged men are more morally compromised than other less-powerful men because if they want to maintain their power, they must perpetrate or support those who perpetrate the most massive forms of violence in the society.

The privileged are also hurt when we look at what is going on at home. In constructing men who are largely undeveloped or underdeveloped in the human potential for nurturance, and in forcing most women to seek wage labor, the sex/gender system of racist, capitalist patriarchy is placing the well-being of increasing numbers of children in jeopardy. This includes the children of privileged groups as more upper-income parents spend more time in the workplace, and as quality child care becomes scarce and expensive.

With parents spending less time at home, children are increasingly vulnerable, especially if men are unable or unwilling to do domestic labor. In her extensive studies of domestic labor, sociologist Arlie Hochschild has found increasing stress in the home. She discovered that many affluent parents are not opting to work part-time, that upper-income new mothers are not any more likely to stay home after three months than low-income new mothers, that job culture disparages parents who put children first, and that quality time in the home is becoming like an office appointment.[54]

Hochschild and coresearcher Anne Machung found that only 21 to 30 percent of men who make more or the same wages as wives share the domestic labor of caring for children. Men who make more money than their partners are *less* likely to do so.[55] Men's continued lack of sharing childcare is confirmed by a 2006 Bureau of Labor Statistics study that found that working women with small children spend more than twice the hours per day caring for their children than their spouses.[56] Men lose out because the relatively few men heavily involved with their children were significantly happier with their family life than less-involved men, and there is some evidence that their children were more empathetic than other children.[57] The fact remains, however, that women who constitute almost half of those who do public labor are responsible for the majority of domestic labor in the United States today.

As to be expected, Hochschild and Machung reported that while the majority of fathers give child care responsibility to mothers, mothers are increasingly giving it to other, more subordinate women. Baby-sitters and childcare center workers are often under pressure to keep their jobs by not bothering harried parents with children's distress. In the words of the authors, "In a time of stalled revolution — when women have gone to work, but the workplace, the culture, and most of all the men have not adjusted themselves to this new reality — children can be the victims."[58] Because of men's enormous fear of nurturing and tenderness, they even more than women are tied to gender roles, to the detriment of themselves and their children.

To make matters worse for children, research indicates that as home life becomes more stressful, women as well as men are seeking refuge in the office. Hochschild says that "increasing numbers of women are discovering a great male secret — that work can be an escape from the pressures of home, pressures that the changing nature of work itself are only intensifying."[59] In other words, not only is wage labor taking up increasing amounts of parents' time, but women are being tempted to give it even more time. Given a partner unwilling to share the second shift, women do not have enough time to be truly successful at home. The loss of a domestic labor force is creating a crisis of care in this society, with the smallest, most vulnerable members paying the biggest price. As children today spend less time with adults than perhaps at any other time in history, the need for quality child care unites people across class and race.

Privileged groups are also hurt, along with everyone else, by the restriction of our capacity for sensuous connection with others, especially through the system of compulsory monogamy. As we have seen, a highly regulated sexual system is one of the pillars of racist capitalism and a de-eroticized industrial morality. Monogamy channels erotic desire into a highly restricted sexual system that is often not equal to the burden.

In the latter decades of the twentieth century, divorce rates soared, peaking at one out of two marriages in the United States ending in divorce.[60] While the reasons are many, human need for nurturing touch and sensual connection cannot be satisfied by genitally focused sex or by one person exclusively. Even when monogamous relationships are rich and satisfying, they are not sufficient to compensate for the loss of erotic connection we experience elsewhere, or balm enough to heal any deep wounds to our self-respect from families of origin, the workplace, and other sites of oppression.[61] Most people need a wide variety of friendships of varying emotional intensity. Yet as the male-dominant family is eroded by the restructured economy, fear increases about unregulated sexual expression. As the economic basis for the family is weakened, the ideology of the male-dominant heterogendered family is promoted for purposes of social control. Racist, capitalist patriarchy, especially as promoted by the religious Right, intensifies the demonization of sexual expression other than heterosexual monogamy.

Privileged people are hurt, as are most in the society, through increasing loss of access to our deepest selves. As the cultural ethos increases restrictions on sexual passion, people experience a more general shutdown of feelings and emotions. As Buddhist educators Joanna Macy and Molly Brown remind us, repression cannot be isolated to certain areas of our capacity to feel. "Repression," they say, "takes a mammoth toll on our energy and also on our sensitivity to the world around us. Repression is not a local anesthetic."[62] In other words, if we must shut down in one area, we shut down at the central nervous system. If we cannot feel deep friendship including sexual passion, we cannot feel much else either, including deep joy, compassion, or pain for our world. Beverly Harrison notes the perplexity of progressive Christian activists at the growing political apathy of many in the churches and traces social passivity to the impoverished dynamics of our interpersonal, primary relationships.[63] Highly regulated male genital sexuality not only shuts down many dimensions of the erotic; it deadens our potential to be justice makers. We become numb to social pain and are unable to feel outrage about what is going on in the world. People who are good at censuring their feelings do not know what they feel and do not have access to compassion for themselves and others.

In addition, a highly restrictive sexual system intensifies authoritarianism in people's relations to themselves and others and thereby reinforces the very systems that are doing us in. As Ellison points out, when people's physical and emotional needs are not being met, when they are divorced from sensuous connection to others and the natural world, people "tend to become more repressive about sex, more judgmental about differences, and more unforgiving toward themselves and others."[64] The more deprived we are of sensuous connections to others in work and play, the more we experience scarcity and the need to protect our "supply." We increase our dependency on exceptionless rules, such as compulsory heterosexual monogamy, which keep us moral infants, unable to engage in the self-critical ethical reflection that comes with the freedom to engage deeply with others.[65]

It is important for dominants to see that compulsory heterosexual monogamy hurts not only heterosexual women and gay, lesbian, bisexual, and transgendered people. As Nicola Field says, the sex/gender system "is a powerful weapon preventing people of all sexualities from realizing their potential, socially as well as sexually."[66] The requirement to achieve a heterogender in order to secure normative status in this society hurts most people, who become truncated human beings, restricted from expressing or developing the widest possible range of human attributes. So, too, the demonization of most sexual relationships hurts most people who are told their feelings and desires are illegitimate. Any expression outside a restrictive ownership pattern may result in social, political, and/or economic punishment for any of us. All of us are damaged because eros and sexual fulfillment are essential to human well-being, and when they are diminished, so are we.

The Contribution of Christian Teachings

The Christian churches, including the Roman Catholic Church, have been the major architects and chief enforcers of compulsory heterosexual monogamy.

Even though Jesus lived in a discipleship of equals with women and other subordinates in his society, hatred of women and hatred of sexuality have been "an active force profoundly deforming Christianity's own internal structure and ideology for centuries."[67] No connection between religion and sexual repression was inevitable or fated.

Christianity began in the first century as a revolutionary movement of women, slaves, and poor people who were joined by socially dominant allies. In the fourth century, Christianity became a powerful state religion in service of elite interests. When the church capitulated to Constantine and supported the religion of empire, ordinary Christians had to discard their roles of opposing oppressive power relations, including opposition to Roman war-making. The emerging church leadership abandoned egalitarian models and adopted Roman hierarchy and the social relations of feudalism, thereby establishing a new identity for Christians.

Historical theologian Samuel Laeuchli dates the origin of the church's anti-sexual code to the Council of Elvira, Spain, in 309 C.E. Laeuchli explains, "By establishing sexual codes the synod meant to define the particular character of Christian life; by setting sexual taboos the synod meant to create the image of an ascetic clerical leadership."[68] Living by restrictive sexual codes gave a new definition to being a Christian, as it also gave the hierarchy the role of enforcing these codes. Identifying the Council of Elvira as the starting point for the church's preoccupation with a repressive "pelvic theology," Catholic ethicist Daniel Maguire argues that regulated sexuality became the litmus test to define orthodoxy and the focus of church authority.[69]

Drawing on anti-body and erotophobic attitudes from classical antiquity, the Christian churches have been primary cultural conduits of hatred, fear, and ignorance about sexuality. The Catholic Church's sexual ethic is a highly regulated marriage ethic organized around child rearing and detailed in Pope Pius XI's 1930 encyclical, "On Christian Marriage" (*Casti Connubii*). The church's version of compulsory heterosexual monogamy requires sacramental marriage and excludes birth control, abortion, sterilization, and divorce.[70] The marriage ethic requires women to be either virgins or properly married mothers, and to follow the example of such saints as Maria Goretti, who chose death rather than rape. Catholic women have learned that without their intact hymens or multiple experiences of married motherhood, they have no right to exist. For men, church teaching reinforces male socialization, especially the repression of emotions and desires. However, room is given men to believe that sexual desire is beyond their control. This belief is supported by traditional moral theology that defined birth control as more sinful than rape because with rape procreation, the only legitimate purpose of sexual desire, was at least possible.

This sexual teaching is foundational to many ills. It enslaves women and makes our very existence subservient to the condition or fruitfulness of our sexual and reproductive organs. By equating women with a (sinful) sexuality, this teaching denies our personhood and violates our bodyright. It gives men implicit permission for sexual violence as it outlaws most sexual expression. It has been a chief ally to industrial morality and racist, capitalist managerial control.

Perhaps worst of all, this sex-negative legacy leads Christians to believe that our bodies are alien forces. The marriage ethic teaches that sexual desire is highly suspect, an enemy of the true self that is at war with spiritual well-being. The history of Christian asceticism shows how pain, especially the deprivation of sensual pleasure, is viewed as the foundation for the moral and spiritual life. Christianity becomes a handmaiden of the exploitative and oppressive status quo as it conditions people to desire pain, subordination, and powerlessness and to fear pleasure, self-assertion, and personal power.[71]

The scandal of this tradition has been acknowledged in recent decades by many Catholic ethicists. Certainly, Daniel Maguire has long been a critic of obsessive pelvic theology. Moral theologian Margaret A. Farley observes that "nearly every traditional moral rule governing sexual behavior in Western culture is today being challenged."[72] Ethicist Barbara Hilkert Andolsen found an examination of "my church's moral memories" to be "profoundly alienating." Andolsen says that "the materials concerning sexuality usually encompassed by the phrase 'the Roman Catholic tradition' are a painful and sometimes repulsive collection."[73] Christine Gudorf looks to more hopeful signs in the Dutch Reformed Church's public repentance for its teaching on apartheid, and the repentance of the Catholic Church at Vatican II for its historic anti-Semitism. Gudorf contends that "the same kind of renunciation of traditional teaching in sexuality, followed by repentance, is necessary on the part of all Christian churches today in response to the suffering and victimization it has long supported and legitimated."[74] There is great need for churches to affirm an ethical eroticism that supports desire and pleasure as essential for human well-being and personal empowerment. One immediate task is to sketch some general outlines of such an ethic, and then as Catholic ethicist Mary Hunt suggests, the churches should "leave the rest up to the good sense of faithful people to be self-directive in these matters."[75]

Sketching an Ethical Eroticism

An ethical eroticism would support our need, as social beings, to connect sensually with ourselves, with the natural world, with human work, and with the many others with whom we share passionate interdependence.

An ethical eroticism would transform our relations to ourselves. It would recognize that we, like all living systems, evolve in variety and resilience the more we are open to our environment. Joanna Macy and Molly Brown remind us that we are beings who do not have armor for exterior covering, but soft and sensitive skin, lips, tongues, ears, eyes, fingertips, and genitals, all of which enable communication and interaction with our environment. Severe regulation of our communicative capacities through power-over dynamics is dysfunctional because it prevents feedback and diversity. Such regulation prevents our growth and well-being as relational selves able to engage in moral reflection and self-critical evaluation. Our capacity to respond to our environment with passion and compassion, if unblocked, will flow forth from our profound mutuality.[76] An ethical eroticism would nurture passion, and its progeny compassion, instead of fearing, loathing, and regulating it.

Because we are embodied beings, an ethical eroticism would respect the gifts that the body, and only the body, can give to the spirit. As infants, we would not have survived had we not been surrounded by loving, careful touching and caressing from other human beings. No matter how well fed, an infant will not survive, let alone flourish, without warmth, comfort, and continual flesh-to-flesh contact with other human bodies.

Many people mistakenly believe we leave the need for touch behind in childhood. Our increasing divorce from the natural world, the alienating nature of the capitalist workplace, the racist coding of sexual desire, and the restrictions of heterosexual monogamy leave little opportunity for sensuous human contact in most areas of our lives. As seen in the anthropological research discussed in this chapter, many societies would evaluate ours as one in which most people are starved for touch and pleasure deprived. An ethical eroticism would value nurturing touch, including but by no means exhausted by mutual sexual pleasuring. Nurturing touch is a major resource for the energy needed to make peace and justice.

An ethical eroticism would support our learning about, experimenting with, and developing a symbolic and physical language about our bodies as sources of communication, nurturant interaction, and passionate expression. It would help us think about coitus as only one possibility (and often not the best possibility) among sexual options. Psychologist Sandra Lipsitz Bem has redefined sex as "an open-ended interaction that needs to be custom choreographed by every new set of participants."[77] Such sexuality requires leisure, permission for experimentation, trust in our bodies, and belief in our right to pleasure. However, all these claims are repugnant to an erotophobic workaholic culture that makes people believe they deserve subordination and pain.

When patriarchal, racist, capitalist culture uses and abuses bodies for its vested interests, it teaches people to distrust their bodies. As a result, even dominants are shut off from themselves, suffer deep distortions of the body's wisdom, and are alienated from personal power. An ethical eroticism would challenge this situation and *trust in our ability to critically evaluate it.*

For example, an ethical eroticism would respond differently from the authorities in my child's day care center years ago. Impelled by a widely publicized trial of a center operator who was accused of sexually molesting children in her care, the director of my child's center prohibited the care-givers from holding the children on their laps during story time or giving the children back rubs before naps. This touch deprivation was very hard on both the adults and the children. The employees were no longer the "aunts and uncles" from whom the children expected physical nurturance at the center and during their visits to the home. Because touching in our culture is too often violent and life-threatening, it takes courage to insist that we need *more* nurturant touching, not less. I agree with theologian Mary Pellauer, who encourages us to "talk at length about the gifts the body gives to the spirit."[78]

The human body is not the only source of spiritual gifts. Even the most expansive sexual experiences will not fully satisfy human erotic needs. As beings who emerged from the amniotic waters of the sea, we need visceral experiences of water, earth, air, sky, forest, mountains, and other earth creatures for emotional balance and for a sense of basic well-being. In contrast to the violent touching of plunder and exploitation, an ethical eroticism would transform our relationship to the natural world to that of nurture, listening, sensuous interaction, and respectful interdependence. An ethical eroticism rejects abusing the earth as supply house and sewer; it recognizes that earth, air, and water flow through our veins and organs, and that we are body extensions of our mother the earth. When she is healthy, so are we, and when she is diseased, we suffer and die prematurely. We need close, harmonious interaction with the earth not only to sustain our bodies but also to maintain emotional and spiritual equilibrium. An ethical eroticism challenges overconsumption, capitalism's life root of profit-making that requires massive ecological abuse and destruction.

An ethical eroticism would challenge the work ethic and the capitalist workplace. Under current arrangements, most bodies at work are divorced from their erotic needs and become appendages of machines. Human instruments of profit-making must be numbed to their desire for communion with others in order to sustain nonsensuous, nongratifying, isolating labor. An ethical eroticism would challenge this situation. It would support democratic control over work, including what is made, the process by which it is made, the resources used, and where the profits go. An ethical eroticism would make work a source of gratification in and of itself, as people do socially useful, self-gratifying, sensuous labor together.

An ethical eroticism will also be resisted because it challenges dominant/subordinate relations and puts them into crisis. An ethical eroticism challenges heterogender and the formation of truncated human beings. It challenges the reproduction of women as an unpaid and underpaid laboring class. Even as the waste from capitalist abundance suffocates the planet, an ethical eroticism challenges the ubiquitous belief that we must live in an economy of scarcity — in jobs, education, health care, and love. An ethical eroticism challenges racism and the identification of shared sexual power with lewdness and promiscuity. It challenges submissiveness and conformity because people in touch with their desire are less likely to tolerate victimization of themselves or others.

An ethical eroticism expands the erotic to include far more than the sexual, and it expands the sexual to include more than heterogendered, male-focused orgasm. An ethical eroticism enlarges the stunted roles for loving that the culture requires of us. It affirms the material world and teaches that our very survival depends on listening to the wisdom of our bodies and the ecosphere. It affirms our reality as species-beings who are interdependent on other bodies and rely on passionate, sensuous, mutual, and self-critical interactions for our well-being.

An ethical eroticism challenges the dangerous homogenization in nature and culture. It affirms the goodness of a variety of life forms in the human and natural worlds, including the multiple ways people need to express ourselves as sexed, gendered, sexual, and erotic beings. It honors multiple relationships of varying emotional intensity. It makes space for rich, lifelong egalitarian partnerships, especially those that renegotiate the terms of fidelity according to the evolving friendship and intimacy needs of the partners. It affirms radically reconstructed work where sensuous interdependent beings spend most of their lives, often in antiseptic environments and alienated isolation.

Finally, an ethical eroticism *helps us be forgiving when we make mistakes.* It anticipates that we will make errors of judgment, perhaps even be driven by jealousy and pettiness. It *trusts our capacity to be self-critical* as we slowly work our way out of nonmutual, abusive, and possessive ways of interacting. This trust is grounded in the belief that as species-beings in profound interdependence for our survival and flourishing, compassion is possible for us. An ethical eroticism knows that unearthing this treasure will take conflict, resistance, risk-taking, and courage. Though often blocked by our sex/gender system and the vested interests it promotes, compassion, essential to our survival as interdependent beings, is a possibility that flows through us all.

Relational Labor and the Politics of Solidarity

Relationships... are the essence of life and morality.
— ANTHONY CORTESE

AS WE HAVE SEEN throughout the previous chapters, systems of privilege and oppression divide people into groups so that social, political, and economic power remains unshared. Dominant groups monopolize privileged access to the benefits of the society. Subordinate groups bear a disproportionate share of society's burdens. The privileged are also in charge of knowledge-making and create an all-pervasive ideology that justifies this set of unjust arrangements as "commonsense" in the everyday workings of the society. At the same time, however, dominant groups share a common vulnerability because they depend on the labor and caretaking roles of subordinates as well as the rapidly diminishing resources of the biosphere. It is also true, as this analysis has shown, that people in privileged positions are shrinking in numbers as maleness, whiteness, and class location protect fewer people from the harsh fallout of the restructured global economy.

Given this situation, elites who take Christian vocation seriously have much to do in building a moral world. As previous chapters have argued, we need to understand the dimensions of unshared class, race, and gender power so that we can intervene in our lives and resist reproducing unjust social relations. The difficulty of this task is intensified by the ambiguity and complexity of our moral agency. We find claiming our power for social transformation difficult because we occupy multiple social locations, live in relative isolation from other groups, and are overexposed to the logic of current arrangements through elite forms of education.

Even so, we can learn much from observing dominant groups. The most powerful elites maintain and increase their power by being superorganized within their groups. As has been noted, the economic, political, and cultural power enjoyed by elites enables them to exercise disproportionate influence in such sectors as business, government, academia, media, and religion. Through these institutions, the most privileged define the vested interests, cultural values, and social behaviors imposed on others.

If justice is to increase, the majority who occupy positions of subordination, including many of the elites addressed here, must become as organized as the most powerful. Subordinates, however, remain largely divided even when they organize to increase their power. Focused primarily on their individually subordinate identities, groups representing low-income people, communities of color, white women, and gays and lesbians, for example, often remain separated and isolated from other subordinate groups.

Philosopher Janet Jakobsen argues that the potential challenge to the status quo represented by these groups is largely contained as each group focuses only on those with power at the center. White women, low-income people, people of color, and gay people often ignore one another while struggling to become more like the norm — white, affluent, heterosexual, and male. Each group, says Jakobsen, becomes co-opted and "trapped in difference" when it advocates for its interests within the terms and norms set by dominants.[1]

Why Diverse Subordinates Are Natural Allies

A primary way the most powerful keep subordinate groups from relating to one another is by making them appear homogeneous and distinct when, in fact, they are heterogeneous and overlapping. For example, some may analyze how women are deeply divided among themselves without noting how their internal divisions unite them with other groups. Recognizing the *diversity within* groups can become the basis for discerning the *commonality among* groups.[2] For example, many women share common cause with men who occupy similar subordinate positions in the systems of class, race, and sexuality. This means that women as a group benefit when we recognize our commonalities with working-class men who are also treated as bodies to be used for profits by dominants. Those concerned with gender oppression, therefore, benefit from those working against class exploitation. Low-income groups are natural allies of feminists whenever they challenge the economic exploitation of women who do not have the freedom to choose to live independently from abusive partners or employers.

Groups concerned about class exploitation and the well-being of poor and low-income people need feminist groups when they understand how gender oppression is a basis for class elitism. Deeply ingrained in the social world of children, the gender-polarized and heteronormative family teaches them that dominant/subordinate relations everywhere in the society are normal and natural. In addition, the exploitation of women as a sex class in the home and the labor market is essential for capitalist profit-making and the reproduction of class society. Exploitative class relations are deeply intertwined with abusive gender relations and could not exist without them.

Groups concerned with the racial system benefit from the struggle of low-income groups and those addressing sexual oppression. Groups concerned with racial oppression need alliances with low-income groups because diverse communities of color continue to overserve the economy by being forced into a disproportionate share of the most dangerous and exploited labor as well as the highest amounts of underemployment and unemployment. People of color also benefit from the efforts of gay liberation groups who share common oppression from a sexual system that requires scapegoats to carry the rejected erotic self fundamental to achieving racially and sexually normative status in this culture.

Similarly, those concerned with gay oppression need to dismantle the class, race, and gender systems. This is particularly evident when we realize that the vast majority of homosexuals in the world are working-class women of color.[3] In addition, most whites would benefit from acknowledging their shared interest with nonwhites who are also exploited by the class system and/or oppressed by the sex/gender system. Groups working for ecological justice need to understand that there will be no care for the planet as long as the economic system makes all things into commodities in the service of profits for shareholders. Groups working for environmental justice need to see that capitalist development, ecological degradation, and increasing poverty are different aspects of the same problem.[4] Groups working for environmental justice need feminist, anti-racist, and gay liberation groups as well. There will also be no real caring for the planet itself as long as the sexual system requires the regulation and abuse of everyone and everything associated with the sensual material world and the negative erotic. To work for the environment is to work to transform all social and material relations.

Understanding how these systems feed off and reinforce one another (even as they sometimes work at cross-purposes) makes it evident that there will be no economic justice, gender justice, racial justice, sexual justice, or ecological justice until there is justice for all. Nicola Field observes, "Our most important task is to show how oppressions affect everyone because they divide us . . . [and they] all come from the same system."[5]

When identity groups realize the benefits each will receive from a collective effort to challenge the common system affecting us all, we *increase the possibilities for social movements* that challenge unshared power.[6] Consequently, ethics, as Jakobsen explores it, involves first and foremost the "relational labor" or "moral labor" of working out alliances among social groups.[7] These alliances take advantage of the possibilities for relationship at the intersections of class, race, gender, and sexuality systems. Alliances use diversity *within* groups to make connections *between* subordinate groups, so that new political action can occur with a larger critical mass who share common concerns. Increased challenge to the status quo becomes possible as the marginalized forge complex relationships among their groups.[8]

From this paradigm, moral agency is primarily activated not by the individual who exercises "free choice," but by *groups involved in the relational labor of creating new forms of social relationships* that, in turn, can build new social movements. Building "solidarity across differences," mobilizing differences to challenge our assigned roles as dominants and subordinates and to interrupt the unshared power of dominant groups at various sites of privilege/oppression, is the major site of moral agency.[9]

Why Alliances Are Hard to Build

Alliances are hard to build for many reasons. Most erotically disempowered people are socialized to be passive consumers of what organizations have to offer rather than builders of new, democratically participatory institutions. In addition, major theoretical constructs, such as postmodernism, condition us to accept the fragmentation and isolation surrounding us. Some critics see postmodernism as a form of capitalist crisis management because it teaches us to confine resistance and struggle to regional and isolated sites and to reject all master narratives.[10] Alliances, however, are the only ways to build the critical mass needed to create practices of resistance in order to address the master interlocking system of male-dominant, racist capitalism that works against most people's real interests.

Alliances are also hard to build because the religious Right has been working arduously over the past decade to increase the divide along the separations that alliances need to overcome. Using racism in white communities, sexism in gay communities, and homophobia in communities of color, the Right has been successful in organizing masses of ordinary people by increasing fear among voters so they will roll back civil rights and social services that benefit everyone. Educator and activist Suzanne Pharr observes that "while the Right is united by their racism, sexism and homophobia in their goal to dominate all of us, we are divided by our own racism, sexism and homophobia — and divided we are falling. . . . We have to understand that if any one group can be left out, then reasons can be found to leave any other group out."[11]

Here it is evident that alliances are hard to build because many people need enemies upon which to project those nonnormative parts of themselves that must be rejected in order to maintain the present disorder. As has been discussed, surviving the systems of male-dominant, racist, class-stratified society requires most people, and perhaps especially the privileged, to reject our vulnerability, spontaneity, and sensuality. As we suffer, we often feel a need to punish and control others. We also expect them to put up with their own pain and suffering. Only when we can generate compassion for our own bodily needs, vulnerability, and dependence upon others will we experience the compassion for others that is necessary for solidarity work.

Only when those in privileged groups perceive exactly how *even we deserve better* will we be released from our need to punish and control others, so we can form alliances with them.

The need for external enemies, and the related assumption that our agenda has no moral ambiguity, is probably the major obstacle to alliance formation. Alliances help groups acknowledge that the enemy resides not only without but also within us and the collectives we forge because all the dominant/subordinate dynamics of society are present within the alliance itself. As much as alliance formation requires self- and group-affirmation in a society that demands self-negation from most, alliances also require humility. Alliances will not happen if affluent males do not control their propensity to take over, or if white women do not challenge our desire to run from conflict. Similarly, just as the enemy is within, so the ally may be without. In gaining recognition that we are deeply flawed, we may gain recognition that our enemy may be capable of wisdom and insight. Living ethically means becoming alert to our own self-righteousness as well as giving credit to the opposition's capacity for compassion.

Jakobsen and Pharr agree that we must go beyond the notion that diversity is a threat to effective action. In fact, Jakobsen contends, alliances of diverse constituencies are the *only* means to challenge dominant culture and its rigidity, conformity, and unshared power arrangements. As long as subordinates and their potential allies from dominant groups remain isolated in their differences, they pose no threat to the status quo. What is a threat is not difference but similarity in cause. When diverse subordinates and their dominant allies discover common cause together, the status quo will not continue. Allies may and do disagree, they do not have a common identity, and they may lack a single normative framework. However, when they understand common concerns, sorrows, and joys as the real connections among them, they can work together to interrupt exploitation and oppression even if disagreements remain.[12]

Common cause, then, does not require sameness. As has been discussed, discovering common cause includes discovering how *homogenizing trends in nature and culture are dangerous to all*. Alliances focus not on creating similarity, but on challenging the norms and behaviors that support the privileges of dominant groups and maintain the systems of unshared power that hurt most. As complex networks constructed in and between differences, alliances cross borders in search of practical solidarity even as each group within the alliance maintains its particular claims.[13]

However powerful the social forces working against solidarity, major thinkers of the last century credit less-powerful groups with the ability to think and act creatively for their well-being and flourishing. Theorists such as Italian Marxist Antonio Gramsci and Frankfurt School theorist Jürgen Habermas recognize the enormous power of the status quo to shape people into conformity and consensus. Given the experiences of fascism, Soviet dictatorship, and American mass culture, it would have been easy for them to be pessimistic about social emancipation. Nevertheless, they insisted that while people are socially constructed, they are also capable of critical evaluation and intervention in the social world. For Habermas, communicating subjects are capable of creative accomplishments independent of the social forces directing the society.[14]

Gramsci also focused on ideological and cultural factors in bringing about social change, stressing the counterhegemonic (or subordinate) knowledge found in ethical frameworks and religious views at the margins of society. He believed that a massive collective movement could achieve hegemonic status if it emerged from grassroots democratic energy rooted in local traditions and willing to engage in long-term struggle.[15] Theorists such as these support the possibility of a democratic reconstruction of society through the communicative interaction of "unruly subjects" in coalition politics.[16]

Despite all the difficulties working against solidarity, alliances need to happen. No matter our degree of vulnerability, everyone's "distance from economic necessity is dwindling."[17] According to Jakobsen, the work of alliance formation is never finished, but remains "constitutive of ongoing moral and political life."[18] This relational labor, as labor activist Kim Moody describes, increases our understanding of society, hones our collaborative skills, and expands the sense of the possible.[19]

Relational Labor and the Prophetic Imagination

The possibility for solidarity also finds support in religious tradition, which further illuminates the relational labor necessary for solidarity work. One such tradition is what Scripture scholar Walter Brueggemann calls "the prophetic imagination." The work of the Hebrew prophets, as well as the ministry of Jesus, brought people together to *identify their suffering and engage their longing* for social transformation. The prophet engages in the work of grieving and refusing to deny or numb oneself to the suffering in society. When people grieve together, they challenge the notion that feeling pain for the world is only a matter of personal maladjustment. When people grieve, they challenge society's propensity to cover up structures of privilege and oppression, violence and death. The prophet unveils "the barriers and pecking orders that secure us at each other's expense, and the fearful practice of eating off the table of a hungry brother and sister."[20] The prophets who weep and mourn call people out of their apathy, numbness, and isolation, all of which are essential to protect unshared power arrangements and maintain the enormous suffering of the status quo. Without numbness to protect them from their own and others' suffering, people begin to see their interdependence, face their vulnerabilities, identify the common roots of their suffering, and enter into a grieving process. Like the work of Amos and Jeremiah before him, Jesus' work of solidarity involved weeping over the self-deception of Jerusalem and claiming that only those who mourned would find comfort.[21]

The comfort brought about by the prophetic work of grieving is the result of coming to terms with one's loss by acknowledging a vision of life that has yet to be realized. Grieving is "the public expression of those very hopes and yearnings that have been denied so long and suppressed so deeply that we no longer know they are there."[22]

In recent decades many people in the United States have lamented what is perceived to be a widespread loss of concern for public affairs and for the common good among the citizenry. Certainly, the preoccupation by the affluent with individual gain in the marketplace, as well as the preoccupation of those losing economic ground with the very survival of their families, is on the rise. Many in Congress have thought that people's preoccupations with individual issues is such that politicians can govern without taking into account voters' concerns. Former senator Alan Simpson from Wyoming reflects this view when he says that what citizens think is expendable to people in government because "the attention span of Americans is which movie is coming out next month and whether the quarterly report on their stock will change."[23] While Simpson is certainly correct that voters tend to be those who own stocks, not all would agree that preoccupation with oneself and one's family is the last word.

It is certainly not so for the religious Right, which has enlisted hundreds of thousands to promote the anti-democratic agenda that Suzanne Pharr noted above. As a response to the political apathy that followed Vietnam and Watergate, the superorganized religious Right moved into the vacuum and infiltrated all levels of politics. By the early 1990s there were forty-eight state units of the Christian Coalition with seventeen thousand neighborhood coordinators, thirty thousand local workers, and contacts in sixty thousand churches. Since no one else is organized to this degree, the religious Right has been able to wage a politics of hate with between 17 and 34 percent of the electorate.[24] Those of us interested in a politics of compassion have much to learn from the organizational strategies of the Right.

However, 17 to 34 percent of the electorate does not a majority make. Many people still experience the need for the kind of compassion affirmed in classical antiquity, the Catholic tradition, feminist theory, and the work of Marxists such as Gramsci and critical theorists such as Habermas. Sociologist Richard Sennett is among those who demonstrate hope about the human person as fundamentally a self-in-relation with a compassionate potential. Among the workers he studied in various American cities, Sennett witnessed indifference and a lack of interest in civic affairs, but also outrage at the lack of commitment, accountability, and responsibility in contemporary life. Sennett believes that "one of the unintended consequences of modern capitalism is that it has strengthened the value of place, aroused a longing for community . . . for some other scene of attachment and depth."[25] This longing is also demonstrated by the reservoir of resistance to the current political climate being played out at the international, national, and community levels in such places as the growing number of grassroots organizations across the United States and in the Two-Thirds World.[26] It is possible that the economic crisis that began in 2007 will only intensify these efforts.

We will consider important stirrings of resistance in Africa and Latin America in the last chapter. In the United States important groups that are challenging the status quo and deserve our ongoing support and study include the Kensington Welfare Rights Union in Philadelphia, Mothers on the Move Against Slums in Chicago, and the Coalition of Immokalee Workers in Florida, to name only a few. The Kensington Welfare Rights Union (KWRU) is an organization of, by, and for impoverished people, working in alliance with other groups to build an international poor people's movement for economic human rights. The Coalition of Immokalee Workers (CIW) is an anti-NAFTA democratic organization that eschews the traditional hierarchies of labor unions and has launched an eleven-year organizing effort including boycotts, hunger strikes, marches, and shareholder resolutions in conjunction with student and other national anti-poverty organizations. Mothers on the Move Against Slums was a militant movement by women in a Southside Chicago neighborhood to prevent the further decline of their housing project by self-organizing its functions.[27]

There are also important stirrings in education, including the "freedom schools" or social justice schools operated by the Children's Defense Fund, governed independently, or run as public charter schools in New York, Chicago, Los Angeles, and Oakland. These schools focus on basic skills and literacy as well as critical inquiry into society. Rooted in an understanding that teaching to "command-and-control testing ignores the critical skills needed to improve the communities that government and the private sector have all but abandoned," these schools engage urban students who are alienated from mainstream education.[28]

Other imaginative examples of local democracy and the public control of social wealth include the public ownership of telecommunications in Glasgow, Kentucky, and a highly successful employee-owned telecommunications equipment business in Harrisonburg, Virginia. In California, the state pension fund plays a significant role in state development, in Alabama the state pension fund helps finance worker-owned firms, and in Alaska oil revenues are invested on behalf of the public at large, with dividends going to every state resident.[29] These are a few of the national stirrings that contain seeds of the knowledge we need to deepen social transformation.

Grounds for hope persist insofar as people are capable of acknowledging loss, *capturing a vision of life that is yet to be realized*, and displaying the power of ordinary people to develop practices that resist the relations of rule. The biblical prophets are relevant here in that they remind us that a certain comfort comes from publicly mourning "against permanent consignment to chaos, oppression, barrenness and exile."[30] This comfort is a gift that comes only with "decisive solidarity with marginal people and the accompanying vulnerability required by that solidarity."[31]

The prophetic imagination brings comfort because in their solidarity and shared vulnerability with suffering people, those who mourn can uncover the violation and human pain that dominant groups must deny to remain in power. The work of solidarity brings comfort because it insists that much social suffering is not normal or natural, it challenges all norms and behaviors that support unshared power, and it struggles for a community where there are no excluded ones. Brueggemann argues that because of Jesus' solidarity with poor and marginalized people, and because of his conflict with the powers that be, he was able to birth an alternative consciousness and stake out possibilities for a new age, a new social order.[32]

In his insistence on *compassion and solidarity as the foundation of social relations*, Jesus promoted not liberal do-goodism, but harsh criticism and a radical threat to the structures and worldviews that promote and justify suffering.[33] Groups who monopolize power can tolerate charity, but they cannot survive masses of exploited and oppressed people, as well as their allies, standing in solidarity with one another as they resist structures of violence.[34] Precisely because it will no longer tolerate unnoticed pain, the work of solidarity signals a social revolution. Only when suffering is identified, and resisted, is the status quo discredited and transformation made possible.

Where is the hope for people with elite privilege? Only when we can grieve about the fact that in order to maintain our lifestyles we cannot have full access to ourselves and to the friendship of others can we begin to move forward. Only when we can grieve about the cultural, political, economic, and sexual structures that deeply distort our own potential as human beings can we move forward. Only in the process of mourning and sharing the pain with others will we be able to unearth the loving connections that still remain possible in the emotional underground of this society. Making these connections is essential to the work of solidarity and social transformation.

Relational Labor and Christian Ethics

In a similar vein, Christian ethicist Ada María Isasi-Díaz suggests that solidarity through alliance-building is the new name for genuine love of the neighbor. Alliance-building is a discernment of mutuality and a practice of lifelong political struggle. When we work to discern the structures that alien-ate us from one another, as this book tries to do, we come to understand how justice-making benefits everyone. People in dominant groups can *be-friend* subordinates, and together they can form alliances that enable all to see that vengeance is not the goal of the struggle, but the achievement of solidarity. Through alliances, subordinates and the privileged can change their history so that the entire "Kindom" of God can flourish together. As Isasi-Díaz affirms, new structures supportive of liberation are a historical possibility; allies must create them together in lifelong political action.[35]

The work of solidarity, therefore, is not only the work of forging new alliances among subordinates. It also involves the relational labor of forging dominant-subordinate alliances. If the creation of a more just society de-pends upon expanding the arena of democratic struggle across class, race, gender, and sexuality lines, this will happen only when the privileged can grieve about our own losses and become clearer about how solidarity bene-fits us as well. The work of solidarity can be embraced by elites who know we are damaged by present arrangements and realize what is at stake for us in collective action for social transformation.

Even so, relational labor remains hard work for everyone. Finding ways to challenge our assigned positions as dominants and subordinates and to resist hierarchical power arrangements often seems an impossibility. For we live in a world where people are giving up *what power they have* all the time as corporate, religious, and cultural authorities consolidate control over an increasingly homogenized society. Dualistic thinking also inhibits us when we are tempted to believe that some people monopolize virtue and others monopolize vice. We think that if we can identify and challenge the opposition, there will be certitude on the road to a just society.

In her provocative study about the struggle to achieve alliances, ethicist Sharon Welch offers jazz as an important model for thinking and strategizing about solidarity. Welch is especially interested in jazz because this African American art form can help us remain aware of the moral ambiguity that always accompanies struggles for justice.

Drawing extensively from her political work, Welch shows how dualistic ways of thinking can be deadly to the creation of mutuality and account-ability in relationships. Jazz is a significant counterpoint here because this musical tradition defies dualistic ways of being in the world (us against them, joy versus sorrow, the moral versus the immoral). Jazz is a model of relational labor since it "emerges from the interplay of structure and im-provisation, collectivity and individuality, tradition and innovation." Jazz gives clues about the positive power of grieving as it *holds together pathos and joy* and refuses to accept societal limits. Jazz is full of risk-taking; it is open ended and never completed. Jazz is serious but always ready to laugh at itself. Jazz is intensely mutual and not afraid of failure. Some of the best jazz has to do with improvisations on people's mistakes. "The worst thing that can be said of a jazz player," says Welch, "is that he or she doesn't listen."[36]

Welch finds jazz a helpful model for justice-seekers in order to open us to risks and to the fact that we are as capable of deep moral failure as our opposition is capable of compassion and justice. Jazz is attuned to the fact that there are no guaranteed outcomes, and that we can deepen relationships with one another by working through conflicts. Jazz is a helpful model for justice-seekers when it most values the integrity of the process as well as the outcome. What is most important and moral is not our agenda or goals. Of most value is *the struggle to achieve balanced and just relationships* and to acknowledge our interdependence as we grow in accountability to one another. For Welch, solidarity and compassion are possible not because they are ethically mandated, but because they bring human beings so much joy.[37]

In a talk about his work to close the U.S. School of the Americas, as its successor, which trains Latin American military in torture and assassination methods used against the resisting poor, Father Roy Bourgeois exemplifies the values articulated in Welch's notion of relational labor. Bourgeois tells how he and his companions in the School of the Americas Watch dress up in army fatigues, bearing the names of those tortured and disappeared on their lapels. In Charlie Chaplin style, they dutifully practice the military salute. Sneaking into the school's courtyard, they plant a boom box in a tree opposite the dormitory where the soldiers-in-training have retired for the night. The boom box blares out Archbishop Oscar Romero's last sermon before his assassination at the hands of the School's graduates. In the sermon Romero pleads with the military to "stop the killing" of the multitudes of poor who resist exploitation and oppression.

Bourgeois and the other resisters end up in prison, of course, with the harshest possible sentence meted out by a southern segregationist judge they affectionately call "Maximum Bob." When the judge gives them a minute to speak at the end of the sentencing, Bourgeois and his companions invite the judge to join them in their next protest, which the judge has guaranteed they will have plenty of time to plan carefully while in prison.

Such playful but serious resistance, which refuses to honor the dualisms rampant in the culture, entices people to join such movements and use their own dramatic energy to imagine creative change. Imaginative resistance seems especially important as we work to take advantage of what the current situation — intensified ecological crisis and economic meltdown — can offer us in terms of an opportunity to create more just social relations (see chapter 6).

As we better understand the construction of social relations and the process of creative, nondualistic relational labor, we can see how liberal individualism and Christian altruism are inadequate guides to our social reality and moral agency. A moral analysis of current arrangements and an understanding of the ethics of relational labor are necessary to move into broad-based coalitions and solidarity work.

Analysis Is Not Politics

For genuine solidarity to become a reality, social analysis alone is not sufficient. As previously argued, the energy to imagine and seek a new future can come only through grief work and collective resistance, both foundational for a politics of compassion and solidarity. Indeed, people can be morally and emotionally disgusted with what the system is doing, but still cooperate because they see no alternative. To address the massive monopolization of power and the steadfast erosion of securities, securities that a just society would confer on everyone, we must be willing to experiment with a new future and move through analysis to the politics of solidarity work. Building on the work of such ethicists and activists as those cited in this chapter, we need to develop strategies for alliance-building and for developing a comprehensive array of pragmatic actions that can work in everyday life to energize us for further struggles to increase power sharing.[38]

Those who write books also need to log in our hours in the struggle to build alliances. We must join or create constituencies in addition to our academic audiences. Educator Henry Giroux writes that we need to specify "the leaky and contradictory nature of dominant power," we need to "reframe the debates," we need to move into "the spaces of resistance within dominant forums," and we must "hijack such sites as talk radio."[39] We must learn from the religious Right and their superior organizational ability, even as we use such models as jazz to critique their deep dualism and our self-righteousness. We must identify, resist, and transform the relations of unshared power that promote class stratification, racism, sexism, and other oppressive conditions. We need to study the creative, nondualistic movements already in process and play more jazz with one another.

To maintain integrity and faithfulness, the churches themselves must be part of the politics of solidarity and alliance formation. Theologian Delores Williams says that when the church ignores economic, racial, sexual, and other forms of violence and abuse of power, "it forfeits its right to be identified as the church of Jesus Christ." Williams asserts that "without a viable commitment to help stop the violence whites do to blacks, men do to women, economically powerful people do to poor people, the Christian church loses its marks of apostolicity, catholicity, unity and holiness."[40] Here is indeed a challenge for Christian institutions that too often promote the hierarchical status quo. Churches must also be transformed in order to create spaces and opportunities for us to analyze, grieve, imagine, be playful, strategize, and *not become discouraged when our mistakes are large.* We know that privileged people, even privileged churches, are capable of changing our theory and our politics. If we are to survive, we must be able to grieve and mourn the ignorance, arrogance, isolation, and destruction spawned by lives based on unearned advantages. Elites must mourn the pseudovalues and impoverished social relations that define most aspects of our privileged lives. We must grieve the loss of our integrity and the threat to the very survival of the planet itself that is posed by current arrangements. Only then will we be able to change the way we see ourselves and our religious traditions, the way we view others, and the way we behave. We must understand that solidarity and new alliances forged within concrete projects for social change are not a utopian dream. Rather, *solidarity is the extension of our fundamental interdependence,* as inherently social beings, as members of the one body of Christ, and, yes, as persons who collectively are increasingly subordinate to our market value in generating profits.

Perhaps most important of all, solidarity and alliance-building provide the means for us to recover our fundamental humanity. Our very humanity is at stake when we see how profoundly damaged we are by internalized superiority and by systems that exploit and oppress most of the people on the globe today. When we no longer deny the environmental destruction that threatens us all, we know that nothing less than fundamental social change will give even the privileged a future.

The Nature of Authentic Privilege

To strengthen solidarity, we can draw on dangerous historical memories as well as on current examples that show the capacities of human beings to defy social hierarchies and care for one another and the earth. We are not only people who benefit from white unearned advantage; we also fight police brutality, economic exploitation, redlining, unequal access to education and health care, and the toxic waste of current production. We are not only practicing heterosexuals, but supporters of gay, lesbian, bisexual, and transgendered persons and their rights, we resist ownership patterns in our own intimate relations, and we do not assume that our children are straight. We are not only privileged men; we also scrub toilets, nurture children, educate about male violence, and challenge hierarchy at home, at work, in politics, and in the churches. We are not only economically affluent; we work for clean elections, progressive taxes to support the common good, unions, and welfare rights, and we oppose the global system of war-making. We are not only affluent white women, but we are allies of women of color and of lower-working-class/poor women of all races.

This work of fighting for a better life continues in large and small ways in local communities and throughout the globe. We need to find these experiments in freedom, extend them, and create more of them. Elites need to decide the groups or communities to which we will be accountable with our limited social power and financial resources. Even as we take baby steps, we change and grow and become capable of bigger steps.

We have considered a variety of religious, ethical, and intellectual traditions that analyze our privilege and mounting peril for all, affirm a politics of compassion, and challenge us to work out the necessary strategies needed to arrive there. Some suggest that the more complex solidarity becomes, and the more sectors of the population are drawn into it, the more clearly will the present disorder become apparent. As a consequence, more alternatives to the status quo, largely invisible to us now, will emerge as possibilities. The very process of grieving and resisting in new spaces, constructed in and between differences, will generate hope.

Others caution that profound change is possible only if we remain wary of dualisms that contaminate even our best analyses, strategies, and goals. The challenge includes living more humbly, carefully — and playfully — in the midst of moral ambiguity and, yes, even failure. This requires focusing our primary energies not only on outcomes, but on the *quality of relationships we can build and enjoy along the way.* As Elisabeth Schüsler Fiorenza has commented similarly about the earliest Christians, the journey is more to the point even than the goal.

To begin, we need to be wherever people are "fighting for a better life — no matter how basic that fight might seem."[41] The late Sr. Marjorie Tuite, educator and activist for people in the margins, once announced: "I am working for a world I will never see. But it is a privilege to be part of the struggle." The privilege that elites must embrace is the privilege belonging to solidarity struggle. If we are to have a future on the planet, this work must become our own.

SIX _____

Intellectual and Political Struggle:
An Agenda for Accountable Disciples

He not busy being born is busy dying.
— BOB DYLAN

WRITER CHARLES BOCK, whose parents ran a Las Vegas pawnshop, recalled childhood memories of the inevitable scenes when desperate adults came to hock their most precious possessions:

> From the back of the store I'd watch as the customers exploded and called my parents dirty Jews and cursed at them and threatened them at the top of their lungs. It's impossible in situations like that not to feel for everybody involved — to be horrified for sure, but more than that, to be saddened by the spectacle, to want so much more than that out of life for everyone.[1]

The previous chapters have explored a critical understanding of the world we live in because intellectual struggle, in addition to political struggle, is necessary to achieve more of life for everyone. I have argued that living in social, political, and economic relations that are *not* defined by domination and subordination is its own reward and achieves more of life for everyone. One can find consensus, from contemplative/activists like the late Dorothy Day, founder of the Catholic Worker movement, to psychologists and philosophers like Paul Bloom and Kwame Anthony Appiah, that *moral potential is best activated in human-friendly contexts*. It is in situations of mutual power sharing that people's best selves are allowed to flourish.[2]

Therefore, movement toward more just and joyful life contexts requires the best possible analysis of the structures that inform our lives. Then, if we understand the points of contradiction and vulnerability within these structures, we will be better able to intervene and interrupt injustice. This is the goal as we imagine ways of living and loving that are more mutual than current arrangements. Courage and boldness are required because the hierarchical status quo has such a tight grip, not only on our social institutions and our assumptions about them, but also on our political imaginations.

150

Consequently, the simple desire to respond to our vocation to create a moral world is not enough. It is also necessary that we interrogate our ideology, our understanding of the structures we inhabit, to see if it is the most representative one available. That is why I have argued that we cannot move toward a more moral world if we have a less than adequate understanding of how the world actually works. As Mohandas Gandhi wrote: "Goodness must be joined with knowledge. Mere goodness is not of much use as I have found in my life."[3]

How can moral agents think about interrupting the injustice that Charles Bock remembers in the daily encounters made in his parents' pawnshop? How do we understand the roots of these encounters or social relations? How do we go about fashioning strategies that foster social relations of mutuality and justice? Do community-based struggles exist that provide schooling for those who wish to build effective movements for greater justice?

To guide our subsequent exploration of these questions, this chapter undertakes three tasks. First, it uses the example of the "pawnshop economy" as an opportunity to summarize the critical social theory in previous chapters. Second, it argues, also based on discussions in previous chapters, that ecological crisis, especially climate meltdown, rooted in the runaway global economy, is currently our most pressing moral challenge. Third, the chapter looks to specific policy recommendations on what we need to do to address climate change. Finally this chapter examines political struggles in the United States, Africa, and Latin America for inspiration and instruction about the concrete strategies required to implement these recommendations and to plant the seeds of a more just society.

In the work of evaluating the morality of social relations, we locate our ideology and interrogate its adequacy by discerning the difference between dominant (conservative or liberal) and critical (liberationist or radical) forms of social analysis. As they respond to the economic context and ethical relations of the pawnshop, people on the conservative (or neoliberal) end of the ideological spectrum would likely say that nothing really can or should be done. Humans are limited in their efforts and potential, and most people do not deserve much more in life than they already have. The assumption behind this evaluation is that despite the experiences of people with hardships, capitalism is the best possible economic system because through the "invisible hand" of the market, it coordinates production, distribution, innovation, and efficiency. Consequently capitalist social relations, especially when government does not use welfare to interfere with the negative fallout from the market, are just because people basically get what they deserve.

In evaluating the economic context and social relations of the pawnshop, liberals, like conservatives, also judge the economic system as basically good and just, and the best one possible. However liberals often acknowledge an "invisible hand" of manipulation by the wealthy to rig the economy in their favor. Therefore, unlike most conservatives, liberals believe welfare policies and other forms of social spending are also necessary when, for example, the market system lays people off from their jobs or when wages are too low. In judging the economy as basically just, liberals assume that the capacity of the powerful to rig markets is *not fundamental to the system,* but can be managed by elected officials more responsible to the commonweal. In other words, liberals believe that inequality is rooted primarily in unaccountable politicians and legislators and in bad public policy.

In contrast, as we have explored in previous chapters, those who ascribe to critical social theory and to liberation readings of Scripture and tradition would challenge most conservative assumptions and approaches while supporting many liberal policies. However, since liberationists discern the unjust power operating in class, race, and sex/gender relations as inherent to the system itself, their view would be that liberal responses, while good beginnings, are limited. Those who believe that critical social theory gives the more adequate (even though always evolving) explanation of the political economy would argue that impoverishment is primarily rooted in basic capitalist dynamics, not unaccountable or incompetent leaders or bad policy. While conservative leaders and policies may exacerbate inequality, and liberal leaders and legislation may ameliorate inequality, liberal policies and more accountable *leaders do not stop the structural reproduction of injustice* by the capitalist system itself.

For example, the liberal responses of anti-racism work and expanding affirmative action so that fewer Jews or people of color have to make their living off the impoverished might help individuals like Charles Bock's parents. But, as we have seen in chapter 3, these liberal policies would not keep the capitalist labor market from generating increasing amounts of low-wage work so that some people would need to support themselves by owning pawnshops. Similarly, expanding the welfare state so that fewer people would be driven to sell whatever valuables they had might keep some customers out of pawnshops, but critical theorists and liberationists hold that welfare policies do not keep workers from being downsized, outsourced, or mechanized.

Kim Phillips-Fein explains that Democrats and Republicans alike have dismantled the (very partial) New Deal welfare state because liberal policies are no match for the dynamics of capitalism.[4] Capitalism, according to the critical theory explored in previous chapters, will always be *reproducing inequality faster than liberal policies can ameliorate it.* Indeed, conservative (or neoliberal) policies (like tax breaks for the wealthy) passed by federal and state governments *increase* the inequality structurally reproduced by capitalism, while liberal policies (like raising the minimum wage and giving people access to more and better education) *soften* the impact of inequality for some. But government policies, in the liberationist view, will never *stop* the reproduction of, not only inequality but also ever increasing income and wealth polarization, because this is the *inherent fallout* from a capitalist, male dominant, and white racist system. That said, it is also true that work to pass liberal public policies may lead to more fundamental structural change, as the discussion below will reveal, showing the unanticipated democratic consequences of a Venezuelan effort to pass a hydrocarbon tax.

In short, what one considers effective moral action substantively changes depending on the degree to which one believes the core political economy itself is ethical. Princeton moral philosopher Kwame Anthony Appiah makes a similar point when he writes: "In life the challenge is not so much to figure out how best to play the game; the challenge is to figure out what game you are playing."[5]

In figuring out this "game," we must be able to explain how, for example, racial divisions empower the class structure by not only hiding it, but also immunizing it from the challenges that the solidarity of the multiracial working class would create. For example, because of racism Bock's parents and their customers, many of whom were likely from diverse communities of color, could not see how they all shared (even if not equally) economic vulnerability in the capitalist labor market. Lacking this understanding, it remains more difficult for people to move together in solidarity as they blame one another for their troubles. Therefore, a closer, critical look at the structures and practices that create us as persons and organize our ideas about the world is essential for the work of social transformation. Liberationists would say that, until we understand how the logic of this interlocking system is opposed by its very nature to the survival of the planet and to the satisfaction of the needs of increasing numbers of human beings and the growth of their human potential, we will not be able to move forward.

Ecologizing the Economy: The Most Pressing Moral Assignment

I have argued that our vocation to build a moral world involves not only the intellectual struggle of comprehending the political economy, but also the political struggle of transforming this huge web of immoral relations. As has been discussed, political struggle is unlikely when unjust social relations remain invisible to us even as they deeply shape who we are, including allowing us to accept privilege and subordination as "natural," and constraining our potential to embody rightly related community. Depending on our willingness to take responsibility for our lives, we can go along with being shaped by allegiance to the class-elitist, racist, and sexist relations of domination and subordination. Or we can work to begin shaping ourselves in allegiance to the self who hungers for love and connection and mutual relations with all creation. If we choose the latter we know that small steps lead to bigger ones. More just social relations will create more just human beings who can in turn create even more just communities and ecological practices.

Political struggle is also unlikely if people do not discern why, no matter our social location or degree of privilege, unjust social relations profoundly damage each one of us. For example, the forms of structural analyses we have pursued in previous chapters to describe the logic of the interlocking system we inhabit illuminate how whites are damaged by racism, how males and heterosexuals suffer from the sex/gender system, how the economic futures of middle- and upper-income people are inextricably tied to those of the already impoverished, and how all of life is imperiled by ecological warming, poisoning, and destruction. Therefore, no matter our degree of privilege, *all of us* have a stake in social, political, and economic transformation.

I have argued that our vocation to create a moral world involves the intellectual and political struggle necessary to transform society into one that is more in harmony with our fundamental interdependent reality. Because our well-being is at stake whenever those on whom we depend are vulnerable, our survival hangs on whether or not we can move from individualism to interdependence in a new phase of human evolution. (Why do we think evolution is only a phenomenon of the past?) This realization was articulated by the Dalai Lama when he said: "As people see their predicament clearly — that our fates are inextricably tied together, that life is a mutually interdependent web of relations — then universal responsibility becomes the only sane choice for thinking people."[6]

Given this radical interdependence on one another and the planet itself, I agree with ethicists like Larry Rasmussen and others, that ecological crisis, "a product of the destructive uncontrollability of a rapidly globalizing capitalist economy," is the most immediate moral challenge and occasion for universal responsibility to the common good.[7] While ecological forms of injustice are sometimes not the primary targets of people who suffer abject impoverishment in the Two-Thirds World, I look to their activism for pedagogical tools to inform First-World movements for social justice, including ecological justice. Of course the struggle for ecological justice is simultaneously a struggle for economic, racial, and sex/gender justice because the same political economy in need of transformation grounds them all. When we understand the interlocking nature of the unjust systems that inform our lives, we know that political struggle around *any* set of justice issues is really a challenge to *all* of them.

Earth Healing and Human Evolution

Indeed, as the twenty-first century unfolds, the need for universal responsibility to the common good is getting increasing attention due to ecological crisis. Among all the interlocking points of contradiction and structural abuse that critical analysis has illuminated in our political economy, it is fair to say that one of the most, if not *the*, most pressing problems at stake for everyone in this historical moment is the overheated planet (the scarcity of potable water is surely a close contender). Uncontrolled heat-trapping carbon emissions are producing erratic weather patterns and increasing climate meltdown. One can argue that this is the most pressing issue because the world's food (and water) supply depends on rainfall cycles and dependable seasons. Demand on the world's food supply continually increases, and already 1 billion people do not have access to clean water. In addition, all living species perform functions valuable to the ecosystem's health and proper functioning, and by the end of this century if climate change escalates, half of the species now alive may be extinct.[8] We in the United States have even more accountability than others for the deleterious global effects of heat-trapping gasses because with only 5 percent of the world's population, we produce a quarter of the earth's carbon emissions.

As Christian ethicist Larry Rasmussen says: "Addressing Earth and its distress is *the* moral assignment of out time."[9] This is such a challenging assignment because our ecological crisis is rooted in our social crisis. We will not succeed in responding to this crisis until we can move out of social isolation and class, race, sex/gender, ideological, and other divisions that alienate us from one another and destroy community. Only then can we collectively organize and claim our power to respond in meaningful ways to the earth's distress and our deep interdependence upon it.

Therefore, it is becoming clearer that social transformation is essential to ecological transformation. As previous chapters have argued, the poisoning of the planet and the poisoning of social relations work in tandem. Bill McKibbon says it is becoming more apparent that living in a society that effectively divides us and ignores our fundamental need for one another is at the root of our escalating ecological crisis. Reflecting on the issue of global warming, he writes that the greatest problem incurred by the burning of fossil fuels is not climate meltdown but the fact that fossil fuel burning has allowed the affluent to live without community. He says:

> The greatest problem of the fossil fuel era on this planet is not that it is destroying everything around us. The greatest problem is that cheap coal and gas and oil have allowed us to live in such independence of each other that we have largely forgotten what community means, what neighbor means. We don't depend on each other for anything real anymore.[10]

This situation has retarded human development. It is reflected in a 2006 Duke University study that found that from 1985 to 2004, while the number of cell phones proliferated, the number of people who have no one to talk to doubled. Entitled "Social Isolation in America," the study concluded that with all our technology, we are both increasingly in touch *and* isolated, both more united and more divided.[11] Unfortunately if collectively responding to ecological crisis is our most pressing task, nothing in our individualist, profit-driven, consumer-oriented, and entertainment-centered culture has prepared us for the restraint on material desire and the mutual cooperation and joint action that addressing global warming, and our own survival, requires. For example, an April 2007 news poll found that only 45 percent of respondents were willing to tolerate personal sacrifices in lifestyle changes to combat global warming. Meanwhile no less than former vice president Al Gore was quoted as saying in 2007: "I can't understand why there aren't rings of young people blocking bulldozers and preventing them from constructing coal-fired power plants."[12]

The inertia of the U.S. population is not surprising given that the economic system constantly increases the amount of energy and raw materials used as part of the requirement for limitless profits, that consumer culture promotes ever more of this state of affairs, and that corporate polluters are major contributors to candidates' campaigns. Nevertheless, we must face the contradictions between the economy's bottom-line profits, or "short-haul wealth," *and* the care of the earth that demands "long-haul reciprocity."[13] Because the very survival of creation is at stake, we have no choice but to find strong, effective, and immediate ways to reverse the calamities that are already upon us.

As has been stated, it seems clear that this moral assignment involves our own human evolution. We do well to remember that only those species capable of meeting the next epochal challenge by developing the necessary physical, emotional, and spiritual attributes survived the planet's evolutionary process. Perhaps we need reminding that 99 percent of species that have ever appeared in the last few billion years have not lasted.[14] As long as we are far more absorbed with tabloid news, reality TV, and being digitally plugged in, the more we remain out of it and in great danger with regard to climate change and our current economic peril. As long as our consciousness remains static and rooted in past eras, a future for the human species is unlikely.

Moving beyond where we are requires considering some important proposals about what we need to do (behaviors and policies) and how we might enact them (strategies and collective action) so that we can move toward ecologizing the economy. For example, it will take a great deal of courage, creativity, and learning from the expertise of others to implement strategies that effectively challenge the coal and oil industries. The powerful forces they exert toward increasing climate meltdown are indicated by the fact that the 2007 U.S. Congress was unable to pass a tax bill that would have rolled back a $13.5 billion tax break for oil companies and used the funds for conservation and wind, solar, and biomass energy development.[15] The technology exists now to *double* national fuel efficiency in vehicles, but we continue to have gridlock in Detroit while taxpayers' encourage increasing carbon emissions by allowing government to subsidize fuel costs (and corporations) at roughly $3–$10 per gallon.[16]

For specific policy proposals to reduce heat-trapping carbon emissions and threats from climate meltdown, I look to NASA's chief, James Hansen. For strategy and forms of collective action in how to get these policies and recommendations implemented, I look to recent stirrings in Africa and Latin America as well as to some of the history of political struggle in the United States. These stirrings not only demonstrate how to achieve immediate political goals in this most pressing moral assignment of becoming accountable to our abuse of the global common. They also demonstrate that people's work for social change involves moving beyond current stages of human alienation and transforming themselves as human beings in this process. When we collectively organize to heal the earth, we also transform ourselves as well.

Climate Meltdown and Earth-Healing Policies

To address the escalating rise in temperature, intensification of storms and coastal tragedies, reduction in available land mass, droughts and crop failures, species extinction, and the spread of pandemics, the United States must act quickly and meaningfully both to curtail the emission of carbon greenhouse gases currently being poured into the atmosphere and to respond to the crises that will ensue from the emissions *already* stored in the atmosphere (for decades to come) and the oceans (for centuries to come).

This was the conclusion of the scientific report issued by the Intergovernmental Panel on Climate Change (IPCC), which met in Brussels in April of 2007. Environmentalist Mark Hertsgaard reports that the two thousand climate change scientists and governmental representatives of IPCC stressed the need for significant *mitigation*, or reduction of current emissions, as well as *adaptation*, preparing to deal with future environmental violence already in the pipeline due to emissions already released.[17] Given this crisis, Congressman Henry Waxman and Senators Bernie Sanders and Barbara Boxer set the national goal of 80 percent in reduction of carbon emissions from their 1990 levels by 2050.[18] Hertsgaard writes "the longer we wait to make the 80 percent cuts that are required, the hotter and stormier our future will be."[19]

In order to achieve this goal of reduction of carbon emissions significant enough to slow down global warming, specific policy proposals have been offered by Dr. James Hansen, director of NASA's Goddard Institute for Space Studies. Hansen believes serious attention to the following five recommendations could "solve the problem."[20]

The first recommendation is a moratorium on building new coal-fired power plants because those already in existence may not be able to be retrofitted.[21] Coal-fired power plants are responsible for about 40 percent of all carbon emissions (and are the principal man-made source of a nerve-system poison, mercury).

The second policy recommendation Hansen makes is a tax on the carbon emissions from burning coal, gasoline, and other fuels. This would be a gradually rising carbon tax that would allow businesses and consumers to plan ahead while spurring the creation of cleaner forms of energy. The tax would subsidize not only alternative forms of energy research and production, but also a rebate for lower-income households untowardly affected by the tax.[22] Environmentalists recognize that the tax system is a "hugely powerful lever" for green politics. It is one of the most precise tools green politics possesses because it forces all of us to do what needs to be done.[23]

Hansen's third policy recommendation is to set national energy efficiency standards for buildings and vehicles, including planes (whose carbon emissions get magnified by other atmospheric gasses by 270 percent) and passenger ships (that produce 7.6 times more carbon than jets).[24]

The fourth recommendation is attention to the stability of Antarctic ice sheets (since, for example, for every millimeter the ocean rises, the shoreline retreats by fifteen hundred meters, or almost a mile).[25]

Hansen's final policy recommendation is to address the gap between what the scientific community knows and what the public, including policymakers, are allowed to know. This includes, of course, effective campaign finance reform.[26]

James Hansen's policy recommendations are supported by many scientists and environmentalists because they move beyond the cosmetic reforms like so-called carbon offset practices and dependencies on dubious quick-fix technologies that have been suggested by big business to protect their quarterly profit sheets. Especially important is his carbon tax recommendation because it seeks to "alter fundamentally the trajectory of greenhouse emissions" in order to stabilize the ice sheets in Greenland and Antarctica, the "greatest immediate threat to humanity from climate change."[27] Such a tax will increase the cost of energy while encouraging less use of it and the development of cleaner energy sources. It would also address carbon emissions often under the radar screen like those produced by deforestation and livestock production. Deforestation puts 1–2 billion tons of carbon into the atmosphere per year, and growing and killing cattle for meat produces a fifth of the world's greenhouse gasses, more than transportation.[28]

It is clear that Hansen's policies are valuable not only for climate stabilization, but also for immediate economic relief. If implemented, these recommendations will employ millions of people in higher paying, high tech jobs, harness surplus capital in constructive endeavors, stimulate consumption, and generate tax revenue while returning profits to businesses that make a positive contribution to the situation of climate meltdown. In working toward energy interdependence, these policies will increase our national security and help our balance of payments.[29]

Needed: Disciples Savvy about Power and Responsibility

However, given the current power arrangements of the class system, Hansen's policies, however fundamental and modest, will not be enacted easily. For example, coal is a large industry in twenty-seven states and profits remain to be made on the huge amounts of coal still to be mined.[30] Such policies will also disrupt the abilities of countless businesses to make superprofits from products and services that are currently based on dirty energy. They will change the lifestyles of millions of Americans who feel entitled to their SUVs, McMansions, multiple and ever running TVs and computers, lawnmowers, leaf blowers, and jet-setter lifestyles. Besides, it is positively un-American to want to pay taxes and accept limits on consumption. As has been noted, nothing in the U.S. individualistic, entertainment-oriented, and consumer-driven lifestyle has prepared individuals to use less energy, vacation closer to home, or travel less frequently. And nothing in our corporate culture based on "short-haul profit," as Larry Rasmussen says, has prepared businesses for "long-haul reciprocity."[31] And so Rasmussen asks: "When privilege continues to reign, as it does, instead of rightly ordered relationships of mutuality, is there a worldly discipleship savvy about the play of power and human responsibility?"[32]

To respond "no" to Rasmussen's challenge is to end the human planetary experiment. Therefore, as worldly disciples become accountable and prepare to enact policies that will save us, we are not naïve about the challenge entailed here, given what we know about capitalist dynamics and ideology and the history of U.S. refusal to address ecological destruction. This includes the penchant in U.S. political discourse not to value sacrifice for the common good. Tony Juniper, a spokesperson for a coalition of environmentalists at the UN Climate Conference in Bali, Indonesia, in 2007 made clear the dangerous irony of this situation when he said: "The United States in particular is behaving like passengers in first class in a jumbo jet, thinking a catastrophe in economy class won't affect them."[33]

In addition, despite their importance, we also need to be clear that even these policy recommendations are limited. For they address the mitigation aspects of global warming, but not the adaptation aspects. Challenging as they are, they do not include policies that respond to the fallout of climate violence now in the offing due to carbon emissions *already released* and present in the atmosphere and the oceans. Neither do Hansen's policies address broader aspects of ecological crisis like continuing (noncarbon) toxic pollution of earth, air, and water, or the increasing scarcity of potable water or proliferation of nuclear waste. Indeed, it is difficult to assess who, in the current capitalist system, would take meaningful responsibility for this enormous part of ecological crisis beyond global warming.

It most likely will not be the Democrats. For example, as we have previously noted, military production (let alone war-marking) is one of the greatest polluters on the planet. Yet U.S. military spending, responsible for just under half of the entire planet's trillion dollar military budget, is heading toward $651 billion in 2009.[34] It seems that Democratic legislators cannot be counted on to challenge this state of affairs when, according to Taxpayers for Common Sense and the Center for Responsive Politics, six of the top ten senators in defense campaign contributions in the 2006 elections were Democrats, and four of the top five "ear markers" for military spending were not Republicans, but Democrats.[35] The fossil fuel industry is also a major contributor to the campaigns of members of both parties. Exxon-Mobil contributed $19 million by 2007 to dispute the conclusions of six hundred scientists from forty countries that human-made global warming is "unequivocal."[36] Political scientist Adolph Reed's observation is important here: "Elected officials are only as good or as bad as the forces they feel they must respond to."[37] Regardless of their personal convictions, will legislators feel more pressure from their corporate donors or from an organized citizenry? Only the latter can ensure that those who have profited from globalization will begin to pay back on the "social mortgage," as the late pope John Paul II taught.

It may be true that Hansen's recommendations are an important place to start because they challenge business as usual in meaningful ways. Yet it is also clear that capitalism's culture of indulgence and entitlement, as well as elected officials' (including Democrats') unwillingness to bite the corporate hands that feed them, make the challenges that face us difficult. While ever escalating business profits depend on increasing amounts of dirty energy and most affluent Americans continue destructive lifestyles in ignorant bliss, *New York Times* editorialist Thomas L. Friedman writes: "Today's global economy has become like a monster truck with the gas pedal stuck and we've lost the key."[38] Yet a *Newsweek* poll found in 2007 that as many as

54 percent of Americans dispute the science of climate change.[39] Currently, liberals and liberationists have no coherent vision or strategy for resisting the forces that drive American foreign and domestic policy, including ecological policy. That is why people who are accountable to intellectual and political struggle in light of capitalism's logic, people who are savvy worldly disciples, are in great demand at this historical moment.

Learning from Africa and Latin America

While our assumptions, behaviors, and structures of political economy make social transformation formidable, significant stirrings in global social justice struggle provide inspiration and instruction. As we attempt to take seriously the implementation of policies like James Hansen's to curb the heating up of the planet, accountable disciples can take courage from emerging challenges to global capitalist policies taking place in the Two-Thirds World, especially in places like Latin America and South Africa.

As the system of race functions to hide the class structure, the current struggle in South Africa makes clear the apartheid system hid the reality of encroaching capitalism. Since the African National Conference (ANC) came to power in 1994 after what appeared to be a successful struggle against apartheid, impoverishment has only increased. Since 1994, the ANC has shed its socialist roots, opened its domestic markets to foreign capital, decreased public spending, privatized public goods, and exchanged the savagery of apartheid for that of globalization. As a result, in 2007 unemployment had nearly doubled, about 40 percent are jobless and nearly half of South Africans live below the official poverty line. Of those poor families who do have housing, most cannot afford water or electricity.[40] Writer Michael Wines says that as many as one in four South Africans live "in a level of squalor that would render most observers speechless."[41]

John S. Saul, Canadian professor emeritus of political science and long-time activist in South Africa, writes that capitalist neoliberal economic policies "forced down the throats of African peoples" has only engendered "growing inequality, ecological degradation, de-industrialization and poverty." He celebrates the emergence of increasingly radical social, labor, and environmental communities that are forming local and international alliances and are the main agents of progressive global change.[42]

These South African political stirrings are drawn from a range of grassroots initiatives that have formed in recent decades to resist the neoliberal policies of the current government. Such home-grown organizations privilege unity of action over ideological conformity. Emerging from sectors that are more heterogeneous than the traditional working-class union movement, the core of their fighting units is the family, and their tactic of direct action has been called "quiet encroachment." Ashwin Desai, professor at the Workers' College in Durban, quotes writer A. Bayat to describe quiet encroachment as:

> the silent, protracted and pervasive advancement of ordinary people on those who are propertied and powerful in a quest for survival and improvement in their lives. It is characterized by quiet, largely atomized and prolonged mobilization with episodic collective action — open and fleeting struggles without clear leadership, ideology or structured organization.[43]

These community mobilizations, averaging about sixteen actions per day in 2007, challenge the traditional political system of state power, political parties, and social institutions in South Africa. The mobilizations include, among others, the Anti-Privatization Forum, the Soweto Electricity Crisis Committee, the Treatment Action Campaign, the Western Cape Anti-Eviction Campaign, the Durban Concerned Citizens Forum, Education Rights Project, Environmental Justice Networking Forum, Youth for Work Campaign, and the Shack Dwellers' Movement. Women are often at the forefront of this organized resistance by people who do not believe they must resort to sweatshops or sex work to pay their bills.[44]

Richard Pitthouse, a research fellow at the University of KwaZulu-Natal in Durban writes that what are being created in these stirrings are profoundly democratic and heterogeneous groups that struggle against an opposition (black) government with the help of (white) middle-income activists in Durban.[45] A common action is the use of the road blockage, a way of disrupting business as usual to hold elected leaders accountable when they ignore their campaign promises. Pitthouse describes how one group, arrested while blocking a road, realized "their aspirations for dignity had become criminal." This realization began to move them from a liberal to a more radical consciousness. He writes: "On the day of the road blockade, they entered the tunnel of the discovery of their betrayal [by the anti-apartheid black government]. Nothing has been the same again."[46]

In addition to blocking roads, another common tactic of resistance is hotwiring turned off electricity. John Saul writes about his conversation with a Soweto resident, Agnes Mohapi, age fifty-eight, who said the following as a resister hot-wired her electricity:

> "We shouldn't have to resort to this" . . . but for all its wretchedness, apartheid never . . . laid her off from her job, jacked up her utility bill, then disconnected her service when she inevitably could not pay. "Privatization did that," she said . . . "and all this globalization garbage our new black government has forced upon us has done nothing but make things worse . . . but we will unite and we will fight this government with the same fury that we fought the whites in their day."[47]

The consciousness pervading this political struggle by ordinary mostly impoverished citizens is that people are entitled to food, water, electricity, and shelter without having to endure exploitative labor. Growing numbers believe that with a movement that is massive enough, and pursued with sufficient imagination and vigor, ordinary people can enact social change. These stirrings are not rooted in specific ideological dogma but emanate from the simple belief that government and business have *no right to charge people for the privilege of living*.[48] Writer William Johnson says that "mass actions to hold the government accountable to its citizens show that democracy in South Africa is alive and well in ways that should make American progressives envious."[49]

Perhaps it is too soon to call these community mobilizations a new "social movement." But John Saul observes that, while it is impossible to know what these "fresh stirrings of popular discontent will achieve," he believes these grassroots initiatives are the beginnings of "a sea change" in South African politics. Despite temptations to "overestimate the strength and unity" of these mobilizations, he thinks "we are entering novel and complex political terrain in South Africa, terrain that is extremely dangerous but also marked by genuine promise."[50]

Surely the justice struggle of such ordinary Africans is both inspirational and instructional for people preparing for the role of worldly discipleship and active moral agency in the United States. So too are the uprisings of impoverished people and their allies in Latin America that are similar backlashes to neoliberal economic policies like increasing cuts in social spending and escalating privatization of public goods. Like the cases in South Africa, these stirrings, in a continent where 43 percent live in poverty, are heterogeneous in origin, from indigenous communities to student networks to labor and neighborhood organizations.[51] They also constitute a wide range of ideological challenge, from those like the leaders in Brazil who concede in varying degrees to financial elites, to forms of grassroots direct rule like the people power of the Zapatista movement in Chiapas, Mexico.

These challenges to global neoliberalism, at both the grassroots and state levels, include the elections of Bolivarian revolutionist Hugo Chavez as president of Venezuela in 2002; the election of Evo Morales of the Movement Toward Socialism in Bolivia in 2005; and the election of Rafael Correa, a proponent of "socialism for the twenty-first century," as president of Ecuador. Latin American challenges to capitalist neoliberalism are also found in the alliance of Venezuela, Cuba, and Bolivia in ALBO, the Bolivarian Alliance for Latin America and the Caribbean; the dramatic electoral social revolutionary struggles in Mexico to protest the stolen 2006 election; the consistent challenge of the Landless Workers' Movement in Brazil; Argentina's repudiation of external debt in defiance of the World Bank, and the Association of Indigenous Councils of Northern Cauca, Colombia.[52]

Such examples are only some of the upsurges in representative democracy where millions of students, indigenous, and other poor people are participating actively in political life so that people (or in some cases the state) can recover some power in the economy that was previously relinquished to foreign economic elites.

The background to these stirrings, of course, is the increasing economic polarization in global capitalism and the use by governments and international financial institutions of neoliberal economic policies to intensify impoverishment of the many and the wealth of the few. As researcher and professor Raul Zibechi explains, what is happening is that, in destroying the (liberal) welfare state that mitigated some of the negative fallout from capitalist dynamics, economic elites are also destroying their ability to maintain hegemony and control over populations. Since increasing numbers of people in the world are no longer tied in any way to the state and to the mainstream economy, they are *creating new forms of community organization* in order to survive. The exclusion of the marginalized from the political economy in this historical phase of capitalism is so deep, that autonomous stirrings to control living conditions are replacing external control by states. Zibechi writes that the marginalized have become so disenfranchised they have "rejected submission" and "transformed the streets" into "new forms of social organization." He says in many of these stirrings the "roadblock" has become a common political tool as a way to "defend spaces controlled by new subjects." Increasing numbers, he writes, are refusing "to accept the role of subordinates or 'excluded' that the system has reserved for them."[53]

The Bolivarian revolution in Venezuela, the fourth largest oil importer to the United States, is perhaps the most inspirational, though still ambiguous and contradictory, example to date of such resistance to neoliberalism.[54] Professor of economics Michael Leibowitz, who has lived and worked there, claims a real alternative to capitalism may be emerging. Leibowitz suggests that, while Venezuela did not start out to build a socialist alternative, in the process of implementing strategies that challenged the logic of capital, Venezuelans may have begun to mobilize themselves to build that alternative.

In contrast to capitalism's logic of profits without limit for relatively few investors regardless of the destruction entailed, some aspects of Venezuela's Bolivarian revolution are characterized by decentralization of power that puts human beings, not profits, machines, or the state, ahead of everything. Venezuela has clearly demonstrated the right of the state to regulate the economy and control a region's resources in the interests of the people. Since Venezuela has socialized the nation's oil profits, as well as the telephone and electricity companies, poverty has dropped by 25 percent.[55]

But in the work of liberation, *human emancipation is even larger* than moves toward economic empowerment. Leibowitz is also interested in how the Venezuelan people are in the process of *personal emancipation* and human evolution as they collectively work to transform their society. He claims, for example, that, while mobilizing to implement a new hydro-carbon tax, people began to organize in ways that pushed them beyond ordinary modes of operating. The dynamic effects of the carbon tax mobi-lization, among others, provided some of the basis for "radical endogenous development, oriented to *building new human capacities* by both teaching specific skills and preparing people to enter into new productive relations through courses in cooperation and self-management."[56] These new social relations, exercised in new organizations like worker councils and commu-nity councils, began to develop new kinds of people. New social relations of self-management, worker-management, and community management cre-ated "forms of association guided by mutual cooperation and solidarity."[57] As a result of these new institutional structures, writes Leibowitz, "people produce not only solutions to their needs, but they also produce themselves as collective workers for themselves."[58] Leibowitz argues that new social relations, the basis of which lay in part in the original organizing to pass a hydrocarbon tax, was the basis for creating new social subjects, that is new men, new women and the institutional seeds of a new society. In this process, a reform *within* capitalism (passing the hydrocarbon tax) led to a transformation *of* capitalism (building new institutions that are creating new forms of people who have values and commitments to the common good that challenge business as usual). Here we see that people develop themselves (and evolve) by participating in the major decisions that impact their lives.[59] We also see that, while it is important to distinguish between liberal and liberationist forms of social analysis, it seems that liberal political work may lead to liberationist forms of structural change. As liberal poli-cies become increasingly insufficient to address problems, or are jettisoned altogether, there is rising consciousness about the undemocratic nature of "capitalist democracy." People are demanding health, housing, education, and social security *apart from the vagaries of capitalism*. Atilio A. Boron, professor of political theory at the University of Buenos Aires, writes that people are beginning to measure the degree of social justice and effective democratic citizenry in a country by "the extent of 'de-commodification' in the supply of basic goods and services to satisfy fundamental human needs," or the degree to which people can survive without being vulnerable to the exclusionary operations of markets.[60]

Leibowitz is clear there are still formidable capitalist barriers to a more democratic alternative in Venezuela. Nevertheless, he claims, something is moving. He gives the example of how a recent rejection by capitalist owners to price controls on food was challenged by communal councils that were ready to take over the supermarkets! What all of this demonstrates is that slight changes in conditions *can* produce dramatic results. Like the transformation (from liberals to liberationists) in those South Africans when their road blockade was met with their arrests, so work on the carbon tax reform contributed to the transformation of Venezuelans and their institutions.[61]

It is important to recognize that people in Venezuela have been building this movement long before Hugo Chavez's ascendancy. Historically, social justice movements are created by the participation of multitudes of ordinary people, often for decades if not centuries, which then harness leaders to bring their movements even further. Indeed, it is these *civil society organizations that created Chavez.* So as he rises in power and prominence in the country and the region, many are cautious. They know that, while the eighteen thousand community councils that decide how to spend government allotments of over $1.5 billion may demonstrate rising grassroots empowerment in Venezuela, these democratic developments need to be read against authoritarian tendencies in the government itself. These include packing the legislature, judiciary, and military with pro-Chavez supporters as well as the defeated referendum then subsequently passed to give Hugo Chavez the presidency for life. The fact that Venezuelans, including many of Chavez's supporters, initially voted against the referendum speaks to the health of Venezuelan democracy.[62] But it shows that a charismatic leader can be a threat to democracy as much as an asset, particularly one who uses inflammatory rhetoric, some of which is misogynist.[63]

It is clear that Venezuela is addressing aspects of the class elitist system and is challenging forms of globalization and neoliberalism. But as long as patriarchy uses sex/gender repression, fundamental also to the class and race systems, society will not be liberated because domination and subordination continue to code human relations. Since women as a group bear more of a burden in the task of reproducing society than men as a group (especially if women also suffer class and race subordination), patriarchs will not lead half the human race to liberation. (They also will be compromised in what they can do to implement class and racial justice since the systems are fundamentally interlocking.) Given that women's impoverishment and lack of emancipation are rooted not only in the capitalist class structure and the race system but also in the sex/gender system, men who uncritically enjoy male privilege will not facilitate genuine, inclusive democracy. As of this writing, the Venezuelan revolution is very much in process and, in terms of both internal and external challenges to this experiment, much remains to be determined. But nothing is ever final because of the possibilities inherent in collective political action, especially if the intellectual analysis of oppression has been well done.

While such stirrings may be possible because of specific conditions in Venezuela — like the presence of visible, deep impoverishment existing alongside arrogant privilege, a leadership that urges the masses to challenge this state of affairs, and time to experiment because the U.S. military has been monopolized in the Middle East — I believe these examples are instructive as well to us in the United States. As Jean Hardisty and Deepak Bhargava observe, such movements demonstrate "the centrality of developing ordinary people as agents of change rather than charismatic leadership or coalitions of elites.... What ultimately forces change is human beings seeing fellow human beings act [in big and small ways] from a place of deep conviction."[64] And even when postcapitalist experiments founder or fail (as they often do from outside opposition by capitalist banks and military invasions, or poor structural analysis, corruption, and backbiting from within, or all of the above), every experiment offers something to learn about social transformation.

Venezuela shows that (however compromised or for whatever limited amount of time) a state *can* support parallel organs of people-power. According to political theorist George Ciccariello-Maher, it also warns us, however, that parallel organs like community councils will be successful *only if* the state can facilitate them rather than control them. He claims the future of the Venezuelan experiment depends on whether the councils can assert their autonomy from the state as they themselves aid the development of other autonomous social forces.[65] Ciccariello would agree with American University economist Robin Hahnel, who says that postcapitalist twentieth-century experiments failed (in the Soviet Union and China, for example) because most people's economic activities were planned *for* them, not *by* them. I would also add that these countries were and still remain male-dominant societies where domination and subordination code the most fundamental human relations.

Political scientist Yiching Wu further observes that in countries such as these we have "neoliberal capitalist development in postsocialist contexts" today because former (so-called) socialist "power holders" who are now "capital owners" have appropriated socialist capital accumulation.[66] These governments, even though identified as "socialist" or "Marxist," did not allow *democratic economic planning* by workers and consumers and communities, because they owned and controlled the wealth of their country's labor force. They did not allow alternative forms of democratic organizations to replace the traditional powers of the state. In similar vein, New York University professor Greg Grandin points out the challenge Venezuela faces is "how to institutionalize this relationship between a fortified executive and an empowered citizenry."[67] Without organs that foster genuine inclusive economic self-management, as well as mutuality in the relations between men and women, really challenging goals, Venezuela will fail too.[68] But as Leibowitz observes, Venezuela has at least begun.

The concrete social stirrings of millions in South Africa and Latin America may inform and inspire U.S. worldly disciples because they may lead us to wonder about what might happen to institutions in the United States if they too were challenged in organized ways. What, for example, might happen to social institutions and to the evolution of moral agents if the enormous coal industry is halted, if most businesses are forced to cut profits when they are produced by dirty energy, if new forms of clean energy become ubiquitous, and if the wealthy loosen their easy control over the U.S. government through genuine campaign finance reform? Since *we re-create ourselves through our actions,* just where might these "reform" measures eventually lead, not only in terms of changes to U.S. institutions, but also to changes in the social construction of U.S. people? What kinds of people will we become when we work to actively transform society in ways that are more accountable to the common good?

Political Strategies in U.S. Justice Struggle

As accountable, worldly disciples commit themselves to collective engagement in the work of enacting meaningful public policy that significantly decreases heat-trapping gas emissions, how do we think about the strategies we use to accomplish this? What kinds of political struggle are attractive and more likely to lead multitudes to engage in using them? What are more likely to begin to reshape institutions, behaviors, and values toward human and planetary well-being? We have briefly explored stirrings that may instruct us from abroad. Now I turn to examine some strategies by activists in the United States that may also serve as pedagogical tools for us today. For a start I suggest the following forms of collective action to get us thinking about moral ways to interrupt violence, especially escalating carbon toxicity, at its roots. I argue that such strategies should be prefigurative, address group-based harm, including ecologically based harm, embody assertive forms of resistance, interrupt injustice at vulnerable points in the system, and be pleasurable to enact. They require knowledge, discipline, and planning, and they also can bring fun and joy.

Before moving to these particular strategies, however, it is important to note that in recent decades it has actually been conservative evangelicals and the political Right who have waged the most effective recent grassroots movement in the United States. While liberals and liberationists have been dealing with the escalating negative fallout of capitalist dynamics by running soup kitchens, homeless shelters, domestic violence programs, living wage campaigns, and labor and community organizing projects, among other programs, religious and political conservatives have been effectively organizing churches, schools, and neighborhoods and taking over the Republican Party. Sometimes using strategies from the labor, civil rights, and feminist movements of the 1950s through the 1970s, the religious and political Right was a backlash to these movements' critique of dominant economic, racial, and sex/gender structures and values. The amazing effectiveness of the Right's grassroots organizing strategies, harnessed to the latest developments in telecommunications and fortified with generous funding from corporate America, has provided enormous social, political, and economic support for globalization, conservative sexuality, and the U.S. privileged status quo. Savvy accountable disciples do well to learn from these effective organizers who even though *seemingly* on the wane in 2009 have dominated U.S. politics and pro-business culture since the 1980s.

We also do well to learn from those who challenged business as usual in the labor, civil rights, and feminist movements of the earlier 1950s–1970s. Many participants in these struggles were grounded in the conviction that *the seeds of the desired end lay in the political means* to achieve that end. This applied not only to the public strategies used, but also to the nature of the organization itself. As a consequence, organizations that work for social change should, in both the public strategies used and the way their organizations are internally structured, prefigure the desired society. In other words, an organization that seeks ecological forms of social justice should not only be identified by its ecologically sound practices that respect the body of our mother the Earth. It should also embody just relations to all material bodies, including classed, raced, and gendered bodies. It does this by paying attention to the diverse dynamics of domination and subordination that inform the day-to-day operations of the organization.

This certainly follows the logic of the Jesus movement as articulated in previous chapters. Like Jesus, his earliest followers lived as if God's will of justice in heaven had already been done on this earth. Consequently, the Jesus movement attracted great numbers because of it discipleship of equals. In the twentieth century, Martin Luther King Jr. also understood that the end existed in embryo form in the means; he understood that the larger society would be converted to civil rights if the movement resisted segregation in ways that were morally consistent with the justice ends they were pursuing.[69] In her book on strategies for social change, Cynthia Kaufman calls the embodying of the intimate connection between how we act in the present and what we seek to achieve in the future "prefigurative politics."[70]

Another dimension of just political struggle has to do with being clear about the *nature of group-based harm*. This means recognizing that some people and the earth itself are easier targets for forms of exploitation and oppression because they belong to groups that are overidentified with their physical bodies (including their emotions and sexuality), which are undervalued in Western political culture and made subordinate in its social relations. While liberals, who tend to focus on individuals, often disparage "identity politics" and believe that it is harmful to see people as members of groups, those informed by a structural analysis of political economy as well as liberation theology believe that the basic dynamics in the society function to reproduce group-based harm. For liberals, exploitation and oppression are *"mistakes"* that can be addressed by educating people. For liberationists, exploitation and oppression are *necessities* that are systematically reproduced by the political economy in order to increase control over people and profits for investors. Many Marxists, like Antonio Gramsci and some liberation theologians, acknowledge, as Kaufman says, "how social power operates in constructing and restricting people based on these types of group memberships."[71] A just political strategy, then, is one that identifies with exploited and oppressed groups, including the planet itself, finds meaningful ways to address their suffering, and is accountable to work for their well-being.

Consequently, just political strategies emanate from organizations that take group privilege and oppression seriously. Such organizations embody new social relations between and among groups that interrupt suffering and prefigure new kinds of social relations. In their own micro communities and organizations, moral agents live so as to prefigure the justice they are collectively organizing to extend to the larger society. As a result, they are transforming not only institutions in society, but more fundamentally they are *transforming themselves*. As we see, addressing the need for prefigurative politics and addressing group-based harm leads to the same transformation. It is not so much that people need more individual rights (often understood to be at the expense of others) but rather they need a transformed society of people and institutions as well as balanced eco-relations, where individual, communal, and ecological well-being are more fully integrated.

Taking power seriously is another form of the same equation. Theorists, like Frantz Fanon, Paulo Freire, and Frederick Douglass, for example, who have thought long and hard about how to do political struggle justly and effectively, also know, as Douglass said, "power concedes nothing without a demand."[72] Douglass also noted that if you "find out just what any people will quietly submit to, then you have found out the exact measure of injustice and wrong that will be imposed upon them."[73] This means subordinates are *morally required to resist* their subordination. Here we can learn from the many South Africans who are exchanging quiet submission for "quiet encroachment." We also implement the moral claim that the end is embryonic in the means in connection with active resistance, not passivity or weakness, in order to be effective. The justice created always remains unfinished as people continually work to transform themselves through their active responsibility for the common good, including all the major decisions that affect their lives.

As we have said previously, in being responsible for the just sharing of power, moral agents must engage in structural analysis so they can create serious plans for action that include withdrawing consent and cooperation with the system of injustice, *and* applying pressure that targets the vulnerabilities in the system. Environmentalist Lierre Keith writes that unjust "power depends on obedience...and the moment [we] withdraw our consent, the powerful are left with nothing." Keith says we need to both withdraw consent and apply pressure with forms of militant action that respond to the question: "Where are the vulnerable targets on this monster that's devouring our planet alive?" She further asks, are predatory corporations most vulnerable around electricity and computers? Be creative, she suggests, about interrupting the injustice at the roots.[74] As Kaufman says, "short of violence, there are many ways that those advocating for social justice can put pressure on those with power."[75]

Finally, strategies that are often the most effective in implementing necessary policies are not only ones that demand knowledge, discipline, sacrifice, and planning but are also strategies that are the most fun to enact. In the 1970s, community organizer Saul Alinsky wrote that the best way to apply pressure is to use tactics "that your people enjoy."[76] This is vividly illustrated in the tradition of the School of the Americas protests as described in the previous chapter. Economist and social activist Michael Albert agrees when he says that the best political strategies are those that apply pressure through tactics that resisters enjoy while raising the costs for unjust policymakers and their institutions. Albert writes, "Change occurs when movements raise the social costs that policymakers are no longer willing to endure and that they can escape only by relenting to the movement's demands."[77]

It is clear that effective strategies for implementing more just social policies like those of James Hansen require sophisticated structural analysis, as well as creativity and imagination as moral agents embody a micro-politics of subtle transformation, or "quiet encroachment." As the new social relations being embodied in Venezuela and South Africa suggest, more just social relations create new forms of social consciousness for the people involved in these new forms of social relations. And when new social relations transform human subjects, they will create new institutions and new societies without which we, and the planet, cannot survive.

The Universe Bends toward Justice

Many people have given up on the possibility of social change today because they believe the United States has sold out to popular conservatism. Whether or not a conservative America is capable of achieving more justice, it surely seems to be possible for thousands of groups throughout the world, as the small number of stirrings covered in this chapter alone begins to suggest.

It is also a matter of some debate as to the degree this evaluation is based on solid data of a uniformly conservative America. For example, researcher Rick Perlstein surveyed a wide range of polls in 2006, including Pew, National Election Studies, Gallop, NBC News/Wall Street Journal,

CNN Opinion, Kaiser Family Foundation/Harvard, Public Agenda/Foreign Affairs, CBS/New York Times, and Annenberg, among others. He found that the data simply does not support the view, widespread in the media and among Democrats, that we live in a conservative America. Even before the 2008 economic emergency began, Perlstein concluded that these polls point to the fact that Americans by and large are anxious about the economy, believe that corporations have too much power, are making too much profit, and that the income gap will continue to widen. His thesis is that while voters have increasingly progressive sympathies on everything from the economy to war to sex education, Democrats in particular, probably due to the media that amplifies conservative views, believe the country has been captured and frozen by the rise of 1990s popular conservatism. Perlstein suggests that opportunities for passing progressive social policy and the energy to implement these policies will increase if this mistaken view of a conservative America is rectified.[78] The election of Barack Obama in 2008 only adds to Perlstein's argument.

Whether Perlstein's reading of the pulse of America is correct, or whether Americans are closer to Dee Graham's thesis (congruent with William Tabb's in chapter 3) that what is mostly at work is "societal Stockholm syndrome" in which the oppressed bond with their predators, it is certainly true there are millions who would join a mobilization with a serious strategy of social change if they believed it had some chance of succeeding.[79] Hence, savvy worldly disciples should feel great incentive to continue to do the analysis, strategizing, and collective political action that will enact policies that begin to tame capitalism and environmental degradation by establishing new ground rules.

The last part of our moral assignment is to pray and "get right with the universe."[80] The need for individual moral agents to "get right with the universe" shows the injustice we target is not only in the public arena; it is within ourselves. We are the ones with a sense of entitlement for what does not belong to us; we are the ones who don't feel responsibility for the impoverishment and ecological devastation our affluence reproduces; we are the ones who shift responsibility for our work and our sexuality onto others; and we are the ones who simply do not know how to engage in democratic social relations. We are the ones who praise the communal values we learned in kindergarten, but wouldn't have a clue as to how to embody them as adults, including extending the logic of democracy into the allocation of social goods. In an interview about his film *Sicko*, Michael Moore said, "When you share the pie, sometimes you have to *wait for your slice*. Sometimes you get the first slice, sometimes you get the third slice. Sometimes ... you get the last slice. But the important thing is you get a slice and *everybody gets a slice* of this [healthcare] pie. That's not what happens in this country."[81]

We are also the ones who interact with digital gadgets and other commodities more than with people and nature, and, if we do not continue to evolve, we are headed for falling victim to the inability of people to pay sufficient attention to us. Loneliness and isolation that come from insufficient attention, let alone nurture and care, from other human beings is what psychologist George Ainslie says will be the most serious and enduring mental health problem of the future.[82] In short, we are the ones, as Leibowitz says, who are the "fragmented, crippled human beings that capitalism produces."[83] The most formidable challenge that disciples seeking accountability face is not the massive power of the elite, but the thwarted human potential of the disciples themselves because of their nondemocratic acculturation, their obsession with commodities, their divorce from one another and nature, all aspects of their stagnation in the process of human evolution.

This does not mean we cannot learn and grow and change, or that there are no others who can instruct us. Even the fact that we are holding ourselves accountable shows we are on the way to recovery and transformation. In fact, *resistance* to injustice is itself *a therapy for what ails us*. Moral philosopher Roger Gottleib says there can be great joy and liberation in confronting a moral task that seems so challenging it fills us with dread. He shows how, in the act of resisting injustice, we no longer let what frightens us determine us and shrink our humanity. Gottleib says that resistance, especially collective resistance, is a spiritual practice that gives us energy and joy. He suggests that when we resist injustice we are fully open to what is going on and to who we really are, active moral agents, who enjoy solidarity with others as we create our futures and ourselves anew.[84] This is the activity that distinguishes us from nonhuman nature. As we have seen from the social stirrings emerging in Latin America and Africa, people who engage in them not only get specific needs met and policies passed; they also *re-create themselves* as collective agents for themselves and for one another and the earth itself.

If we want a future for ourselves, our children, our grandchildren, and all God has made, our ongoing task is no less than this. Our success is never guaranteed, but we are supported by the way the universe bends, for if the God of Exodus, the Prophets, and Jesus created the universe, then justice is at its heart.[85]

Notes

Introduction to the Second Edition

1. Beverly W. Harrison, "The Dream of a Common Language: Toward a Normative Theory of Justice in Christian Ethics," *The Annual of the Society of Christian Ethics*, 1983, ed. Larry L. Rasmussen (Waterloo, Ontario: Council on the Study of Religion, Wilfrid Laurier University, 1983), 4.

2. From 1950 to 1970 federal spending on infrastructure renewal was over 3 percent of GDP. After 1980 the figure was reduced to less than 1 percent. In 2005, the American Society of Civil Engineers estimated it would cost 1.6 trillion over the next five years to repair U.S. infrastructure. This estimate is noninclusive of the need for widespread high-speed broadband and major expenditures to reduce carbon emissions. Editorial, "Things Fall Apart," *The Nation*, August 27–September 3, 2007, 3.

3. Michael Grunwald, "The Threatening Storm," *Time Magazine*, August 13, 2007, 30–39.

4. Gary Younge, "New Orleans Forsaken," *The Nation*, September 18, 2006, 17–20.

5. Christopher Shea, "Colorblinded," *Boston Globe,* September 3, 2006, D3.

6. Grunwald, "The Threatening Storm," 32.

7. Derrick Z. Jackson, "Earmarking the War Machine," *Boston Globe*, July 21, 2007, A9.

8. Chalmers Johnson, *Nemesis: The Last Days of the American Republic* (New York: Metropolitan Books, 2007).

9. Frank Rich, "Ronald Reagan Is Still Dead," *New York Times,* January 20, 2008, WK11.

10. See Jean-Claude Paye and Michael E. Tigar, "A New Form of State: War and Criminal Law," *Monthly Review* 59, no. 4 (September 2007), esp. 15.

11. Chuck Collins and Felice Yeskill, *Economic Apartheid in America: A Primer on Economic Inequality and Insecurity* (New York: New Press, 2005), 100.

12. Elizabeth DiNovella, "Amy Goodman: The Progressive Interview," *The Progressive* (February 2008): 39, and Frank Rich, "McCain Channels His Inner Hillary," *New York Times*, March 12, 2008, WK12.

13. James Carroll, "60 Years of Faulty Logic," *Boston Globe*, March 12, 2007, A11.

14. Barbara Ehrenreich, "Bush's Old Warfare State," *The Progressive* (August 2006), *http://progressive.org/node/831,* and Kathy Dobie, "Denial in the Corps," *The Nation,* February 18, 2008, 12.

15. Dobie, "Denial in the Corps," 11–19.

16. Quoted in ibid., 13.

17. See Arc Ecology: Environment, Economy, Society, and Peace, online at *www.arcecology.org*.

18. John Bellamy Foster and Brett Clark, "Rachel Carson's Ecological Critique," *Monthly Review* 59, no. 9 (February 2008): 5–7.

19. Ibid., 1–17.

20. Joshua Muldavin, "China's Not Alone in Environmental Crisis," *Boston Globe,* December 19, 2007, A23.

21. William K. Tabb, "Resource Wars," *Monthly Review* 58, no. 8 (January 2007): 32–42.

22. Quoted in Atilio A. Boron, "The Truth about Capitalist Democracy," in *Telling the Truth: Socialist Register 2006,* ed. Leo Panitch and Colin Leys (New York: Monthly Review Press, 2006), 55.

23. Pamela K. Brubaker, *Globalization at What Price? Economic Change and Daily Life* (Cleveland: Pilgrim Press, 2001), 39.

24. Editorial, "1,000 Heroines," *Boston Globe,* November 11, 2005, A22.

25. Swanee Hunt, "The Three Lessons of Sebrenica," *Boston Globe,* July 11, 2005, A11.

26. See Parag Khanna, "Waving Goodbye to Hegemony," *New York Times Magazine,* January 27, 2008, 35–66, and H. D. S. Greenway, "An Asian Century?" *Boston Globe,* January 29, 2008, A15.

27. Jamie Gass, "Rounding Out Our Future Workforce," *Boston Globe,* January 24, 2006, A13.

28. James Randerson, "World's Richest 1 Percent Own 40 Percent of All Wealth," *The Guardian,* December 6, 2006, 1–2, *www.guardian.co.uk.*

29. Kim Phillips-Fein, "Deal Breakers," *The Nation,* December 10, 2007, 17.

30. New Economic Foundation, "World Economy Giving Less to Poorest in Spite of Global Poverty" (January 23, 2006): *www.globalpolicy.org/socecon/develop/quality/2006/0123growthpoverty.htm.*

31. Tina Rosenberg, "Reverse Foreign Aid: Why Are Poor Countries Subsidizing Rich Ones?" *New York Times Magazine,* March 25, 2007, 16.

32. New Economic Foundation, "World Economy Giving Less to Poorest in Spite of Global Poverty."

33. Martin Hart-Landsberg and Paul Burkett, "China, Capitalist Accumulation, and Labor," *Monthly Review* 59, no. 1 (May 2007): 17–18.

34. Jacob S. Hacker, "The Rise of the Office-Park Populist," *New York Times Magazine,* December 24, 2006, 24.

35. Jared Bernstein and Lawrence Mishel, "Economy's Gains Fail to Reach Most Workers' Paychecks," *Economic Policy Institute* (September 3, 2007), *http://epi.org/content.cfm/bp195,* and Robert Kuttner, "Here's a Job Americans Would Do," *Boston Globe,* May 27, 2006, A15.

36. Eyal Press, "The Missing Class," *The Nation,* August 13–20, 2007, 22.

37. Current Population Reports, "Income, Poverty, and Health Insurance Coverage in the United States: 2006," *U.S. Census Bureau* (August 2007): A13.

38. Anna Badkhen, "A Warehouse for the Poor," *Boston Globe,* February 9, 2008, A1.

39. Megan Woolhouse, "Attempted Kidnapping Unsettles Belmont," *Boston Globe,* February 9, 2008, B3.

40. Sasha Chanoff, "Tribal Hatred Didn't Cause Violence in Kenya," *Boston Globe,* January 19, 2008, A13.

41. Michael Fitzgerald, "Militarism and the American Way of Life," *Utne Reader, The Humanist* (March/April 2005): 6.

42. Robert McAfee Brown, *Theology in a New Key* (Philadelphia: Westminster Press, 1978), 80.

43. Quoted in Christopher Leslie Brown, "Little Ships of Horror," book review of Marcus Rediker, *The Slave Ship: A Human History* (New York: Viking, 2007) in *The Nation,* February 4, 2008, 24.

44. Quoted in Stuart Klawans, "A Hard Man," *The Nation,* January 28, 2008, 32.

45. John Perkins, *Confessions of an Economic Hit Man* (San Francisco: Berrett-Koehler Publishers, 2004), 48–49.

1. An Ethical Agenda for Elites

1. David Harvey, *Justice, Nature, and the Geography of Difference* (Cambridge, Mass.: Blackwell Publishers, 1996), 334–38.

2. Paul Krugman, "The Great Wealth Transfer," *Rolling Stone,* no. 1015 (December 14, 2006): 48; Robert Kuttner, "Here's a Job Americans Would Do," *Boston Globe,* May 27, 2006, A15, and David Cay Johnston, "Income Gap Is Widening, Data Shows," *New York Times, www.newyorktimes.com/2007/03/29/business/29tax.html.*

3. Peggy McIntosh, "White Privilege and Male Privilege: A Personal Account of Coming to See Correspondences through Work in Women's Studies," working paper 189, Wellesley College Center for Research on Women, Wellesley, Mass., 1988.

4. Even though I reject the opposition in postmodernism to critical theories of class exploitation, racism, and gender subordination, as well as postmodernism's indifference to institutional change and social transformation, I follow its logic here in asserting that class, race, and gender differences are not essential but are social constructions. See Stephen Best and Douglas Kellner, *Postmodern Theory: Critical Interrogations* (New York: Guilford Press, 1991).

5. Patricia Hill Collins, *Fighting Words: Black Women and the Search for Justice* (Minneapolis: University of Minnesota Press, 1998), 102–3.

6. Michael Zweig, "Six Points on Class," in *More Unequal: Aspects of Class in the United States,* ed. Michael D. Yates (New York: Monthly Review Press, 2007), 174.

7. Michael Parenti, *Power and the Powerless* (New York: St. Martin's Press, 1978), 11.

8. William K. Tabb, "The Power of the Rich," in *More Unequal: Aspects of Class in the United States,* ed. Michael D. Yates (New York: Monthly Review Press, 2007), 41, and Jared Bernstein and Lawrence Mishel, "Economy's Gains Fail to Reach Most Workers' Paychecks," *Economic Policy Institute,* September 3, 2007, *www.epi.org/content.cfm/bp195.*

9. Historical Income Table, Households, *U.S. Census Bureau, www.censusgov//hhes/www/income/histinc/h01ar.html.*

10. Parenti, *Power and the Powerless,* 12.

11. Himani Bannerji first used the word "commonsense" to denote the ubiquitous taken-for-granted assumptions undergirding racism. See Himani Bannerji, *Thinking Through: Essays on Feminism, Marxism, and Anti-Racism* (Toronto: Women's Press, 1995).

12. Francis Fox Piven and Richard A. Cloward, "Eras of Power," *Monthly Review* 49, no. 8 (January 1998): 11–23.

13. Parenti, *Power and the Powerless,* 5.

14. Michael Albert and Robin Hahnel, *Unorthodox Marxism: An Essay on Capitalism, Socialism, and Revolution* (Boston: South End Press, 1978), 61.

15. Parenti, *Power and the Powerless,* 13, 223.

16. Antonio Gramsci, *Selections from the Prison Notebooks of Antonio Gramsci,* ed. and trans. Quinton Hoare and Geoffrey Nowell Smith (New York: International Publishers, 1972).

17. Colin Nickerson, "Canadian Executive Returns as Hero from Colombia Ordeal," *Boston Globe,* January 13, 1999, sec. A.

18. Beverly W. Harrison, "The Fate of the Middle 'Class' in Late Capitalism," in *God and Capitalism: A Prophetic Critique of Market Economy,* ed. J. Mark Thomas and Vernon Visick (Madison, Wisc.: A-R Editions, 1991), 55.

19. Bannerji, "But Who Will Speak for Us?" in *Unsettling Relations,* ed. Himani Bannerji et al. (Boston: South End Press, 1991), 84.

20. Critical theory in a narrow sense refers to the intellectual tradition established by the Frankfurt School for Social Research in 1923 and includes the more recent work of Jürgen Habermas. While I draw on some of these theorists, I use a broader definition of critical social theory that draws on bodies of knowledge that actively engage the central issues facing groups who live in contexts characterized by class, race, and gender injustice. See David Held, *Introduction to Critical Theory: Horkheimer to Habermas* (Berkeley: University of California Press, 1980), and Collins, *Fighting Words,* 124–54.

21. Philip Cushman, *Constructing the Self, Constructing America* (New York: Addison-Wesley, 1995), 10, 57–61, 281.

22. David Harvey, *The Condition of Postmodernity* (Cambridge, Mass.: Basil Blackwell, 1989), 14.

23. Gunnemann, as cited in Elizabeth M. Bounds, *Coming Together/Coming Apart: Religion, Community, and Modernity* (New York: Routledge, 1977), 32–33.

24. Ibid., 33.

25. Mary E. Hobgood, *Catholic Social Teaching and Economic Theory: Paradigms in Conflict* (Philadelphia: Temple University Press, 1991). See esp. chapter 2.

26. Susanne Kappeler, *The Will to Violence: The Politics of Personal Behavior* (New York: Columbia Teachers College Press, 1995), 29–32.

27. Judith V. Jordan, "Clarity in Connection: Empathic Knowing, Desire, and Sexuality," in *Women's Growth in Diversity,* ed. Judith V. Jordan (New York: Guilford Press, 1997), 51.

28. Harrison, "The Fate of the Middle 'Class' in Late Capitalism," 55.

29. Contrary to those who hold, on the one hand, that we have an essential human nature or, on the other hand, that we are socially constructed in every aspect, I am persuaded by the view that who we are is what we have been able to do (some laboring under far more constraints than others) with our species-nature and

our concrete environmental particulars. The content of our species-nature seems to be relevant in all historical and cultural contexts (e.g., basic material needs, love, friendship and respect, self-management). Our concrete environment, however, is culturally and historically specific. See Albert and Hahnel, *Unorthodox Marxism*, 118–25, 136.

30. Elizabeth Bettenhausen, "Embracing Identity: Creativity and Security" (ms., AIDS and Religion in America Convocation Papers, 1999), 4, published on the *AIDS National Interfaith Network* web site at *www.anin.org*.

31. Kristin Waters, review of *Revisioning the Political: Feminist Reconstructions of Traditional Concepts in Western Philosophy*, by Nancy J. Hirschmann and Christine Di Stefano, eds., *American Philosophical Newsletters* 96, no. 2 (Spring 1997): 39–42.

32. Joanna Macy and Molly Young Brown, *Coming Back to Life: Practices on Recovering Our Lives* (Philadelphia: New Society Publishers, 1998), 49.

33. Kappeler, *The Will to Violence*, 24–28.

34. Suzanne Pharr, *In the Time of the Right: Reflections on Liberation* (Berkeley: Chardon Press, 1996), 45.

35. Eric Mount Jr., *Professional Ethics in Context: Institutions, Images, and Empathy* (Louisville: Westminster/John Knox, 1990), 142.

36. Bettenhausen, "Embracing Identity," 3.

37. Pharr, *In the Time of the Right*, 21.

38. I am grateful to Susanne Kappeler, whose lead I am following in framing this discussion. See Kappeler, *The Will to Violence*, 20–23.

39. Pharr, *In the Time of the Right*, 1.

40. Harrison, "The Fate of the Middle 'Class.'"

41. Priscilla Pope-Levison and John R. Levison, *Jesus in Global Contexts* (Louisville: John Knox/Westminster, 1992).

42. These scholars are too numerous to list. The best-known include Gustavo Gutiérrez, Jon Sobrino, Juan Louis Segundo, Leonardo Boff, Jose Míguez Bonino, Aloysius Pieris, Chung Hyun Kyung, C. S. Song, Justin S. Ukpong, Mercy Amba Oduyoye, and John S. Mbiti.

43. Marcus J. Borg, *Jesus in Contemporary Scholarship* (Valley Forge, Pa.: Trinity Press, 1994), 9. In addition to Borg, these scholars include John Dominic Crossan, Elisabeth Schüssler Fiorenza, Richard Horsley, Norman Gottwald, Bernard Lee, and Richard J. Cassidy.

44. Ibid., 101–17.

45. Ibid., 29.

46. Robert A. Ludwig, "Reconstructing Jesus for a Dysfunctional Church," in *Jesus and Faith: A Conversation on the Work of John Dominic Crossan*, ed. Jeffrey Carlson and Robert A. Ludwig (Maryknoll, N.Y.: Orbis Books, 1994), 64–67.

47. Catherine Keller, "The Jesus of History and the Feminism of Theology," in *Jesus and Faith*, 71–82.

48. Quoted in Borg, *Jesus in Contemporary Scholarship*, 25.

49. Hobgood, *Catholic Social Teaching*. See esp. chapter 6.

50. Ibid., 154–55.

51. This is true of the entire tradition of Catholic social teaching. See Hobgood, *Catholic Social Teaching*.

52. Gloria H. Albrecht, *The Character of Our Communities: Toward an Ethic of Liberation for the Church* (Nashville: Abingdon Press, 1995), 148.

53. Bounds, *Coming Together/Coming Apart*, 38.

54. Henry Giroux, *Fugitive Cultures: Race, Violence, and Youth* (New York: Routledge, 1996), 184.

55. Stanley A. Deetz, *Democracy in an Age of Corporate Colonization* (Albany: State University of New York Press, 1992), 159.

56. Donna Bivens, quoted in Marian Meck Groot, "The Heart Cannot Express Its Goodness," *The Brown Papers* 3, no. 5 (February 1997): 1.

57. Norman K. Gottwald, "Values and Economic Structures," in *Religion and Economic Justice,* ed. Michael Zweig (Philadelphia: Temple University Press, 1991), 53–77.

58. Hannah Arendt, *Eichmann in Jerusalem: A Report on the Banality of Evil* (New York: Viking, 1963).

59. Beverly Wildung Harrison, "Theological Reflection in the Struggle for Liberation," in *Making the Connections: Essays in Feminist Social Ethics,* ed. Carol Robb (Boston: Beacon Press, 1985), 260.

2. Dismantling Whiteness

1. For additional analysis on the links between racism and the economic and erotic disempowerment of white people see Mary Elizabeth Hobgood, "White Economic and Erotic Disempowerment: A Theological Exploration in the Struggle against Racism," in *Interrupting White Privilege: Catholic Theologians Break the Silence,* ed. Laurie M. Cassidy and Alex Mikulich (Maryknoll, N.Y.: Orbis Books, 2007), 40–55.

2. Robert S. Boynton, "The Plot against Equality: Review of Walter Benn Michaels," *The Nation,* December 25, 2006, 24.

3. Elizabeth M. Bounds, "Gaps and Flashpoints: Untangling Race and Class," in *Disrupting White Supremacy from Within: White People on What We Need to Do,* ed. Jennifer Harvey, Karin A. Case, and Robin Hawley Gorsline (Cleveland: Pilgrim Press, 2004), 123–41.

4. Ibid., 125.

5. People of color are diverse and heterogeneous groups in the United States that include African Americans, Latinos, Chicanos, American Indians, Asian Americans, and Arab Americans, among others.

6. Written communication to Mary E. Hobgood, February 18, 1999. Reprinted by permission.

7. Maria Lugones, *"Hablando cara a cara*/Speaking Face to Face: An Exploration of Ethnocentric Racism," in *Making Face, Making Soul: Creative and Critical Perspectives by Feminists of Color,* ed. Gloria Anzaldúa (San Francisco: Aunt Lute Books, 1990), 48–49.

8. Peggy McIntosh, "White Privilege and Male Privilege: A Personal Account of Coming to See Correspondences through Work in Women's Studies," working paper 189, Wellesley College Center for Research on Women, Wellesley, Mass., 1988.

9. Beverly W. Harrison, "The Fate of the Middle 'Class' in Late Capitalism," in *God and Capitalism: A Prophetic Critique of Market Economy,* ed. J. Mark Thomas and Vernon Visick (Madison, Wis.: A-R Editions, 1991), 55.

10. Ada María Isasi-Díaz, "Solidarity: Love of Neighbor in the 1980s," in *Feminist Theological Ethics,* ed. Lois K. Daly (Louisville: Westminster/John Knox, 1994), 82.

11. Himani Bannerji, "But Who Will Speak for Us?" in *Unsettling Relations,* ed. Himani Bannerji et al. (Boston: South End Press, 1991), 116.

12. Iris Marion Young, "Asymmetrical Reciprocity: On Moral Respect, Wonder, and Enlarged Thought," *Constellations* 3, no. 3 (1997): 349.

13. Ibid., 360.

14. For example, even poorer working-class white males benefit from race-segregated and gender-segregated labor and the lower relative income received by people of color and white women.

15. Ruth Frakenberg, "When We Are Capable of Stopping, We Begin to See: Being White, Seeing Whiteness," in *Names We Call Home: Autobiography on Racial Identity,* ed. Becky Thompson and Sangeeta Tyagi (New York: Routledge, 1996), 15.

16. Noel Ignatiev, *How the Irish Became White* (New York: Routledge, 1995), 115–16. See also Karen Brodkin, *How Jews Became White Folks and What That Says about Race in America* (New Brunswick, N.J.: Rutgers University Press, 1999).

17. David R. Roediger, *The Wages of Whiteness: Race and the Making of the American Working Class* (New York: Verso, 1991).

18. Ibid., 151–54.

19. Philip Cushman, *Constructing the Self, Constructing America* (New York: Addison-Wesley, 1995), 50.

20. Ibid., 16.

21. Roediger, *The Wages of Whiteness,* 115–31; and Cushman, *Constructing the Self,* 41–52.

22. Herbert Marcuse, *One Dimensional Man* (Boston: Beacon Press, 1964), 59.

23. Ibid., 70. Contrary to another member of the Frankfurt School, Jürgen Habermas, who is discussed in the fifth chapter, Marcuse did not believe in the possibility of social emancipation. He held that social forces had created a "one-dimensional society" in which bureaucratic control and cultural manipulation produced the "decline of the individual."

24. Cushman, *Constructing the Self,* 52.

25. Walter Brueggemann, *The Prophetic Imagination* (Minneapolis: Fortress Press, 1978), 45.

26. Herbert Marcuse, *Eros and Civilization: A Philosophical Inquiry into Freud* (Boston: Beacon Press, 1955), 203–8.

27. Cushman, *Constructing the Self,* 52; Roediger, *The Wages of Whiteness,* 97.

28. Roediger, *The Wages of Whiteness,* 58.

29. Ibid., 12.

30. Ann Withorn, "Why My Mother Slapped Me," in *For Crying Out Loud: Women's Poverty in the United States,* ed. Ann Withorn and Diane Dujon (Boston: South End Press, 1996), 13–16.

31. bell hooks, *Killing Rage: Ending Racism* (New York: Henry Holt, 1995), 31–50.

32. Ibid., 54.

33. Marilyn Frye, "White Woman Feminist," in *Overcoming Racism and Sexism,* ed. Linda A. Bell and David Blumenfeld (Lanham, Md.: Rowman & Littlefield, 1995), 119.

34. Quoted in Elizabeth M. Bounds, *Coming Together/Coming Apart: Religion, Community, and Modernity* (New York: Routledge, 1977), 96.

35. Roediger, *The Wages of Whiteness,* 177.

36. Barbara Fields as quoted in Rose M. Brewer, "Theorizing Race, Class, and Gender," in *Materialist Feminism: A Reader in Class, Difference, and Women's Lives,* ed. Rosemary Hennessy and Chrys Ingraham (New York: Routledge, 1997), 239.

37. Paul Kivel, *Uprooting Racism* (Philadelphia: New Society Publishers, 1996), 79.

38. Robert John Ackerman, *Heterogeneities: Race, Gender, Class, Nation, and State* (Amherst: University of Massachusetts Press, 1996), 1–7.

39. McIntosh, "White Privilege and Male Privilege."

40. Ibid., 5–9.

41. Manning Marable, *How Capitalism Underdeveloped Black America: Problems in Race, Political Economy, and Society* (Boston: South End Press, 1983).

42. Kivel, *Uprooting Racism,* 133, 143.

43. Marc Cooper, "The Heartland's Raw Deal: How Meatpacking Is Creating a New Immigrant Underclass," *The Nation,* February 3, 1997, 11–17.

44. Kivel, *Uprooting Racism,* 29–30.

45. Ackerman, *Heterogeneities,* 36.

46. Arthur Brittan and Mary Meynard, *Sexism, Racism, and Oppression* (New York: Basil Blackwell, 1984), 50.

47. bell hooks, *Black Looks: Race and Representation* (Boston: South End Press, 1992), 21–39.

48. Ibid., 39.

49. Kivel, *Uprooting Racism,* 137–38.

50. Ibid., 167.

51. About 39 percent of AFDC families have been white; 37 percent black; 18 percent Latino; 3 percent Asian; and 1 percent American Indian. See Holly Sklar, *Chaos or Community: Seeking Solutions, Not Scapegoats for Bad Economics* (Boston: South End Press, 1995), 94.

52. Ibid., 126.

53. Young, "Asymmetrical Reciprocity," 345.

54. Ann Ferguson, *Sexual Democracy: Women, Oppression, and Revolution* (San Francisco: Westview Press, 1995), 115.

55. Stephanie M. Wildman, *Privilege Revealed: How Invisible Preference Undermines America* (New York: New York University Press, 1996), 85–102.

56. bell hooks, *Killing Rage,* 224.

57. Sharon D. Welch, *Sweet Dreams in America: Making Ethics and Spirituality Work* (New York: Routledge, 1999), 131.

58. Kate McKenna, "Subjects of Discourse: Learning the Language That Counts," in *Unsettling Relations: The University as a Site of Feminist Struggle* (Boston: South End Press, 1996), 121.

59. Joni Seager, "Creating a Culture of Destruction: Gender, Militarism, and the Environment," in *Toxic Struggles: The Theory and Practice of Environmental Justice,* ed. Richard Hofrichter (Philadelphia: New Society Publishers, 1993), 63.

60. Robert D. Bullard, "Anatomy of Environmental Racism," in *Toxic Struggles,* 30.

61. Seager, "Creating a Culture of Destruction," 63.

62. Ibid.

63. Cynthia Hamilton, "Environmental Consequences of Urban Growth and Blight," in *Toxic Struggles,* 71.

64. Daniel Faber and James O'Connor, "Capitalism and Crisis of Environmentalism," in *Toxic Struggles,* 14.

65. Larry L. Rasmussen, *Earth Community, Earth Ethics* (Maryknoll, N.Y.: Orbis Books, 1996), 75–110.

66. Kivel, *Uprooting Racism,* 36–37, 50.

67. Toni Morrison, quoted in Susanne Kappeler, *The Will to Violence: The Politics of Personal Behavior* (New York: Columbia Teachers College Press, 1995), 54.

68. Gloria H. Albrecht, *The Character of Our Communities: Toward an Ethic of Liberation for the Church* (Nashville: Abingdon Press, 1995), 164.

69. Kivel, *Uprooting Racism,* 36–37.

70. Barbara Smith, "Between a Rock and a Hard Place," in *Yours in the Struggle: Three Feminist Perspectives on Anti-Semitism and Racism,* ed. Elly Bulkin, Minnie Bruce Pratt, and Barbara Smith (Ithaca, N.Y.: Firebrand Books, 1984), 74.

71. Quoted in Becky Thompson, "Time Traveling and Border Crossing: Reflections on White Identity," in *Names We Call Home,* 103.

72. Bryan N. Massingale, "The Ethics of Racism," *Origins* 28 (November 26, 1998): 425–26.

73. National Conference of Catholic Bishops, *Brothers and Sisters to Us: U.S. Bishops' Pastoral Letter on Racism in Our Day* (Washington, D.C.: U.S. Catholic Conference, 1979).

74. Massingale, "The Ethics of Racism," 424–28.

75. National Conference of Catholic Bishops, *Brothers and Sisters to Us,* 6.

76. Ibid., 3.

77. Ibid., 10–13.

78. See also Black Bishops of the United States, "What We Have Seen and Heard: Pastoral Letter on Evangelization," *Origins* 14 (October 18, 1984): 282; National Conference of Catholic Bishops, *Heritage and Hope: Evangelization in the United States* (Washington, D.C.: U.S. Catholic Conference, 1991), 2; Massingale, "The Ethics of Racism," n. 18.

79. Cynthia Garcia Coll, Robin Cook-Nobles, and Janet L. Surrey, "Building Connection through Diversity," in *Women's Growth in Diversity,* ed. Judith V. Jordan (New York: Guilford Press, 1997), 187.

80. Ferguson, *Sexual Democracy,* 127.

81. Kappeler, *The Will to Violence,* 234.

82. bell hooks, *Killing Rage,* 263–65; Gloria Yamato, "Something about the Subject Makes It Hard to Name," in *Making Face, Making Soul,* 24.

83. John Anner, ed., *Beyond Identity Politics: Emerging Social Justice Movements in Communities of Color* (Boston: South End Press, 1996). See also chapter 6 here.

84. Becky Thompson and Sangeeta Tyagi, "Story Telling as Social Conscience," in *Names We Call Home,* xv.

85. Kivel, *Uprooting Racism,* 205.

86. Bounds, *Coming Together/Coming Apart,* 21.

87. Welch as cited in ibid., 89.

88. Ibid., 120.

89. W. E. B. DuBois, *The Gift of Black Folk,* quoted in Roediger, *The Wages of Whiteness,* 180.

90. Sharon D. Welch, "Dreams of the Common Good: From the Analytics of Oppression to the Politics of Transformation," in *New Visions for the Americas: Religious Engagement and Social Transformation,* ed. David Batstone (Minneapolis: Fortress Press, 1993), 187.

91. Melanie Kaye/Kantrowitz, "Jews in the U.S.: The Rising Costs of Whiteness," in *Names We Call Home,* 134.

3. An Economic Ethics of Right Relationship

1. William Greider, *One World Ready or Not: The Manic Logic of Global Capitalism* (New York: Simon & Schuster, 1997), 337–38.

2. David Harvey, *Justice, Nature, and the Geography of Difference* (Cambridge, Mass.: Blackwell Publishers, 1996), 334–38.

3. John O'Connor, "The Promise of Environmental Democracy," in *Toxic Struggles: The Theory and Practice of Environmental Justice,* ed. Richard Hofrichter (Philadelphia: New Society Publishers, 1993), 47.

4. Robert Reich, "The New Rich–Rich Gap," *Common Dreams News Center,* December 13, 2005, 1–3. *www.commondreams.org/views05/1212-20.html.*

5. Ibid.

6. Norman K. Gottwald, "Values and Economic Structures," in *Religion and Economic Justice,* ed. Michael Zweig (Philadelphia: Temple University Press, 1991), 55.

7. Michael Lerner, "Jewish Liberation Theology," in *Religion and Economic Justice,* 131–33.

8. Gottwald, "Values and Economic Structures," 55–56.

9. Ibid., 57.

10. Marcus J. Borg, *Jesus in Contemporary Scholarship* (Valley Forge, Pa.: Trinity Press, 1994), 104, 117.

11. Gottwald, "Values and Economic Structures," 58.

12. Carol S. Robb, *Equal Value: An Ethical Approach to Economics and Sex* (Boston: Beacon Press, 1995), 142–45.

13. See Mary E. Hobgood, *Catholic Social Teaching and Economic Theory: Paradigms in Conflict* (Philadelphia: Temple University Press, 1991), esp. 228–37.

14. *Sollicitudo Rei Socialis* (1987), 42. The official English texts of Catholic documents can be found in David J. O'Brien and Thomas A. Shannon, eds., *Catholic Social Teaching: The Documentary Heritage* (Maryknoll, N.Y.: Orbis Books, 1992).

I follow the standard convention of using Latin names for documents originating in Rome and standard paragraph or section numbers for all documents.

15. *Centesimus Annus* (1991), 40.

16. *Laborem Exercens* (1981), 12, 14.

17. *Ethical Choices and Political Challenges* (1983), 13.

18. Ibid., 6.

19. Third General Conference of the Latin American Bishops, Puebla, Mexico (1979), 96, 733, 1134, 1136, 1142, 1145, 1217.

20. Hobgood, *Catholic Social Teaching,* 159–60.

21. Gottwald, "Values and Economic Structures," 67.

22. Max Weber, *The Theory of Social and Economic Organization,* ed. Talcott Parsons (New York: Free Press, 1964), 424–29.

23. Historical Income Table, Households, *U.S. Census Bureau, www.censusgov/hhes/www/income/histinc/h01ar.html.*

24. For Marx's discussions on class, which are scattered throughout his work, see David McLellan, *Karl Marx: Selected Writings* (New York: Oxford University Press, 1977). See subsequent elaborations by Marxist theoreticians such as Maurice Dobb, *Studies in the Development of Capitalism* (New York: International Publishers, 1964); Harry Braverman, *Labor and Monopoly Capital* (New York: Monthly Review Press, 1974); Michael Albert and Robin Hahnel, *Unorthodox Marxism: An Essay on Capitalism, Socialism, and Revolution* (Boston: South End Press, 1978).

25. Ann Ferguson, *Sexual Democracy: Women, Oppression, and Revolution* (San Francisco: Westview Press, 1995), 35. Ferguson says that the notion of work here involves not only the production of things and services but also the production of people. However, we separate the two since they have different "logics" and feminist and class theoreticians still have work to better elucidate how the production of things and services and the production of people are deeply intertwined. Ibid., 69.

26. Michael Zweig, "Six Points on Class," in *More Unequal: Aspects of Class in the United States,* ed. Michael D. Yates (New York: Monthly Review Press, 2007), 173–74.

27. Quoted in David Leonhardt, "Larry Summers's Evolution," *New York Times Magazine,* June 10, 2007, 22.

28. David Cay Johnston, "Income Gap Is Widening, Data Shows," *New York Times,* March 29, 2007, *www.newyorktimes.com/2007/03/29/business/29tax.html.*

29. Robert Kuttner, "Survival of the Richest," *Boston Globe,* June 24, 2006, A17.

30. See ibid., 3; Paul Krugman, "The Great Wealth Transfer," *Rolling Stone,* December 14, 2006, 48; Rick Klein, "Senate Backs 5 Year 70 Billion Tax Cut," *Boston Globe,* May 13, 2006, A2; Robert Kuttner, "Tax Cuts: Shameful Sham," *Boston Globe,* August 5, 2006, A15.

31. See Barbara and John Ehrenreich, "The Professional-Managerial Class," in *Between Labor and Capital,* ed. Pat Walker (Montreal: Black Rose Books, 1978), 5–45. While the Ehrenreichs, like Robert Reich and Michael Zweig, among many others, see this group as a separate class, I prefer to emphasize the common class position that professionals and managers share with laborers vis-à-vis capital.

32. Stephanie Luce and Mark Brenner, "Women and Class: What Has Happened in Forty Years?" in *More Unequal: Aspects of Class in the United States,* ed. Michael D. Yates, 119–20.

33. John Irons, "Typical Families See Income and Earnings Decline," *Economic Policy Institute* (September 5, 2007), *www.epi.org/content.cfm/webfeatures_snapshots_20070905.*

34. Ibid., 121–22.

35. Myra H. Strober, "Two-Earner Families," in *Feminism, Children, and the New Families,* ed. Sanford M. Dornbush and Myra H. Strober (New York: Guilford Press, 1988): 161–90; Man-yee Kan, "Gender Asymmetry in the Division of Domestic Labor," paper presented at the British Household Panel Survey, 2001, Institute for Social and Economic Research, University of Essex, *www.iser.essex.ac.uk/activities/conference/bhps-2001/docs/pdf;* Suzanne M. Bianchi, "Maternal Employment and Time with Children: Dramatic Change or Surprising Continuity?" *Demography* 37 (November 2000): 401–14, and Ellen Goodman, "Getting Over the Mommy Wars," *Boston Globe,* May 12, 2006, A17. It is important to be clear that capitalism means something different for women than for men because capitalist relations of production are built upon patriarchal relations of reproduction. Women who work harder for less in the public workforce also work for nothing in the home, bearing the burden of a double working day. How capitalism and patriarchy are intertwined will be addressed in chapter 4.

36. Stephanie Luce and Mark Brenner, "Women and Class: What Has Happened in Forty Years?" in *More Unequal: Aspects of Class in the United States,* ed. Michael D. Yates, 122–23.

37. Sabiyha Prince, "Will the Real Black Middle Class Please Stand Up," in *More Unequal: Aspects of Class in the United States,* 99; Current Population Reports, "Income, Poverty and Health Insurance Coverage in the United States: 2006," *U.S. Census Bureau* (August 2007): 11; Algernon Austin and Jared Bernstein, "Don't Blame Black Culture," *Economic Policy Institute* (November 8, 2006), *www.epi.org/content.cfm/webfeatures_viewpoints_don't_blam.*

38. Current Population Reports, "Income, Poverty and Health Insurance Coverage in the United States: 2006," *U.S. Census Bureau* (August 2007): 4–7; David Roediger and Michael Zweig, "Race and Poverty: An Exchange," *Monthly Review* 58, no. 7 (December 2006): 61–63; Economic Snapshots, "Minority Wealth Gap: Net Worth Gap Twice That of Income," *Economic Policy Institute* (March 15, 2006). *www.epi.org/content.cfm/webfeatures_snapshots_20060315.*

39. Jared Bernstein and Lawrence Mishel, "Economy's Gains Fail to Reach Most Workers Paychecks," *Economic Policy Institute* (September 3, 2007): 1–6, *www.epi.org/content.cfm/bp195.*

40. Ruth Conniff, "The Progressive Interview: Elizabeth Edwards," *The Progressive* (August 2007): 33, and Ralph Whitehead Jr., "Colleges and the Numbers Game," *Boston Globe,* February 4, 2008, A15.

41. Current Population Reports, "Income, Poverty and Health Insurance Coverage in the United States: 2006." *U.S. Census Bureau* (August 2007): A13.

42. Editorial, "When Wages Don't Pay the Bills," *Boston Globe,* November 1, 2007, A12.

43. Kathryn Newman cited in Eyal Press, "The Missing Class," *The Nation,* August 13–20, 2007, 22.

44. See, for example, Joan Greenbaum, *Windows on the Workplace: Computers, Jobs, and the Organization of Office Work in the Late Twentieth Century* (New York: Monthly Review Press, 1995); and Barbara Hilkert Andolsen, *The New Job Contract: Economic Justice in an Age of Insecurity* (Cleveland: Pilgrim Press, 1998).

45. Juliet B. Schor, *The Overworked American* (New York: Basic Books, 1991).

46. Greenbaum, *Windows on the Workplace,* 19–21, 93.

47. Carmen Vasquez, "Walking on Moonsands," in *Racism in the Lives of Women,* ed. Jeanne Adleman and Gloria Enguidanos (Binghamton, N.Y.: Harrington Park Press, 1995), 7.

48. Greenbaum, *Windows on the Workplace;* Andolsen, *The New Job Contract;* and William K. Tabb, "Globalization Is *An* Issue, the Power of Capital Is *The* Issue," *Monthly Review* 49, no. 2 (June 1997): 29 n. 3.

49. Chuck Collins and Felice Yeskel with United for a Fair Economy, Foreword Juliet Schor, *Economic Apartheid in America* (New York: New Press, 2005), 55.

50. Zweig, "Class and Poverty," 208; see also Kim Moody, *Workers in a Lean World: Unions in the International Economy* (London: Verso, 1997), 188.

51. Robert Kuttner, "Health Insurance Dilemma," *Boston Globe,* January 20, 2007, A13, and Alison Bass, "An Underinsured Kick in the Groin," *Boston Globe,* January 21, 2008, A11.

52. Charles Kennedy, "A New Job for Greenspan," *Boston Globe,* January 19, 2006, A11 and Teresa Ghilarducci, "The End of Retirement" *Monthly Review* 58, no. 1 (May 2006): 16.

53. Editorial, "Pump-Priming the Economy," *New York Times,* January 20, 2008, WK10, and Michael D. Yates, "Capitalism Is Rotten to the Core," review of Immanuel Ness, *Immigrants, Unions, and the New U.S. Labor Market* (Philadelphia: Temple University Press, 2005), and Howard Karger, *Shortchanged: Life and Debt in the Fringe Economy* (San Francisco: Berrett-Koehler Publishing, 2005) in *Monthly Review* 58, no. 1 (May 2006): 59.

54. Schor, *The Overworked American,* 22, 150.

55. Collins and Yeskel, *Economic Apartheid in America,* 15.

56. John Bellamy Foster, "The Household Debt Bubble," *Monthly Review* 58, no. 1 (May 2006): 6.

57. Ibid., 6.

58. Ibid., 173.

59. Greenbaum, *Windows on the Workplace,* 18, 26, 31, 45, 48.

60. Ibid., 96.

61. Martha E. Gimenez, "How Corporations Get Us to Work without Pay," *Monthly Review* 59, no. 7 (December 2007): 37–41.

62. Peter Wagner, *The Prison Index: Taking the Pulse of the Crime Control Industry,* Western Prison Project and the Prison Policy Initiative (2003), *www.prisonpolicy.org/prisonindex/prisonlabor.html.*

63. Vijay Prashad, "Reclaim the Neighborhood, Change the World," *Monthly Review* 59, no. 7 (December 2007): 61, and Jared Bernstein, "Job Market Flashing Recession," *Economic Policy Institute* (January 4, 2008), *www.epi.org/content.cfm?id =2852.*

64. William K. Tabb, "Wage Stagnation, Growing Insecurity, and the Future of the U.S. Working Class," *Monthly Review* 59, no. 2 (June 2007): 24, and David Moberg, "Class Consciousness Matters," *Features* (June 24, 2005): 2.

65. Ibid., 27.

66. Ibid.

67. Harvey, *Justice*, 348.

68. Ibid., 347.

69. Susanne Kappeler, *The Will to Violence: The Politics of Personal Behavior* (New York: Columbia Teachers College Press, 1995), 216.

70. Katha Pollitt, "Let Them Eat Numbers," *The Nation*, December 30, 1996, 8.

71. Elizabeth V. Spellman, *Fruits of Sorrow: Framing Our Attention to Suffering* (Boston: Beacon Press, 1997).

72. Albrecht, *The Character of Our Communities,* 162.

73. Beverly Wildung Harrison, "Theological Reflection in the Struggle for Liberation," in *Making the Connections: Essays in Feminist Social Ethics,* ed. Carol Robb (Boston: Beacon Press, 1985), 246.

74. Greider, *One World Ready or Not,* 336, 359.

75. Ibid., 45–48.

76. Ibid., 48.

77. David Loy, "The Religion of the Market," *Journal of the American Academy of Religion* 65, no. 2 (Summer 1997): 283.

78. Harvey, *Justice*, 339.

79. Thom Shanker, "Proposed Military Spending Is Highest since World War II," *New York Times*, February 4, 2008, at *www.nytimes.com/2008/02/04/washington/04military.html*.

80. Frank Rich, "Ronald Reagan Is Still Dead," *New York Times*, January 20, 2008, WK11, and Roberta Spivek, "The Cost of War," *Peacework* (November 2007): 8–9.

81. FY 2007 Budget Proposal, "Budget Would Increase Security Spending but Cut or Curb 141 Programs," *Washington Post*, February 7, 2006, A19, online at *www.washingtonpost.com/wp-srv/politics/interactive/budget07/agencies.html*.

82. Holly Sklar, *Chaos or Community: Seeking Solutions, Not Scapegoats for Bad Economics* (Boston: South End Press, 1995), 149.

83. Ramsey Clark, Sean Gervasi, Sara Flounders, Nadja Tesich, Thomas Deichmann and others, *NATO in the Balkans: Voices of Opposition* (New York: International Action Center, 1998).

84. Quoted in Sklar, *Chaos or Community,* 35.

85. Greg Albo, "The World Economy, Market Imperatives, and Alternatives," *Monthly Review* 48, no. 7 (December 1996): 7.

86. Greider, *One World Ready or Not,* 48.

87. Tabb, "Globalization Is an Issue," 22, and Adam Turl, "Is the U.S. Becoming Post-Industrial?" *International Socialist Review* (March–April 2007): 49–50.

88. Piven and Cloward, "Eras of Power," 20.

89. Adam Turl, "Is the U.S. Becoming Post-Industrial?" 50, and Fernando E. Gapasin and Michael D. Yates, "Labor Movement: Is There Hope?" *Monthly Review* 57, no. 2 (June 2005): 35–50.

90. John Bellamy Foster and Fred Magdoff, *The Great Financial Crisis: Causes and Consequences* (New York: Monthly Review Press, 2009), 132.

91. James Grant, "Paying the Price for the Feds Success," *New York Times,* January 27, 2008, WK16.

92. Jenny Anderson and Vikas Bajaj, "Loan Reviewer Aiding Inquiry into Big Banks," *New York Times,* January 27, 2008, A1, A17.

93. Gretchen Morgenson, "O Wise Bank, What Do We Do?" *New York Times,* January 27, 2008, WK1, 10.

94. Grant, "Paying the Price for the Fed's Success," WK16.

95. Anderson and Bajaj, "Loan Reviewer Aiding Inquiry into Big Banks," A17.

96. Robert Kuttner, "It's Time to Save the Housing Sector," *Boston Globe,* January 24, 2008, A11, and Roger Lowenstein, "The Education of Ben Bernanke," *New York Times Magazine,* January 20, 2008, 40.

97. John Bellamy Foster and Fred Magdoff, *The Great Financial Crisis: Causes and Consequences* (New York: Monthly Review Press, 2009), 104–5; John Bellamy Foster and Robert W. McChesney, "A New New Deal under Obama?" *Monthly Review* 60, no. 9 (February 2009): 8, and James M. Stone, "A New Rulebook of Financial Regulations," *Boston Globe,* February 5, 2009, A15.

98. John Bellamy Foster and Fred Magdoff, *The Great Financial Crisis,* 116.

99. Robert Kuttner, *Obama's Challenge: America's Economic Crisis and the Power of a Transformative Presidency* (White River Junction, Vt.: Chelsea Green Publishing, 2008).

100. John Bellamy Foster and Robert W. McChesney, "A New New Deal under Obama?" *Monthly Review* 60, no. 9 (February 2009): 8.

101. Ibid., 5.

102. Victor Wallis, "Capitalist and Socialist Responses to the Ecological Crisis," *Monthly Review* 60, no. 6 (November 2008): 29, 33.

103. John Bellamy Foster and Fred Magdoff, *The Great Financial Crisis,* 125.

104. George Ritzer, *The McDonaldization of Society* (Thousand Oaks, Calif.: Pine Forge Press, 1996), 79–99.

105. David Harvey, *The Condition of Postmodernity* (Cambridge, Mass.: Basil Blackwell, 1989), 107.

106. Ibid., 147, 153, 174.

107. Ibid., 159.

108. Ynestra King, "Feminism and Ecology," in *Toxic Struggles,* 77.

109. Harvey, *The Condition of Postmodernity,* 229.

110. Stanley A. Deetz, *Democracy in an Age of Corporate Colonization* (Albany: State University of New York Press, 1992), 226, 294.

111. Harvey, *The Condition of Postmodernity,* 287.

112. Greenbaum, *Windows on the Workplace,* 77.

113. Loy, "The Religion of the Market," 287.

114. Deetz, *Democracy in an Age of Corporate Colonization,* 209.

115. Ibid., 215.

116. Ibid., 210.

117. Beverly Harrison, "The Ideological Spectrum: How Values Are Transformed in the Real World," in *Advocating Justice and Equality: A Policy Resource Guide* (Elkhart, Ind.: National Council of the Churches of Christ USA, 1998), 21.

118. Marc Estrin, "If Not Mean-Spirited, What Are They?" *Peacework* 254 (July–August 1995): 10.

119. Margaret Cerullo and Marla Erlien, "Beyond the Normal Family," in *For Crying Out Loud: Women and Poverty in the United States,* ed. Rachel Lefkowitz and Ann Withorn (New York: Pilgrim Press, 1988), 252.

120. Carole Pateman, *The Sexual Contract* (Cambridge: Polity Press, 1988), 149.

121. Estrin, "If Not Mean-Spirited," 10.

122. Vincent Navarro, "The Worldwide Class Struggle," *Monthly Review* 58, no. 4 (September 2006), 18–33, see esp. 23–28.

123. Ibid., 28.

124. Greider, *One World Ready or Not,* 390, 404–6.

125. Edward S. Herman, *Triumph of the Market* (Boston: South End Press, 1995), 5.

126. Kim Bobo, "Put the Fair Minimum Wage Back on Track," *Interfaith Worker Justice* (June 26, 2006):1, *www.iwj.org/actnow/actnow/give.html.*

127. For more information contact the AFL-CIO at 408-761-7173.

128. Cooper, "The Heartland's Raw Deal," 11–17.

129. Harvey, *The Condition of Postmodernity,* 303.

130. Peter J. Haas, *Morality after Auschwitz: The Radical Challenge of the Nazi Ethic* (Philadelphia: Fortress Press, 1988), 170.

131. Paul Farmer, Margaret Connors, and Janie Simmons, eds., *Women, Poverty, and AIDS* (Monroe, Maine: Common Courage Press, 1996).

132. Stan Grossfeld, "New Dangers Make Way to U.S. Tables," *Boston Sunday Globe,* September 20, 1998, sec. A.

133. Minnie Bruce Pratt, *Rebellion: Essays 1980–1991* (Ithaca, N.Y.: Firebrand Books, 1991), 118–21.

134. Ibid., 121.

135. Deetz, *Democracy in an Age of Corporate Colonization,* 203.

136. Greider, *One World Ready or Not,* 216.

137. Sklar, *Chaos or Community,* 44–46; Greider, One *World Ready or Not,* 64–65; Greenbaum, *Windows on the Workplace,* 120, 129.

138. Greenbaum, *Windows on the Workplace,* 124.

139. Jared Bernstein, "The 21st Century Workplace," *Economic Policy Institute* (May 26, 2005), at *www.epi.org/content.cfm/webfeatures_viewpoints_workplace_testimony/* and Economic Policy Institute, "Economic Snapshots" (February 22, 2006), *www.epi.org/content.cfm/webfeatures_snapshots_20060222.*

140. Facts and Figures: State of Working America 2004/2005, "Jobs," Economic Policy Institute, *http://epinet.org.*

141. Louis Uchitelle, "Retraining, but for What?" *New York Times,* March 26, 2006, Section 3, B1.

142. Ibid., B10, and Adam Turl, "Is the U.S. Becoming Post-Industrial?" *International Socialist Review* (March–April 2007): 53.

143. Diane E. Lewis, "For Educated Workers, Things Are Looking Good," *Boston Globe,* September 30, 2006, B5, and Facts and Figures, State of Working Class America 2004/2005, "Wages," Economic Policy Institute, *http://epinet.org,* and Adam Turl, "Is the U.S. Becoming Post-Industrial?" 55–56.

144. Harrison, "Theological Reflection," 247.

145. Christine E. Gudorf, *Body, Sex, and Pleasure: Reconstructing Christian Sexual Ethics* (Cleveland: Pilgrim Press, 1994), 160–204.

146. Robert N. Bellah, "Class Wars and Culture Wars in the University Today," *Council of Societies for the Study of Religion Bulletin* 27, no. 1 (February 1998): 2.

147. Quoted in bell hooks, *Outlaw Culture: Resisting Representations* (New York: Routledge, 1995), 246.

148. Margaret Talbot, "Attachment Theory: The Ultimate Experiment," *New York Times Magazine*, May 24, 1998, 24–54.

149. Lawrence Mordekhai Thomas, "Power, Trust, and Evil," in *Overcoming Racism and Sexism*, ed. Linda A. Bell and David Blumenfeld (Lanham, Md.: Rowman & Littlefield, 1995), 160.

150. Ibid., 158–61.

151. Loy, "The Religion of the Market," 288.

152. Harrison, "Theological Reflection," 243.

153. Kenneth Westhuis, "Reginald Bibby's Preference for the Market Model in the Sociology of Religion," *The Ecumenist* 3, no. 1 (January–March 1996): 7.

154. Adam Phillips, "Satisfaction Not Guaranteed," *New York Times Magazine*, June 7, 1998, 82.

155. "Measures of Pleasure," *Women's Review of Books* 15, nos. 10–11 (July 1988): 11, 13.

156. Alice Walker, *Anything We Love Can Be Saved* (New York: Ballantine Books, 1997), 55, 196.

157. To identify the potential for working-class solidarity in the highly segmented intermediate sector, see Carolyn Howe, *Political Ideology and Class Formation: A Study of the Middle Class* (Westport, Conn.: Praeger, 1992), esp. chapters 5 and 7.

158. Ibid., 152.

159. Ferguson, *Sexual Democracy,* 175–76.

160. Bleifuss, "Warfare or Welfare," *In These Times* 21, no. 2 (December 9, 1996): 14.

161. Puebla (1979), 525; see also 806, 1046, 1054.

4. Constructing a Compassionate Sexuality

1. Gail Rubin, "The Traffic in Women: Notes on the 'Political Economy' of Sex," in *Toward an Anthropology of Women*, ed. Rayna Reiter (New York: Monthly Review Press, 1975).

2. Chrys Ingraham, "The Heterosexual Imaginary: Feminist Sociology and Theories of Gender," in *Materialist Feminism: A Reader in Class, Difference, and Women's Lives*, ed. Rosemary Hennessy and Chrys Ingraham (New York: Routledge, 1997), 286–87.

3. Some of this expanding work includes Paula Gun Allen, ed., *Spider Woman's Granddaughters: Traditional Tales and Contemporary Writing by Native American Women* (New York: Fawcett Columbine, 1989); Cherrie Moraga and Gloria Anzaldúa, eds., *This Bridge Called My Back: Writings by Radical Women of Color* (New York: Kitchen Table Press, 1981); Gloria T. Hull, Patricia Bell Scott, and Barbara Smith, eds., *All the Women Are White, All the Blacks Are Men, but Some of Us Are Brave* (New York: Feminist Press, 1982); bell hooks, *Feminist Theory: From*

Margin to Center (Boston: South End Press, 1984); Barbara Christian, *Black Feminist Criticism* (New York: Pergamon, 1985); Gloria Anzaldúa, *Making Face, Making Soul: Creative and Critical Perspectives by Women of Color = Haciendo caras* (San Francisco: Aunt Lute Books, 1990); Patricia Hill Collins, *Black Feminist Thought: Knowledge, Consciousness, and the Politics of Empowerment* (New York: Routledge & Kegan Paul, 1991); Elaine H. Kim, Lilia A. Villanueva, and Asian Women United of California, eds., *Making More Waves: New Writing by Asian American Women* (Boston: Beacon Press, 1997); Carla Trujillo, ed., *Living Chicana Theory* (Berkeley: Third Women Press, 1998).

4. Ann Ferguson, *Sexual Democracy: Women, Oppression, and Revolution* (San Francisco: Westview Press, 1995), 114–15.

5. Rose M. Brewer, "Theorizing Race, Class, and Gender," in *Materialist Feminism: A Reader in Class, Difference, and Women's Lives,* ed. Rosemary Hennessy and Chrys Ingraham (New York: Routledge, 1997), 246; Julianne Malveaux, "The Real Deal on Black Unemployment," *Black Issues in Higher Education* (August 12, 2004): 5.

6. Hazel Carby, "White Women Listen! Black Feminism and the Boundaries of Sisterhood," in *Black British Feminism: A Reader,* ed. Heidi Safia Mirza (New York: Routledge, 1982), 115.

7. Arthur Brittan and Mary Meynard, *Sexism, Racism, and Oppression* (New York: Basil Blackwell, 1984), 56.

8. Stephanie Luce and Mark Brenner, "Women and Class: What Has Happened in Forty Years?" in *More Unequal: Aspects of Class in the United States,* ed. Michael D. Yates (New York: Monthly Review Press, 2007), 122–23.

9. Feminist Majority Foundation, "The Economics of Gender and Race, Examining the Wage Gap in the United States" (April 13, 2005). *www.feministcampus.org* and Amy Caiazza, April Shaw, and Misha Werschkul, "Women's Economic Status in the States: Wide Disparities by Race, Ethnicity and Region," Institute for Women's Policy Research (2003), *www.iwpr.org.*

10. Luce and Brenner, "Women and Class: What Has Happened in Forty Years?" 122.

11. Nancy Fraser, *Justice Interruptus: Critical Reflections on the "Postsocialist" Condition* (New York: Routledge, 1997), 228.

12. Cynthia R. Comacchio, "Motherhood in Crisis," in *Materialist Feminism,* 306–27.

13. John D'Emilio, "Capitalism and Gay Identity," in *The Lesbian and Gay Studies Reader,* ed. Henry Ablelove, Michele Aina Barale, and David M. Halperin (New York: Routledge, 1993), 467–78.

14. Feminist Majority Foundation, "The Economics of Gender and Race: Examining the Wage Gap in the United States" (April 13, 2005), *www.feministcampus.org.*

15. Ingraham, "The Heterosexual Imaginary," 283; and U.S. Department of Labor, Women's Bureau, *1993 Handbook on Women Workers: Trends and Issues* (Washington, D.C., 1993), 232–33. Quoted in Gloria H. Albrecht, "The Production of Character," *Welfare Policy: Feminist Critiques,* ed. Elizabeth M. Bounds, Pamela K. Brubaker, and Mary E. Hobgood (Cleveland: Pilgrim Press, 1999), 103.

16. Daniel C. McGuire and Larry L. Rasmussen, *Ethics for a Small Planet: New Horizons on Population, Consumption, and Ecology* (Albany: State University of New York Press, 1998), 3.

17. Meera Nanda, "History Is What Hurts: A Materialist Feminist Perspective on the Green Revolution and Its Ecofeminist Critics," in *Materialist Feminism*, 373–81.

18. Carby, "White Women Listen!" 110–28.

19. Ferguson, *Sexual Democracy,* 40, 115.

20. Beverly Wildung Harrison, "Theological Reflection in the Struggle for Liberation," in *Making the Connections: Essays in Feminist Social Ethics,* ed. Carol Robb (Boston: Beacon Press, 1985), 3–21

21. Marvin M. Ellison, *Erotic Justice: A Liberating Ethic of Sexuality* (Louisville: Westminster John Knox, 1996), 8.

22. Ibid., 45.

23. Christine E. Gudorf, *Body, Sex, and Pleasure: Reconstructing Christian Sexual Ethics* (Cleveland: Pilgrim Press, 1994), 176.

24. Lori L. Heise, "Violence, Sexuality, and Women's Lives," in *The Gender Sexuality Reader: Culture, History, and Political Economy,* ed. Roger N. Lancaster and Michaela di Leonardo (New York: Routledge, 1997), 414.

25. Ibid., 414.

26. Herbert Marcuse, *Eros and Civilization: A Philosophical Inquiry into Freud* (Boston: Beacon Press, 1955), 199–222.

27. Comacchio, "Motherhood in Crisis," 311.

28. Linda Singer, *Erotic Welfare: Sexual Theory and Politics in the Age of Epidemic* (New York: Routledge, 1993), 39.

29. Paul Kivel, *Uprooting Racism* (Philadelphia: New Society Publishers, 1996), 66.

30. Evelyn Brooks Higginbotham, "African-American Women's History and the Metalanguage of Race," *Signs: Journal of Women in Culture and Society* 17, no. 2 (1992): 254.

31. Collins, *Black Feminist Thought,* 174.

32. Patricia J. Williams, "Mr. Lincoln's Legacy," *The Nation,* October 26, 1998, 9.

33. Mary D. Pellauer, "The Moral Significance of the Female Orgasm," in *Sexuality and the Sacred: Sources for Theological Reflection,* ed. James B. Nelson and Sandra P. Longfellow (Louisville: Westminster/John Knox, 1994), 154.

34. Mary E. Hobgood, "Marriage, Market Values, and Social Justice: Toward an Examination of Compulsory Monogamy," in *Redefining Sexual Ethics,* ed. Eleanor H. Haney and Susan E. Davies (Cleveland: Pilgrim Press, 1991), 115–26.

35. Gudorf, *Body, Sex, and Pleasure,* 160–204.

36. Alice Miller, *The Drama of the Gifted Child* (New York: Basic Books, 1994), and *For Your Own Good: Hidden Cruelty in Child-Rearing and the Roots of Violence* (New York: Farrar, Straus & Giroux, 1983), 231.

37. Ellison, *Erotic Justice,* 50.

38. Lise Vogel, "From the Women's Question to Women's Liberation," in *Materialist Feminism,* 144.

39. Leslie Feinberg, "Transgender Liberation," in *Materialist Feminism,* 230.

40. Ingraham, "The Heterosexual Imaginary," 287.

41. Feinberg, "Transgender Liberation," 229.

42. Ibid., 229–30.

43. Maria Mies, "Colonization and Housewifizaton," in *Materialist Feminism,* 177.

44. Heise, "Violence, Sexuality, and Women's Lives," 424–25.

45. Peggy Reeves Sanday, "The Socio-Cultural Context of Rape: A Cross-Cultural Study," *Journal of Social Issues* 37, no. 4 (1981): 5–27.

46. Heise, "Violence, Sexuality, and Women's Lives," 424.

47. James B. Nelson, *The Intimate Connection: Male Sexuality, Masculinist Spirituality* (Philadelphia: Westminster Press, 1988), 80.

48. Classical literature on the origins of the heteronormative monogamous family includes the following: Johann Bachofen, *Das Mutterrecht* (Berlin: Bauhaus-Archiv, 1861); Lewis Henry Morgan, *Ancient Society* (Cambridge, Mass.: Belknap Press, 1877); Frederick Engels, *The Origins of the Family, Private Property and the State* (New York: International, 1884); Eli Zaretsky, *Capitalism, the Family, and Personal Life* (New York: Harper & Row, 1976).

49. Feinberg, "Transgender Liberation," 231.

50. Ingraham, "The Heterosexual Imaginary," 289.

51. Carby, "White Women Listen!" 123.

52. Howard Zinn, *A People's History of the United States* (New York: Harper & Row, 1980), 21.

53. Paul Kivel, *Men's Work: How to Stop the Violence That Tears Our Lives Apart* (New York: Ballantine Books, 1992), 2.

54. Arlie Russell Hochschild, "There's No Place Like Work," *New York Times Magazine,* April 20, 1997, 51–84.

55. Arlie Hochschild and Anne Machung, "Men Who Share the Second Shift," in *Windows on Society,* 4th ed., ed. John W. Heeren and Marylee Mason (Los Angeles: Roxbury Publishing, 1996), 158–68. This is true across class lines. Hochschild and Machung also found that if a husband made *less* than his wife or had no job, he did *no* domestic labor, making up in patriarchal privilege what he lost over his wife in class privilege.

56. Luce and Brenner, "Women and Class: What Has Happened in Forty Years?" 123.

57. Hochschild and Machung, "Men Who Share the Second Shift," 158, 166.

58. Ibid., 166.

59. Hochschild, "There's No Place Like Work," 84.

60. Ruth Sidel, *Women and Children Last: The Plight of Poor Women in Affluent America* (New York: Penguin Books, 1986), 17.

61. Beverly Wildung Harrison, "Sexuality and Social Policy," in *Sexuality and the Sacred,* 244.

62. Joanna Macy and Molly Young Brown, *Coming Back to Life: Practices to Reconnect Our Lives, Our World,* foreword by Matthew Fox (Stony Creek, Conn.: New Society Publishers, 1998), 34–35.

63. Harrison, "Sexuality and Social Policy," 243.

64. Ellison, *Erotic Justice,* 91.

65. Ibid., 57.

66. Nicola Field, "Identity and the Lifestyle Market," in *Materialist Feminism,* 264.

67. Harrison, "Theological Reflection," 225.

68. Samuel Laeuchli, *Power and Sexuality: The Emergence of Canon Law at the Synod of Elvira* (Philadelphia: Temple University Press, 1972), 88.

69. Maguire as cited in Ellison, *Erotic Justice,* 61.

70. Pius XI, "On Christian Marriage," in *Seven Great Encyclicals,* ed. William J. Gibbons, S.J. (New York and Mahwah, N.J.: Paulist Press, 1963), 77–117.

71. Beverly Wildung Harrison and Carter Heyward, "Pain and Pleasure: Avoiding the Confusions of Christian Tradition in Feminist Theory," in *Sexuality and the Sacred,* 131–40.

72. Margaret A. Farley, "An Ethic for Same-Sex Relations," in *A Challenge to Love: Gay and Lesbian Relations in the Church,* ed. Robert Nugent (New York: Crossroad, 1986), 93.

73. Barbara Hilkert Andolsen, "Whose Sexuality? Whose Tradition? Women, Experience, and Roman Catholic Sexual Ethics," in *Feminist Ethics and the Catholic Moral Tradition,* ed. Charles E. Curran, Margaret A. Farley, and Richard A. McCormick, S.J. (New York and Mahwah, N.J.: Paulist Press, 1996), 207, 210.

74. Gudorf, *Body, Sex, and Pleasure,* 2.

75. Mary E. Hunt, "Sexual Ethics: A Lesbian Perspective," *Open Hands* 4, no. 3 (Winter 1989): 10.

76. Macy and Brown, *Coming Back to Life,* 52–59.

77. Sandra Lipsitz Bem, *An Unconventional Family* (New Haven, Conn.: Yale University Press, 1998), 123. People are developing a larger sexual repertoire. But as in the case of Bill Clinton, they are refusing to call it sex. Ironically, in a sexually restrictive culture, this looks like an attempt to "out-orthodox the orthodox" as people claim some semblance of freedom outside male-focused genital sex that, because of oppression, is the only sexual expression with normative status.

78. Pellauer, "The Moral Significance of the Female Orgasm," 161.

5. *Relational Labor and the Politics of Solidarity*

1. Janet R. Jakobsen, *Working Alliances and the Politics of Difference* (Bloomington: Indiana University Press, 1998), 128–31, 144, 153, 169–70.

2. Ibid., 7, 19, 118–19.

3. Nicola Field, "Identity and the Lifestyle Market," in *Materialist Feminism: A Reader in Class, Difference, and Women's Lives,* ed. Rosemary Hennessy and Chrys Ingraham (New York: Routledge, 1997), 264.

4. Daniel Faber and James O'Connor, "Capitalism and the Crisis of Environmentalism," in *Toxic Struggles: The Theory and Practice of Environmental Justice,* ed. Richard Hofrichter (Philadelphia: New Society Publishers, 1993), 22.

5. Field, "Identity and the Lifestyle Market," 264.

6. Jakobsen, *Working Alliances,* 118–19.

7. Ibid., 16, 22.

8. Ibid., 14–15.

9. Ibid., 21, 33, 146–47.

10. See Rosemary Hennessy and Rajeswari Mohan, "The Construction of Women in Three Popular Texts of Empire," in *Materialist Feminism,* ed. Hennessy

and Ingraham, 187; Field, "Identity and the Lifestyle Market," 267–69; Carole A. Stabile, "Feminism and the Ends of Postmodernism," in *Materialist Feminism*, ed. Hennessy and Ingraham, 395–408; David Harvey, *The Condition of Postmodernity* (Cambridge, Mass.: Basil Blackwell, 1989).

11. Suzanne Pharr, *In the Time of the Right: Reflections on Liberation* (Berkeley: Chardon Press, 1996), 79, 81.

12. Jakobsen, *Working Alliances*, 150–72.

13. Ibid., 83, 102–4.

14. See Jürgen Habermas, *The Structural Transformation of the Public Sphere: An Inquiry into a Category of Bourgeois Society*, trans. Thomas Burger and Frederick Lawrence (Cambridge, Mass.: MIT Press, 1989); and Jürgen Habermas, *The Theory of Communicative Action*, vol. 2, *Lifeworld and System: A Critique of Functional Reason*, trans. Thomas McCarthy (Boston: Beacon Press, 1987).

15. Antonio Gramsci, *Selections from the Prison Notebooks of Antonio Gramsci*, ed. and trans. Quinton Hoare and Geoffrey Nowell Smith (New York: International Publishers, 1972); and Carl Boggs, *The Two Revolutions: Antonio Gramsci and the Dilemmas of Western Marxism* (Boston: South End Press, 1984), 243–74.

16. For a critical evaluation of Habermas that contrasts him with Gramsci, see Nancy Fraser, *Justice Interruptus: Critical Reflections on the "Postsocialist" Condition* (New York: Routledge, 1997), 69–98.

17. Stabile, "Feminism and the Ends of Postmodernism," 407.

18. Jakobsen, *Working Alliances*, 27.

19. Kim Moody, *Workers in a Lean World: Unions in the International Economy* (London: Verso, 1997), 304–7.

20. Walter Brueggemann, *The Prophetic Imagination* (Minneapolis: Fortress Press, 1978), 50.

21. See Matthew 5:4 and Luke 19:41. Brueggemann, *The Prophetic Imagination*, 60.

22. Brueggemann, *The Prophetic Imagination*, 67.

23. Bob Hebert, "House of Arrogance," *New York Times*, December 20, 1998, WK13.

24. David M. Schribman, "One Nation under God: How the Religious Right Changed the American Conversation," *Boston Globe Magazine*, January 10, 1999, 27–31.

25. Alan Ehrenhalt, "You Call This Progress?" review of *The Corrosion of Character* by Richard Sennett (New York: W. W. Norton, 1998), *New York Times Book Review*, December 20, 1998, 16.

26. See, for example, John Anner, ed., *Beyond Identity Politics: Emerging Social Justice Movements in Communities of Color* (Boston: South End Press, 1996); Ray M. Tillman and Michael S. Cummings, eds., *The Transformations of U.S. Unions: Voices, Visions, and Strategies from the Grassroots* (Boulder, Colo.: Lynne Rienner Publishers, 1999); Kevin Danaher, ed., *50 Years Is Enough: The Case against the World Bank* (Boston: South End Press, 1994); Jeremy Brecher, John Brown Childs, and Jun Cutler, eds., *Global Visions: Beyond the New World Order* (Boston: South End Press, 1993); Jeffrey S. Juris, *Networking Futures: The Movements against Corporate Globalization* (Durham, N.C.: Duke University Press, 2008); Biorn Maybury-Lewis, *The Politics of the Possible: The Brazilian Workers' Trade*

Union Movement (Philadelphia: Temple University Press, 1994); Gail Omvedt, *We Will Smash This Prison* (London: Zed, 1980).

27. See *www.kwru.org;* Elly Leary, "Florida's Migrant Workers Take Down Taco Bell," *Monthly Review* 57, no. 5 (October 2005): 11–25, and Vijay Prashad, "Reclaiming the Hood, Changing the World," *Monthly Review* 59, no. 7 (December 2007): 60–64.

28. Adam Doster, "The Conscious Classroom," *The Nation,* February 25, 2008, 22.

29. Gar Alperovitz, "America beyond Capitalism: What a 'Pluralist Commonwealth' Would Look Like," *Dollars and Sense* no. 256 (November–December 2004): 30.

30. Brueggemann, *The Prophetic Imagination,* 68.

31. Ibid., 81.

32. Ibid., 81–83.

33. Ibid., 86.

34. Ibid., 88.

35. Ada María Isasi-Díaz, "Solidarity: Love of Neighbor in the 1980s," in *Feminist Theological Ethics,* ed. Lois K. Daly (Louisville: Westminster/John Knox, 1994), 77–87.

36. Sharon D. Welch, *Sweet Dreams in America: Making Ethics and Spirituality Work* (New York: Routledge, 1999), 21, 26.

37. Ibid., 130.

38. Patricia Hill Collins, *Fighting Words: Black Women and the Search for Justice* (Minneapolis: University of Minnesota Press, 1998), 189, 240.

39. Henry Giroux, *Fugitive Cultures: Race, Violence, and Youth* (New York: Routledge, 1996), 153–55.

40. Delores S. Williams, "Straight Talk, Plain Talk: Womanist Words about Salvation in a Social Context," in *Embracing the Spirit: Womanist Perspectives on Hope, Salvation, and Transformation,* ed. Emilie M. Townes (Maryknoll, N.Y.: Orbis Books, 1997), 119–20.

41. Moody, *Workers in a Lean World,* 310.

6. Intellectual and Political Struggle

1. Quoted in Liesl Schillinger, "Leaving Las Vegas," book review of Charles Bock, *Beautiful Children* (New York: Random House, 2007), *New York Times Book Review* (February 3, 2008): 1.

2. Paul Bloom, "Morality Studies," book review of Kwame Anthony Appiah, *Experiments in Ethics* (Cambridge, Mass.: Harvard University Press, 2007), *New York Times Book Review* (February 3, 2008): 22.

3. Quoted in Gerard Vanderhaar, *Why Good People Do Bad Things* (Mystic, Conn.: Twenty-Third Publications, 1994): 34.

4. Kim Phillips-Fein, "Deal Breakers," book review of Paul Krugman, *The Conscience of a Liberal* (New York: Norton, 2007), and Jonathan Chait, *The Big Con: The True Story of How Washington Got Hijacked by Crackpot Economics* (Boston: Houghton Mifflin, 2007), *The Nation,* December 10, 2007, 11–17.

5. Quoted in Paul Bloom, "Morality Studies," book review of Kwame Anthony Appiah, *Experiments in Ethics* (Cambridge, Mass.: Harvard University Press, 2007) *New York Times Book Review* (February 3, 2008): 22.

6. Quoted in Hal Brill et al., *Investing with Your Values* (Gabriola, B.C.: New Society Publishers, 1999), xxii.

7. James Bellamy Foster, "The Ecology of Destruction," *Monthly Review* 58, no. 9 (February 2007): 7.

8. Roxana Robinson, "Watching as the World Vanishes," *Boston Sunday Globe,* January 1, 2006, C11.

9. Larry Rasmussen, "Green Discipleship," in *Reflections: Yale Divinity School* (Spring 2007): 70.

10. Bill McKibbon, "How Big Should People Be? *Reflections: Yale Divinity School*" (Spring 2007): 27.

11. Ellen Goodman, "Friendless in America," *Boston Globe,* June 30, 2006, A17.

12. Quoted in Nicholas D. Kristof, "Uncertainty about Global Warming No Excuse for Inaction," *Worcester Telegram and Gazette,* August 17, 2007, A7.

13. Larry Rasmussen, "Green Discipleship," 70.

14. Wesley Morris, "A Grim Reminder," *Boston Globe,* August 24, 2007, E6.

15. Joseph Hebert, "Congress Backs Fuel Economy Boost," *Boston Globe,* December 19, 2007, A12.

16. Bilal Zuberi, "A Drive toward Fuel Economy," *Boston Globe,* August 13, 2007, A11; and Allen E. Smith, "The Road to Energy Conservation," *Boston Globe,* November 19, 2007, A13.

17. Mark Hertsgaard, "Adapt or Die," *The Nation,* May 7, 2007, 24.

18. Editorial, "Going Green" *The Nation,* May 7, 2007, 3.

19. Mark Hertsgaard, "Adapt or Die," *The Nation,* May 7, 2007, 24.

20. James Hansen, "Why We Can't Wait," *The Nation,* May 7, 2007, 13.

21. Jeff Goodell, "The Dirty Rock," *The Nation,* May 7, 2007, 32.

22. See Doug Henwood, "Cooler Elites," *The Nation,* May 7, 2007, 22, and Editorial, "Coal Miner's Nation," *Boston Globe,* August 23, 2007, A8.

23. Jackie Ashley, "Millions of Us Have to Accept Duller Lives," *Common Dreams News Center* (December 13, 2005), at *www.commondreams.org/views05/1212–29.htm.*

24. George Monbiot, "Flying into Trouble," *The Nation,* May 7, 2007, 33.

25. Lierre Keith, *www.inthewake.org/keith1.html.*

26. Hansen, "Why We Can't Wait," 14.

27. John Bellamy Foster, "The Ecology of Destruction," *Monthly Review* 58, no. 9 (February 2007): 6.

28. Daniel Nepstad, "Diet for a Hot Planet," *Boston Globe,* November 22, 2006, A15, and Mark Bittman, "Rethinking the Meat-Guzzler," *New York Times,* January 27, 2008, WK4.

29. Ibid., 13.

30. Andrew Revkin, "A Bold Step to Capture an Elusive Gas Falters," *New York Times,* February 3, 2008, WK4.

31. Larry Rasmussen, "Green Discipleship," *Reflections: Yale Divinity School* (Spring 2007): 70.

32. Ibid.

33. Charles J. Hanley, "Climate Talks in Bali Take an Extra Day," *Boston Globe,* December 15, 2007, A3.

34. Barney Frank, "Cut the Military Budget – II," *The Nation,* March 2, 2009, 8.

35. Derrick Z. Jackson, "Earmarking the War Machine," *Boston Globe,* July 21, 2007, A9.

36. Derrick Z. Jackson, "When Ignorance Isn't Bliss," *Boston Globe,* August 18, 2007, A11.

37. Adolph L. Reed Jr., "Sitting This One Out," *The Progressive* (November 2007): 27.

38. Thomas L. Friedman, "It's Too Late for Later," *New York Times,* December 16, 2007, WK10.

39. Jackson, "When Ignorance Isn't Bliss," A11.

40. William Johnson, "South Africa's Winter of Disconnect," *The Nation,* October 4, 2007, 3.

41. Michael Wines, "Shantytown Dwellers in South Africa Protest," *New York Times,* December 25, 2005, YT 10.

42. John S. Saul, *The Next Liberation Struggle: Capitalism, Socialism and Democracy in South Africa* (New York: Monthly Review Press, 2005), 258.

43. See Ashwin Desai, "Neo-Liberalism and Resistance in South Africa," *Monthly Review* 54, no. 8 (January 2003): 7.

44. Saul, *The Next Liberation Struggle,* 237.

45. Richard Pitthouse, "Struggle Is a School," *Monthly Review* 57, no. 9 (February 2006): 30–51.

46. Ibid., 36.

47. Agnes Mohapi as quoted in Saul, *The Next Liberation Struggle,* 237.

48. For vivid descriptions of these movements see Ashwin Desai, *We Are the Poors: Community Struggles in Post-Apartheid South Africa* (New York: Monthly Review Press, 2002).

49. William Johnson, "South Africa's Winter of Discontent," *The Nation,* October 4, 2007, 3.

50. Saul, *The Next Liberation Struggle,* 237, 239.

51. Indira A. R. Lakshmanan, "A Growing Fight for Power on Latin American Left," *Boston Sunday Globe,* June 4, 2006, A6.

52. John Bellamy Foster, "The Latin American Revolt," *Monthly Review* 59, no. 3 (July–August 2007): 2, and Naomi Klein, "The Threat of Hope in Latin America," *The Nation,* November 21, 2005, 14.

53. See Raul Zibechi, "Subterranean Echoes: Resistance and Politics from the Basement," *Socialism and Democracy* 19, no. 3 (November 2005): 19, 27–39.

54. Sandra Sierra, "Chavez Threatens to Cut Off Oil Sales," *Boston Globe,* February 11, 2008, A3. Venezuela is behind Canada, Saudi Arabia, and Mexico.

55. Joseph P. Kennedy, II, "Yes, Oil From Venezuela," *Boston Globe,* December 24, 2006, C9.

56. Michael A. Leibowitz, "Venezuela: A Good Example of the Bad Left of Latin America," *Monthly Review* 59, no. 3 (July–August, 2007): 44.

57. Ibid., 45–47.

58. Ibid., 49.

59. Ibid.

60. Atilio A. Boron, "The Truth about Capitalist Democracy," in *Telling the Truth: Socialist Register 2006*, ed. Leo Panitch and Colin Leys (New York: Monthly Review Press, 2006): 52.

61. Leibowitz, "Venezuela," 61.

62. Daniel Wilkinson, "Chavez's Fix," *The Nation*, March 10, 2008, 31–41.

63. Ibid., 32.

64. Jean Hardisty and Deepak Bhargava, "Wrong about the Right," *The Nation*, November 7, 2005, 24.

65. George Ciccariello-Maher, "Dual Power in the Venezuelan Revolution," *Monthly Review* 59, no. 4 (September 2007): 42–56.

66. Yiching Wu, "Rethinking Capitalist Restoration in China," *Monthly Review* 57, no. 6 (November 2005): 62–63.

67. Greg Grandin, "Chavez Galbraithiano," *The Nation*, October 15, 2007, 5–6.

68. Robin Hahnel, "Against the Market Economy: Advice to Venezuelan Friends," *Monthly Review* 59, no. 8 (January 2008): 11–28.

69. Cynthia Kaufman, *Ideas for Action: Relevant Theory for Radical Change* (Cambridge, Mass.: South End Press, 2003), 291.

70. Ibid., 77–278.

71. Ibid., 280.

72. Quoted in ibid., 287.

73. Ibid.

74. Keith, *www.inthewake.org/keith1.html*.

75. Kaufman, *Ideas for Action*, 291.

76. Alinsky as cited in ibid., 292.

77. Albert as cited in ibid.

78. Rick Perlstein, "Will the Progressive Majority Emerge?" *The Nation*, July 9, 2007, 11–16.

79. Graham as cited in Keith, *www.inthewake.org/keithl.html*.

80. Ibid.

81. Christopher Hayes, "Michael Moore's *Sicko*," *The Nation*, July 16, 2007, 14.

82. Ainslie as cited in Robert H. Frank, *Falling Behind: How Rising Inequality Harms the Middle Class* (Los Angeles: University of California Press, 2007), vii.

83. Michael A. Leibowitz, *Build It Now: Socialism for the Twenty-first Century* (New York: Monthly Review Press, 2006), 113.

84. Roger S. Gottlieb, *A Spirituality of Resistance* (New York: Crossroad, 1999), 158–72.

85. Robert McAfee Brown, *Religion and Violence: A Primer for White Americans* (Philadelphia: Westminster Press, 1973).

Index